barefoot ragamuffin curricula

www.barefootmeandering.com

veritas • gnaritas • libertas

liberis meis

Wayfarers

Modern History

Term 3

Kathy Jo DeVore

with Ernest DeVore and Jared DeVore

Table of Contents

Mechanically

Mechanically he rose and proceeded to repack the luncheon-basket, carefully and without haste. Mechanically he returned home, gathered together a few small necessaries and special treasures he was fond of, and put them in a satchel; acting with slow deliberation, moving about the room like a sleep-walker; listening ever with parted lips. He swung the satchel over his shoulder, carefully selected a stout stick for his wayfaring, and with no haste, but with no hesitation at all, he stepped across the threshold just as the Mole appeared at the door.

"Why, where are you off to, Ratty?" asked the Mole in great surprise, grasping him by the arm.

"Going South, with the rest of them," murmured the Rat in a dreamy monotone, never looking at him. "Seawards first and then on shipboard, and so to the shores that are calling me!"

The Wind in the Willows by Kenneth Grahame

One Program, All Stages

P/K   Pre-K and Kindergarten

Grammar Stage, 1st-4th grades
LG   Lower grammar/elementary, 1st and 2nd grades
UG   Upper grammar/elementary, 3rd and 4th grades

Dialectic Stage, 5th-8th grades
LD   Lower dialectic/middle school, 5th and 6th grades
UD   Upper dialectic/middle school, 7th and 8th grades

Rhetoric Stage, 9th-12th grades
LR   Lower rhetoric/high school, 9th and 10th grades
UR   Upper rhetoric/high school, 11th and 12th grades

Introduction

Each Wayfarers book contains a schedule for a complete year of study for all grades. Other books are required to complete this curriculum.

Wayfarers is a complete program with all subjects scheduled for all grades. Because of this, you will find quite a bit of repetition and quite a few choices built into Wayfarers. For instance, the same lower grammar story Bible is scheduled each year. This repetition means that you have that information scheduled for you whenever you have a lower grammar student in need of a Bible story book. You will also choose between two different geography read-alouds and three different composers. These choices mean that when you come back to this book in four years for another trip through this time period, you won't be repeating exactly the same books and composers that you did last time.

Like my other curricula, Wayfarers does not completely follow any particular educational style. My educational philosophy has been influenced by Susan Wise Bauer as much as by Charlotte Mason. I appreciate the neo-classical model of organizing education by the developmental stages of the students, of following a four year history rotation, and of having all the children study the same content areas each year. I appreciate Charlotte Mason's focus on narrations as a method of having the students work with the material they've explored and as a method of evaluating what the student has learned.

I also appreciate Charlotte Mason's focus on high quality literature. If I could keep only one aspect of our homeschooling, if we had to give up everything else and keep only this one thing, I'd keep quality literature. This does not mean that the child has to read everything himself. Read-alouds are acceptable, and so are audio books. But literature is the backbone of all of our studies, and the rest would be pointless without it. With the literature would go the ideas and the knowledge of how others live and have lived. As literature is the backbone to our studies, the assignments are built onto and around it. Read it, talk about it, write about it. That's essentially what this entire curriculum is. With that in mind, I strongly encourage you to avoid the temptation of adding busywork to your day.

I've tried to make Wayfarers simple and flexible. If you have a child who loves to read, there are plenty of book selections included. If you have a child who needs more hands-on, do the minimum level of reading and do the activities, or add projects and lapbooks.

Wayfarers has multiple book lists scheduled to make it easy to tailor the program to your needs. History has a spine and two lists of books scheduled. You can choose either of the lists, or both of them. Science also has multiple lists from which to choose. This way, you can choose how much reading your student will be doing.

I'm going to repeat this part because it's really important...

You Don't Have to Read Everything

The books scheduled are for informing the mind and feeding the imagination, but you don't have to read all the books in a Wayfarers schedule.

I have children who are always looking for a new book, but at least one of my children reads more slowly than his brothers, and he doesn't enjoy reading as much. For him, it is far preferable to read a smaller number of books and interact with the material in other ways. For younger students, this might mean lapbooks, notebooking, or activities. For older students, it might mean the wonderful research suggestions in Diana Waring's History Revealed program.

I've made it easy to leave off an entire list of books if you want. This is also an important consideration if you have a limited budget and a mediocre library.

Strategies for the Reading Lists

There are many different ways a family may choose to do the reading in Wayfarers. I recommend that children begin doing part of their own school reading once they're reading fluently, or by 2nd grade. This will depend on the child, of course, but I do not worry about covering all the books in the lists before my children are old enough to do part of the reading for themselves.

• For our family, the geography literature is currently the preferred read-aloud material, and the Milestones topics are directly related to these books. We do them as our evening read-aloud.

• If you want to do more history and/or science reading together as a family, I recommend choosing one or more lists from the dialectic and/or grammar stage books to do together as a family. Each student can read additional books from the other lists if desired.

• If you'd rather do more story books as a family, you have multiple options. Each level of *English Lessons Through Literature* has reading scheduled three-times per week, and these are on the literature portion of the schedule for your convenience, with the complete list of books in Appendix A. In addition, a second read-aloud is also scheduled three-times per week in Wayfarers.

Signposts and Milestones

Signposts appear at the beginning of the week's schedule, and they tell you something about what's up ahead, including lists of materials necessary to complete the activities and experiments of the week.

Milestones are at the end of the week, and they discuss where you've been. Milestones contain the History Through Art lesson for the week as well as discussions on several topics taken from the geography literature books. For the youngest children, reading the topics in Milestones may be enough. For older children, these can be jumping off points for further exploration, and they may encourage the child to explore other topics he comes across in his reading.

Book Selections

There is no magic list of books which produces educated children. Some books are better suited to this purpose than others, but even the Great Books are not so great when read too soon. And there are certainly enough Great Books to allow us to read the ones we find most interesting rather than slogging through another person's list of favorites.

Books go out of print. Your library may not have a book. You may simply need a break. In such cases, substitute a book or skip one altogether.

Change the Model

Wayfarers schedules lessons for thirty-six weeks, 180 days, so it can be completed in a standard school year. However, as year-round homeschoolers, it would be rare indeed for us to complete 180 days of school in a "normal" September to May school year. If you instead take a full calendar year to complete Wayfarers, you only need to complete three scheduled weeks in each calendar month. That means if you start in September, then in September, you would complete weeks 1-3 of the program; in October, you would complete weeks 4-6; etc. In this way, the following August, you would be doing weeks 33-36, finishing just in time to start the next book in September. In this way, you can either have three full weeks of school followed by a week off, or you can have four more relaxed weeks of school each month.

This brings balance to the traditional model. Instead of cramming a year's worth of education into nine months and a year's worth of relaxation into three months, we can teach our children to balance work and play every month of their lives.

Preschool and Lower Grammar

Pathways is a free two-year reading plan for preschoolers and lower grammar stage children. While I originally wrote it as a placeholder program for people who were waiting to begin *English Lessons Through Literature*, I would not hesitate to use it as a complete curriculum for first or second grade students. I've scheduled it here for convenience, and I've also included the book lists and instructions in Appendix E. With *Pathways*, you choose your path and follow it through the year. That path might give you anywhere from one to five days of reading with one to four books scheduled each day. Take some time to familiarize yourself with the way it works, and choose which part of the schedule you'd like to follow. PLEASE NOTE: when a chapter number is not given, you're just supposed to read the next story.

I also included thirty-six preschool activities, one for each week; these repeat in each Wayfarers book. Many of these are very basic things that you may already do; the idea is not to present an activity for use on a single day, but rather to add some new activities to your repertoire. I decided to include the repeatable ones as a rotating schedule so that little ones have something on the schedule every day, too. You could also print them out and draw one at random each day, or just choose one from the list. Some are based on Montessori activities. Some of the preschool activities may work better for younger children, and some may work better for older ones. Some may include choking hazards, so please evaluate each activity based on your child's age and abilities. Some include print outs or items you may not necessarily have around the house, so you'll want to see the supply list in Signposts each week to prepare. Twice a week, on art days, they have an art lesson from one of the Barry Stebbing's books for preschool children.

I also recommend teaching the phonograms to preschoolers. Phonogram review is mentioned frequently on the Language Arts portion of the schedule as a reminder for all ages. Toddlers are in full language acquisition mode, so it seems wise to take full advantage of it. My daughter started learning them before she was three years old, and she considered it a game. This can be done in a very gentle way using the Montessori three-period lesson, explained briefly in Appendix E.

Narrations and Notebooking

No busywork is built into this program. Instead, oral and written narrations are scheduled for each day of the week to help you make them a regular part of your homeschool. Lower grammar students may draw pictures from the reading instead of telling about it; I like to have the child tell me about his picture as an intermediate step to formal narrations. Older students have both oral and written narrations. I normally have my children start writing their own narrations in 4th grade after teaching them to type in 3rd grade. Before that time, I recommend staying with oral narrations. If you want or need a written record, then play scribe for the child, typing up his words as he tells them to you.

Narration is my preferred method for the student to work with the material he's learning and also my preferred tool for evaluation. It's superior for both of these purposes, and it also serves helps the student practice expressing himself both verbally and in writing. You do not necessarily have to do every scheduled narration. However, oral narrations in particular are very easy to work into life, such as having a child tell you about what he read that day while you take care of tasks around the house or while out-and-about.

Learning styles do play a part in narrations. Some children narrate best when they hear the story (auditory), while others narrate best when they read it themselves (visual). Still others may act out the story while hearing it (kinesthetic). It may take a bit of time to determine the best way to approach the material with younger children.

I've scheduled one creative narration each week. These are intended to add fun and interest to the narration process and to encourage the student to try different ways of writing. It is acceptable to just do straight narrations without any embellishments. However, I encourage you to try the embellishments, at least occasionally.

Narrations can also be combined with notebooking. In many ways, notebooking provides a format for narrations, making it visual as well as language based. These books, created by the student, also provide review.

Language Arts

I've scheduled two grammar options, my own *English Lessons Through Literature* and *Rod and Staff English*. Both of these programs provide grammar and writing lessons. Obviously, I prefer and recommend my own. However, I recognize that some people would prefer a more traditional approach.

If you choose the Rod and Staff option, I recommend waiting to begin until Grade 3. If you really want to do some sort of grammar before that, I suggest doing the first two levels of either ELTL or another gentle program designed for 1st and 2nd grade students.

Rod and Staff is scheduled three to four times per week. I don't recommend doing the tests and additional worksheets, but if you choose to, you have one or two free days per week to include them. Not all of the Rod and Staff books have the same number of lessons, so when you finish the book, additional lessons may still be listed on the schedule. Following the Wayfarers schedule will skip the last chapter of the Grade 6 book.

Unlike ELTL, Rod and Staff does not include a literature selection and copywork for each day. Therefore, along with Rod and Staff, I recommend doing the literature selections from ELTL, and do the copywork from ELTL for Levels 1-4. The reading selections are on the second page of the schedule under "Literature" on Days 1, 3, and 5.

For 5th grade and up, I recommend having the student begin a commonplace book. A commonplace book is a book for copying poetry, passages from literature, and other writings or information. A simple composition book can be used for this purpose. Students can add to the commonplace book from school or free reading. My children choose their own passages to copy, passages which speak to them in some way. For my oldest son, it's often something philosophical or political. For my second son, it's usually something funny.

High School Language Arts

Susan Wise Bauer has an excellent lecture on high school writing available at the Peace Hill Press website (www.peacehillpress.com).

For those who choose to use *Rod and Staff English*, their two high school books are scheduled here as well. For those who use *English Lessons Through Literature*, writing programs have been scheduled for the rhetoric stage. For upper rhetoric, I've included *Writing Great Research Papers* by Laurie Rozakis and scheduled time to write a research paper each year.

For lower rhetoric, I've included a writing program for each year. *Rhetorical Devices* by Brendan McGuigan is scheduled for one of these years, and it should be a useful course of study for any student. *The Power in Your Hands* by Sharon Watson is scheduled for the other year. I recommend *The Power in Your Hands* specifically for those who are uncomfortable teaching high school writing without a guide.

High school students should still write narrations in history and science, but now the narrations should move to a new level. Each written narration should begin with an introduction and end with a conclusion. The student should no longer be merely repeating the information; he should be also be adding his own observations.

He also can, and should, take the basic narration and make it persuasive. After reading one of the Federalists papers, the student can explain why he agrees or disagrees with the author. When his science book proclaims the wonders of chemical fertilizers, the student can make his own assessment and explain why he feels the way he does. This becomes a logical extension of the writing he's already been doing, not a whole new type of writing.

Students can also write persuasively on other topics. I believe that students need to learn to write persuasively, but I also believe that they are perfectly capable of learning to write persuasively with topics which they love and are passionate about. In fact, I believe that they are better able to learn to write well with such subjects. When my oldest son follows me around the house making an argument regarding a topic he's been thinking on, I say, "That sounds like a good topic for an essay." So far, I've read essays on how Star Wars is pro-Jedi propaganda, how the Japanese mythology upon which Pokemon is based has been overly simplified in the franchise, and how one of the Anti-Federalist writers was a time traveler. All of these were very interesting, and he enjoyed writing them, but they would never have been written had I forced him to remain strictly in the realms of science, history, and literature.

For literary analysis topics, occasionally choose an essay topic from Cliffs Notes, Spark Notes, or PinkMonkey.com for one of the books on the reading lists.

History and Science

History and science reading are divided into three parts: spine, core reading, and optional extra reading (for science). The spine and the core reading are scheduled out, and there may be more than one spine from which to choose. Additionally, you may find that you would prefer that your child use the spine from another stage. This is fine. Grammar stage uses *Story of the World* exclusively, dialectic stage uses mainly the H. A. Guerber books, and one option for rhetoric stage is Diana Waring's History Revealed program. Any of these could be used for other stages. We have used SOTW for dialectic stage and History Revealed for upper dialectic.

The same is true for the reading selections. An advanced 4th grader might use some of the dialectic books while his 9th grade brother might use a combination of the dialectic and rhetoric books. Adapt the lists to your circumstances and your students. Please remember that these lists are not rules. They're more like guidelines.

The optional extra reading is only for science, and it is not scheduled out in the same way. It's simply a recommendation that it would be a good week to read that book. Most of the optional extra reading could easily be read in a week.

The books are not divided up to align perfectly with one another. In my opinion, this tends to make a study begin to feel stilted and unnatural. I prefer a more natural method which allows each book to carry on at its own pace and in its own order. In this way, the books reinforce and review one another. In history and science, the spines are divided evenly throughout the year. In science, many of the main reading books may cover the topics in a different order than the spine. The additional reading in history is arranged chronologically. This means that the student may read about the Battle of Hastings in the spine one week, and then read about William the Conqueror in a historical fiction book weeks later.

High School Science

Too often, high school is seen only as a time for college prep. I see this as a problem because high school then becomes a time of mini-college classes, a time to teach exactly the same things that colleges teach in the first two years, using exactly the same methods but at a slower pace. The assumption seems to be that students will not be able to succeed in college without doing mini-college first. And while I do understand the importance of high school preparing students for college, even for students who aren't sure they want to go to college, I still feel like it's a mistake for high school to be nothing more than mini-college. It generally leaves no time for high school to also be a time of exploration, of discovering who the adult will be on the other side.

When my oldest son was young, I had a plan for science. It involved plenty of living science books throughout elementary and middle school. For high school, we'd switch gears and use a Serious Curriculum. That day finally arrived. I bought a popular textbook with an enormous weight and price, and we began using it with some lesson plans that I found online.

A curious thing happened. My biology loving son quit liking the school subject known as Biology. Where he'd always devoured every science book I'd handed him, now I had to remind him to read. My Serious High School Science was sucking the joy out of science for my son.

I decided to re-evaluate my goals. In *Mere Christianity*, C. S. Lewis wrote, "We all want progress. But progress means getting nearer to the place where you want to be. And if you have taken a wrong turning then to go forward does not get you any nearer. If you are on the wrong road progress means doing an about-turn and walking back to the right road and in that case the man who turns back soonest is the most progressive man" (28).

We turned back. The simple fact is that when adults want to learn about a subject, we don't ordinarily go find a textbook and start doing exercises. Instead, we do what I'd had my son do when he was younger—we read living books, written by those who love their fields and enjoy explaining them to laypersons. We read many books written by a variety of authors, not one book written by committee. We explore, covering some topics shallowly while reading more deeply where we're the most interested.

And that is how we study science in high school now—the same way we do in the earlier grades, through good books. Science is one area where vocabulary development is crucial for success. The good news is that plenty of reading quality science books over the years will give children the necessary vocabulary. Just as with history, we use a spine to cover the basics of the subject. Sometimes, when I can find one, the spine might be a living textbook. The spine becomes our safety net with regard to leaving gaps. Though, for the record, there will always be gaps in any education. I don't worry about gaps because they're impossible to prevent.

Will this prepare students for the CLEP test? Maybe, maybe not, but in my opinion, it's about time we made high school mean something on it's own. It's not merely prep time for a test or yet another class. It's NOT that the prep time is unimportant. However, it doesn't have to be the entire point of high school. Instead, our students can read books by people involved in these sciences for a living who love what they do and want to share their enthusiasm with others. And then, if it's necessary to your student's goals and plans, buy a CLEP book and spend a certain amount of time in it each week. Another option is to use community colleges and dual enrollment. In this way, your child will get actual college credit instead of just mini-college time.

For those who are uncomfortable with the idea of covering science in this way, I've scheduled a second option. The second method has a more traditional scope and sequence, but a much different execution. Instead of a dry, boring textbook, Bridget Ardoin's *Science for High School* has students research the answers to a series of questions each week. In this way, students practice researching information and narrating what they've learned. This is far preferable to a standard textbook, yet it covers the same material. If you choose this route, you can still choose to read some of the other books if time allows.

PLEASE NOTE: Science is only scheduled twice a week in Wayfarers, on Tuesdays and Thursdays. Rhetoric students have little to no lessons in language arts on those days. In addition, there is no history reading, and the core science reading is optional for students doing *Science for High School*. That means rhetoric students should have a decent chunk of time free to work on the questions for *Science for High School* on these days. However, be aware that your student might need to work on it more often than it appears on the schedule.

High School History and Literature

Simplicity is part of the beauty of following a Charlotte Mason, classical education. History is learned through literature, so the rhetoric history readings are also the rhetoric literature readings. The rhetoric literature section of the schedule is an optional section which includes poetry and readings from the religion courses.

Wayfarers follows the history divisions presented in *The Well-Trained Mind* and *Story of the World*. These are more like guidelines than actual rules, though.

Ancient: BC 5000 - 400 AD
Medieval: 400 - 1600
Revolution: 1600 - 1850
Modern: 1850 - Present

Religion

Christian Bible study is included each year for all age groups. Rhetoric students who follow the Wayfarers Bible study program will read the entire Bible in three years during high school.

Regarding other religions, for younger students, Wayfarers includes optional geography readings from various religious traditions. For the rhetoric student, we take this to the next level with a comparative religions course. This spans three years in the volumes Ancient through Revolution. The fourth volume, Modern, is dedicated to the history of the Christian church.

Christian Bible Studies

I've given two different options for studying the Bible with young children. The first way has the family reading the Bible together as a read aloud. This is the only plan for 9th grade and up, though of course older students could read the Bible to themselves. The Old Testament is covered in the first and third years. The New Testament and Psalms are covered in the second year, and the fourth year wraps up with a one year overview of the Bible.

Ancient	Medieval	Revolution	Modern
OT—The Law and the Histories	New Testament and Psalms	OT—Prophets and Poetry	Overview of the Bible

I recognize that many people prefer to focus on Bible stories for younger children. With that in mind, I've scheduled Bible story books through 8th grade. Since some of these span two years, and you might start in any year, the schedule just tells how many stories to read each day.

For younger children, Calvary Curriculum (www.calvarycurriculum.com) offers one of the best free resources for teaching Bible on the internet. These lessons and coloring pages can be incorporated into any program you choose to use.

Rhetoric: Comparative Religions
and Christian Church History

The major world religions are covered with additional reading in Wayfarers as follows, though other religions are also touched upon in the spine and the lectures.

Ancient	Medieval	Revolution	Modern
Hinduism, Judaism, Jainism	Buddhism, Confucianism, Daoism, Shinto	Christianity, Islam, Baha'i	History of the Christian Church

These optional readings are found on Days 1, 3, and 5 on the schedule, on the second page under "Literature" since the great religious texts of the world are also Great Books.

In the Supreme Court case Abington Township v. Schempp, Justice Clark delivered the opinion of the Court and said, "It might well be said that one's education is not complete without a study of comparative religion or the history of religion and its relationship to the advancement of civilization." And indeed, so much of history and even the daily news can be incomprehensible without some knowledge of what people believe. Understanding other faiths can supply the necessary background information to these discussions.

Should your household study other faiths? This is a decision that parents will have to consider carefully. Personally, I want my children's initial learning about other faiths to happen while they are still at home and I am in charge of their educations so that we will have a chance to discuss the issues that are bound to arise.

Once you've decided to study other faiths, *how* becomes an issue. In Wayfarers, we tackle this issue in the same way that we tackle all such issues: We read excellent books!

> Do unto others as you would have others do unto you.

I love that most of the world religions contain some version of the Golden Rule. And I can tell you one thing that I do not like. I hate it when non-Christians attempt to tell what Christianity is. Invariably, they get it wrong, sometimes in huge ways and sometimes in small ways, but always in disturbing and distorting ways. And this goes both ways. I recently saw an example of this when I saw some Christian sites which were highly critical of some eastern practices. The problem is not with their criticism—we are called to discernment—but with their obvious misunderstanding of what the eastern practices are and are intended to accomplish. Because of this misunderstanding, they made helpful practices seem like they are inherently anti-Christian.

Discernment requires factual information and an absence of fear.

That is why this course in comparative religions is not from a Christian point of view even though I myself am a Christian. Instead, most of the books in this study are actual scriptures from these traditions with commentary from a positive point of view. If we are going to study other faiths, it is best to do so from a position of respect—which is not the same as agreement—instead of treating those other faiths in a way which we generally do not like to be treated ourselves. Explaining another's faith "from a Christian perspective" is more about Christianity and evangelization than about the other faiths. I'm not saying that there is not a time and a place for such a study. However, in my opinion, such a study would not be about comparative religions. In a comparative religions course, the emphasis is on understanding each individual religion and how they compare to one another instead of attempting to view them all through the lens of one's own faith.

For instance, let's look at Islam. I am sure that anyone reading this is aware that the Qur'an receives a lot of negative attention in the modern United States. In the book scheduled on the Qur'an, the author chooses to look at the shorter and older Suras. These can be compared to hymns or the Psalms in the Hebrew and Christian scriptures. In other words, you will not find some of the verses which can be considered more controversial among Westerners. These verses simply do not appear in this book. Does this show a bias? Perhaps, and perhaps not. The book is merely an introduction to the Qur'an, after all. Some would argue that the Hebrew scriptures (the Old Testament for Christians) contain some equally disturbing verses, but generally speaking, we do not start with these verses when introducing children and unbelievers to our scriptures.

On the other hand, by reading a book which discusses the historical context and the language of the Qur'an and reading some of the Suras, a student is more prepared to go to a translation of the Qur'an and read verses for himself in context, and he is less likely to feel intimidated by such an action since he has already read and understood Suras from the Qur'an. In other words, we are trying to produce students who can explore these sources as they come across them in life and who can form their own opinions instead of being forced to rely on sound bites from others.

At the same time, none of the material included in this course assumes belief in the particular tradition discussed. They are not neutral, and yet they do not proselytize.

> Philip ran up to it and heard him reading the prophet Isaiah. He asked, "Do you understand what you are reading?" He replied, "How can I, unless someone guides me?" And he invited Philip to get in and sit beside him.
> ~Acts 8:30-31 (NRSV)

Most of the books include commentary to help students understand what they are reading. The commentary can discuss such things as the historical setting, alternate translations, and how the verses have been understood over the years. Like the Ethiopian in Acts, we often need a guide when reading scripture from any tradition.

This study also includes three lecture series from the Great Courses. For church history, I've scheduled *The History of Christianity: From the Disciples to the Dawn of the Reformation.* For comparative religions, I've scheduled *Sacred Texts of the World* and *Cultural Literacy for Religion.* There is a great deal of overlap between the two, so while I'm scheduling both, it is fine to use only one—or neither. I love both of these lecture series and find them beneficial to this study, but the books will be enough if time or finances do not allow for the lectures. Traditionally, all of their courses go on sale at least once a year, so it is good to watch for sales the year before you need a course. In addition, these courses are also available through their subscription service, the Great Courses Plus.

Hither & Thither: Geography

Geography is covered each year in Wayfarers through curricula as well as quality literature. The geography literature is the main scheduled daily read-aloud in Wayfarers, and it's also the source material for the topics at the end of each week.

World geography is a two-year program covered in the Ancient and Medieval History books using Knowledge Quest's *Expedition Earth.* World geography is also reviewed in the Revolution and Modern History books. United States geography is a two-year program covered in the Revolution and Modern History books using my own *50 States and Where to Find Them.*

On the schedule each day, you will find two geography literature reading selections from which to choose. The reason for two selections is so that when you return to this book in four years, you'll have a complete second set of books to read for geography. Or, if you choose, you can repeat your favorites from your first time around. For example, the study of Oceania starts with a choice between *Escape to Murray River* or *The Twenty-One Balloons.* The first time through the Ancient History book, you might read *Escape to Murray River.* Four years later, you might choose *The Twenty-One Balloons* instead.

High school students have their own reading selections. I wanted to keep these selections light and fun, so they are mostly travelogues. As with the literature selections for the grammar and dialectic stages, the books recommended are intended to help give the student a better feel for the cultures of other countries while learning geography. If these are not to your student's tastes, please feel free to skip them or substitute with other books.

Nutrition and Sex Ed

Wayfarers includes health books in the Ancient and Revolution books. "Health" here includes both nutrition and sex education books.

For the books on nutrition, there are two options. I've scheduled USDA approved books that discuss the government guidelines for good health. I've also scheduled books from a primal/ancestral health point of view which say exactly the opposite.

All but one of the sex education books are from a Christian perspective. They are all explicit, and they all include explicit illustrations. They are collectively known as "The Book" in our household. My husband says one of them made him blush, and he was only partially joking. I choose to cover sex education with my children while they are still young because they are not as embarrassed by the topic as they become once they near puberty. This is not to say that it becomes an easy topic to discuss, only that it becomes easier. You may choose to use the books a little earlier, a little later, or skip them altogether, based on your views.

Boys, Girls and Body Science is not from a Christian perspective, but there's also nothing anti-Christian about it. One line says, "[S]ome families say that you should be married first, before you have sex. You need to know the rules for your family." This book has an emphasis on knowing the proper names for private body parts and treating this subject as just another area of science.

Optional Activities

The schedule has an activity section which includes art, music, science, and geography activities. These are OPTIONAL. Here's an overview of the activities included so you can decide which, if any, you would like to add to your week.

Remember, these are scheduled for those who love them. Those who don't love them should skip them. I do, however, encourage you to evaluate each of your children as individuals. As one of my children got older, and as I became more experienced as a homeschooler, I realized that he needed fewer books and more hands-on. It's okay to have one child doing both history reading lists and no hands-on activities while another does only one reading list with hands-on activities. Each child is different, and we need to meet them where they are.

I recommend the music and art activities for getting the greatest benefit for the least amount of time invested. It's also easier to add hands-on activities when at least some of the children are older.

Music

Each term (twelve weeks) has a choice between three composers. This way, if you use this book at all three levels, you won't be repeating the same composers each time. I recommend choosing a CD, MP3 collection, or even YouTube.com recordings, and listening to the composer each day. This could be before beginning formal work, while drawing or doing handicrafts, or during a meal.

Art

Twice a week, an art lesson using Barry Stebbing's art books is scheduled.

If you use *English Lessons Through Literature*, you already have picture study every other week. If you do not use ELTL, you can still use the scheduled picture studies by downloading the free art files from my online store.

Geography

Three activity books have been scheduled for geography: *Geography Through Art*, *Eat Your Way Around the World* (Ancient and Medieval years), and *Eat Your Way Through the USA* (Revolution and Modern years). These are added primarily for fun, but if you choose to do them, they'll also add another dimension to the learning about the geography and culture of other lands. The art book is scheduled weekly. The cooking books are scheduled occasionally.

Science

For those who prefer a more hands-on approach, the Great Science Adventures program is scheduled. I recommend the eBook versions for the ease in printing out the consumable portions.

In addition, two science experiments are scheduled each week. I must say that to me, science experiments are optional. They can be educational and fun, but that doesn't make them necessary. This is an area where I've seen a lot of guilt from homeschoolers over the years, the fact that they don't manage to make time for experiments. I say to do them when you can, skip them when you can't, and remember that no child ever failed in life because he didn't get to see baking soda and vinegar blow up a balloon.

Timeline/Book of Centuries

I've scheduled a timeline or Book of Centuries activity each week as a reminder for dialectic and rhetoric students to add people and events from the previous week's studies to a timeline.

Work in Progress

The spine for grammar and dialectic science, *Quark Chronicles*, is scheduled in Wayfarers, but the series is a work in progress. *Quark Chronicles* is an eight-book science adventure series which will be published in the order in which the books will appear in Wayfarers: Botany, Zoology, Anatomy, Astronomy, Geology, Weather, Chemistry, and Physics.

Wayfarers
Modern History

Legend for the Book Lists

[1]	Term 1
[2]	Term 2
[3]	Term 3
#	All terms
*	Scheduled for longer than 6 weeks
†	From a Christian perspective

Curricula and Other

ENGLISH/LANGUAGE ARTS	
GRAMMAR AND DIALECTIC	**RHETORIC**

Appropriate level of the following:
 	
English Lessons Through Literature
    OR Rod and Staff English
    OR your own grammar program
 	
Reading Lessons Through Literature
    OR Spelling Wisdom for dictation
    OR do the scheduled dictation from school reading
	Bulchevy's Book of English Verse by Arthur Quiller-Couch [www.gutenberg.org/ebooks/1304]
	
	LR: The Power in Your Hands by Sharon Watson
	
	LR: Essential Literary Terms by Sharon Hamilton
	
	UR: Writing Great Research Papers by Laurie Rozakis

MATH	

Appropriate level of the following:
 	
Math-U-See
    OR Miquon and/or Singapore Math
    OR Your own math program
	Math-U-See
	    OR Your own math program

ART

Choose the appropriate Barry Stebbing art program [www.howgreatthouart.com].

UD AND RHETORIC: FINE ART, HUMANITIES

How to Look at and Understand Great Art by Sharon Latchaw Hirsh [www.thegreatcourses.com]

DIALECTIC

Upper Dialectic, The Story of Science: # Einstein Adds a New Dimension by Joy Hakim 3, ˙ Science Matters by Robert Hazen [See note after this table.]	**Upper Dialectic, Logic:** # The Art of Argument 1, 2, * How to Read a Book by Mortimer J. Adler and Charles Van Doren 2, 3, * Economics in One Lesson by Henry Hazlitt

READ-ALOUDS

1, * The Hobbit by J.R.R. Tolkien
1, 2, * Charlotte's Web by E. B. White
2, * The Trumpet of the Swan by E. B. White
2, 3, * The Borrowers by Mary Norton
3, * The Neverending Story by Michael Ende

Joy Hakim's *The Story of Science* and Robert Hazen's *Science Matters* are scheduled across two Ꮤayꜰarers books. The first two books are scheduled in Ancient and Revolution while the second two books are scheduled in Medieval and Modern, making it a simple matter to start one year and finish the following year. Ideally, students will begin this progression with *Aristotle Leads the Way* in 6th or 7th grade and finish the last two books the following year in 7th or 8th grade.

In the same way, logic books are scheduled across two Ꮤayꜰarers books. Again, ideally, students will use *The Art of Argument* in 7th to 8th grade, then use *The Argument Builder* and *The Discovery of Deduction* the following year. However, the latter two books can be used even if the student hasn't already used *The Art of Argument*.

Geography Reading

GEOGRAPHY CURRICULA AND ACTIVITY BOOKS (OPTIONAL)

[#] 50 States and Where to Find Them by Kathy Jo DeVore
   Optional literature for 50 States: Minn of the Mississippi by Holling C. Holling
                              The Drinking Gourd by F. N. Monjo
                              The Tree in the Trail by Holling C. Holling
                              Seabird by Holling C. Holling
[1] Maps and Geography by Ken Jennings
[#] Eat Your Way Through the USA by Loree Pettit

GRAMMAR AND DIALECTIC

LIST A—WORLD FOCUS	LIST B—AMERICAN FOCUS
[1] Africa: Journey to Jo'burg by Beverly Naidoo	[1] Kentucky: Tadpole by Ruth White
[1] Africa: Chasing Cheetahs by Sy Montgomery	[1] Mississippi: Glory Be by Augusta Scattergood
[1] Russia: The Endless Steppe: Growing Up in Siberia by Esther Rudomin Hautzig	[1] Florida: Because of Win Dixie by Kate DiCamillo
[1] Russia: Favorite Russian Fairy Tales by Arthur Ransome	[1,2] Florida: Strawberry Girl by Lois Lenski
[1,2] India: Folk Tales and Fairy Stories From India by Sudhin N. Ghose	[2] Oklahoma: Blue Willow by Doris Gates
[2] Middle-East, Afghanistan: The Breadwinner by Deborah Ellis	[2] Oklahoma: Summer of the Monkeys by Wilson Rawls
[2] Pacific Island: Kensuke's Kingdom by Michael Morpurgo	[2,3] Texas: Holes by Louis Sachar
[2] England: Why the Whales Came by Michael Morpurgo	[3] Arizona: Brighty of the Grand Canyon by Marguerite Henry
[2] Czech Republic: Philomena by Kate Seredy	[3] Montana: Smoky the Cowhorse by Will James
[2,3] Hungary: The Singing Tree by Kate Seredy	[3] Nevada: Mustang: Wild Spirit of the West by Marguerite Henry
[3] United States: Moccasin Trail by Eloise Jarvis McGraw	
[3] Germany: An Elephant in the Garden by Michael Morpurgo	

RHETORIC

[#] Geography for Dummies by Charles A. Heatwole
[1,*] A Walk in the Woods: Rediscovering America on the Appalachian Trail by Bill Bryson
[1,2,*] On the Water: Discovering America in a Row Boat by Nathaniel Stone
[2,3,*] Notes from a Small Island by Bill Bryson
[3] A Walk Along the Ganges by Dennison Berwick
[3] Kilimanjaro Diaries by Eva Melusine Thieme

[See "Notes About Books"]

History and Literature Reading

HISTORY SPINES		
GRAMMAR	**DIALECTIC**	**RHETORIC**
Story of the World Vol. 4 by Susan Wise Bauer	Story of the World Vol. 4 by Susan Wise Bauer	See "Notes About Books." **World History:** Western Civilization by Jackson J. Spielvogel OR American History: America: A Narrative History (Brief Edition, Vol. 2) by George Brown Tindall OR [†] History Revealed by Diana Waring World Empires, World Missions, World Wars (last seven units)

HISTORY READING SELECTIONS		
GRAMMAR		**UPPER GRAMMAR**
CORE READING 1	**CORE READING 2**	**CORE READING 3**
World History Focus:	**American History Focus:**	[1,ʼ] The Story of Eli Whitney by Jean Lee Latham
[1] Our Sunburnt Country by Arthur Baillie	[1] Fifty Cents and a Dream: Young Booker T. Washington by Jabari Asim	[1] Soft Rain by Cornelia Cornelissen
[1] (YWWT) You Wouldn't Want to Meet a Body Snatcher! by Fiona MacDonald	[1] Sarah, Plain and Tall by Patricia MacLachlan	[1,2] Who Was Harriet Tubman? by Yona Zeldis McDonough
[1] (YWWT) You Wouldn't Want to Be a Victorian Mill Worker! by John Malam	[1] Elizabeth Leads the Way: Elizabeth Cady Stanton and the Right to Vote by Tanya Lee Stone	[2] Shades of Gray by Carolyn Reeder
[1] (YWWT) You Wouldn't Want to Be an 18th-Century British Convict! by Meredith Costain	[1] The Taxing Case of the Cows: A True Story About Suffrage by Pegi Deitz Shea	[2] Blizzard by Jim Murphy
[2] China, the Culture by Bobbie Kalman	[1] (YWWT) You Wouldn't Want to Live in a Wild West Town! by Peter Hicks	[2,3] Albert Einstein and Relativity for Kids by Jerome Pohlen
[1,2] World War I for Kids by R. Kent Rasmussen	[1] Who Was Sitting Bull? by Stephanie Spinner	[3] Candy Bomber by Michael O. Tunnell
[2] (YWWT) You Wouldn't Want to Be a Suffragist!: by Fiona MacDonald	[1] (YWWT) You Wouldn't Want to Work on the Railroad! by Ian Graham	[3] Who Was Gandhi? by Dana Meachen Rau
[2] Franklin and Winston: A Christmas That Changed the World by Douglas Wood	[1,2] The Story of Thomas Alva Edison by Margaret Cousins	[3] Journey to Jo'burg by Beverley Naidoo

[2] Always Remember Me: How One Family Survived World War II by Marisabina Russo [2] Mercedes and the Chocolate Pilot by Margot Theis Raven [2] Kaspar the Titanic Cat by Michael Morpurgo [2,3] What Was the Hindenburg? by Janet Pascal [3] Burying the Sun by Gloria Whelan [3] Who Was Nelson Mandela? by Meg Belviso [3] (MTH) Magic Tree House Fact Tracker: Heroes for All Times by Mary Pope Osborne [Our Sunburnt Country PDF is available at http://www.currclick.com/product/23683/AustraliaAn-Illustrated-History-Book]	[2] The Wright Brothers by Quentin Reynolds [2] World War I for Kids by R. Kent Rasmussen [2,3] World War II for Kids [3] Grandfather Gandhi by Arun Gandhi [3] Who Was Martin Luther King, Jr.? by Bonnie Bader [3] Neil Armstrong: Young Pilot by Montrew Dunham [3] You Wouldn't Want to Be on Apollo 13! by Ian Graham

DIALECTIC

CORE READING 1	CORE READING 2
World History Focus: [1,*] Optional: Fahrenheit 451 by Ray Bradbury [2,*] Optional: Choice of juvenile books by Robert A. Heinlein (See "Notes About Books") [1,*] The Scarlet Pimpernel by Baroness Orczy [1,2] The War to End All Wars: World War I by Russell Freedman [2] The Good Fight by Stephen E. Ambrose [2] WWII Bio, Hitler OR Stalin by Albert Marrin [2,3,*] The Story of the Trapp Family Singers by Maria Augusta Trapp [3] Hiroshima by John Hershey [3,*] Red Scarf Girl: A Memoir of the Cultural Revolution by Ji-li Jiang	**American History Focus:** [1,*] Optional: Fahrenheit 451 by Ray Bradbury [2,*] Optional: Choice of juvenile books by Robert A. Heinlein (See "Notes About Books") [1] Gettysburg by MacKinlay Kantor [1] Treasure Island by Robert Louis Stevenson [1,2] The Wright Brothers by Quentin Reynolds [2] The Yanks are Coming by Albert Marrin [2] The Good Fight by Stephen E. Ambrose [2] When Hitler Stole Pink Rabbit by Judith Kerr [2] America and Vietnam by Albert Marrin [2,3,*] Where the Red Fern Grows by Wilson Rawls [3,*] Warriors Don't Cry by Melba Pattillo Beals

RHETORIC

CORE READING 1	CORE READING 2
World History Focus:	**American History Focus:**
[#] LR: The Philosophy Book by William Buckingham	[#] LR: The Philosophy Book by William Buckingham
[1,2,·,†] UR: Good Ideas from Questionable Christians and Outright Pagans by Steve Wilkens	[1,2,·,†] UR: Good Ideas from Questionable Christians and Outright Pagans by Steve Wilkens
[3,·] UR: Think: A Compelling Introduction to Philosophy by Simon Blackburn	[3,·] UR: Think: A Compelling Introduction to Philosophy by Simon Blackburn
[#] Optional: Les Miserables by Victor Hugo [See "Notes About Books"]	[#] Optional: Les Miserables by Victor Hugo [See "Notes About Books"]
[1,2,·] The Tenant of Wildfell Hall by Ann Brontë	[1] The Life and Times of Frederick Douglas by Frederick Douglas
[2,·] Tale of Two Cities by Charles Dickens	[1,·] The Adventures of Huckleberry Finn by Mark Twain
[2] Siddhartha by Hermann Hesse	[1,2,·] Red Badge of Courage by Stephen Crane
[2,3] Brave New World by Aldous Huxley	[2] Up from Slavery by Booker T. Washington
[3,·] Nineteen Eighty-Four by George Orwell	[2] The Great Gatsby by F. Scott Fitzgerald
[3] Animal Farm by George Orwell	[2] Of Mice and Men by John Steinbeck
[2,3,·] Optional: A Midsummer Night's Dream by William Shakespeare	[2,3] To Kill a Mockingbird by Harper Lee
	[3] Strength to Love OR A Gift of Love by Martin Luther King, Jr. [See "Notes About Books"]
	[3] Ender's Game by Orson Scott Card
	[2,3,·] Optional: A Midsummer Night's Dream by William Shakespeare

Bible Reading

BIBLE AND THEOLOGY RESOURCES		
GRAMMAR	**DIALECTIC**	**RHETORIC**

LG: The Beginner's Bible
UG: Egermeier's Bible Story Book
	LD: Hurlbut's Story of the Bible
	UD: Golden Children's Bible
	UD: Pilgrim's Progress
	    by John Bunyan
	    Simply Christian by N. T. Wright
		R: The Great Divorce by C. S. Lewis
		LR: The Best Things in Life AND
		    The Unaborted Socrates
		    by Peter Kreeft
		LR: Cross Purposes by Mark Miller
		LR: Cold-Case Christianity
		    by J. Warner Wallace
		UR: Pagan Christianity by Frank Viola
		UR: Letters to a Diminished Church
		    by Dorothy Sayers
		UR: The Orthodox Way by Kallistos Ware
		UR: Are Women Human?
		    by Dorothy L. Sayers

Old Story New by Marty Machowski		
Bible version of your choice.		

Christian Church History

COMPARATIVE RELIGIONS RESOURCES
RHETORIC
CORE READING
#,˙ The 100 Most Important Events in Christian History by A. Kenneth Curtis, J. Stephen Lang, Randy Petersen
#,˙ Church History in Plain Language by Bruce Shelley
² The Ecclesiastical History of the English Nation by Venerable Bede (Aeterna Press)
³ The "Book of Common Prayer": A Biography by Alan Jacobs
³ The Great Courses: Science and Religion

Science Reading

SCIENCE SPINES	
GRAMMAR AND DIALECTIC	**RHETORIC**
The Quark Chronicles: Chemistry AND The Quark Chronicles: Physics by Ernest DeVore The Quark Chronicles is currently being written. It is being scheduled here in advance rather than later producing an "updated" version of Wayfarers. If it is not available when you begin, choose from the Core Reading selections.	Science for High School Physics (SHSPhys) by Bridget Ardoin OR The Manga Guide to Physics by Hideo Nitta The Manga Guide to Relativity by Hideo Nitta Physics I for Dummies by Steven Holzner
Optional experiment and activity books: [1, 2, *] Janice VanCleave's 201 Awesome, Magical, Bizarre, & Incredible Experiments by Janice VanCleave Great Science Adventures: [1, *] The World of Tools and Technology (Lessons 12-24) [1, 2, *] Discovering Atoms, Molecules, and Matter [3, *] The World of Light and Sound [eBook versions, great for printing the consumable parts, are available at www.commonsensepress.com/mm5/merchant.mvc]	**Physics Lab Book, See Note:** [†] Experiences in Physics by Mark Julicher [www.homeschoolsciencepress.com]
SCIENCE READING SELECTIONS	
GRAMMAR	

CORE READING 1	**CORE READING 2**

[1, 2, *] RS4K Focus on Elementary Chemistry
    by Rebecca Keller
[2] Thomas Edison for Kids by Laurie Carlson
[2, 3, *] RS4K Focus on Elementary Physics
    by Rebecca Keller
[3] Isaac Newton and Physics for Kids
	[1, *] The Elements and Carbon Chemistry
	    by Ellen J. McHenry
	[1, 2, *] Fizz, Bubble, and Flash by Brandolini Anita
	[2] Zap!: Wile E. Coyote Experiments with Energy
	    by Suzanne Slade
	[2] Splat!: Wile E. Coyote Experiments with States of
	    Matter by Suzanne Slade
	[2] Smash!: Wile E. Coyote Experiments with Simple
	    Machines by Mark Weakland
	[3] Thud!: Wile E. Coyote Experiments with Forces and
	    Motion by Mark Weakland
	[3] Insiders Inventions by Glenn Murphy
	[3] Insiders Flight by Von Hardesty

DIALECTIC	
CORE READING 1	CORE READING 2

[1,2,·] The Mystery of the Periodic Table
    by Benjamin Wiker
[1,2,·] The Elements by Theodore Gray
[2] Focus on Middle School Chemistry by Rebecca Keller
[2,3] Focus on Middle School Physics by Rebecca Keller
[3] The Time and Space of Uncle Albert
    by Russell Stannard
[3] Black Holes and Uncle Albert by Russell Stannard
[3] Uncle Albert and the Quantum Quest
    by Russell Stannard
	[1,2,·] The Mystery of the Periodic Table
	    by Benjamin Wiker
	[1,·,†] Exploring the World of Chemistry
	    by John Hudson Tiner
	[1] The Elements and by Ellen J. McHenry
	[1,2] Carbon Chemistry by Ellen J. McHenry
	[2,3,·,†] Exploring the World of Physics
	    by John Hudson Tiner
	Secrets of the Universe:
	[3] Objects in Motion by Paul Fleisher
	[3] Liquids and Gases by Paul Fleisher
	[3] Matter and Energy by Paul Fleisher
	[3] Waves by Paul Fleisher
	[3] Relativity and Quantum Mechanics by Paul Fleisher

RHETORIC	
[1,·] For the Love of Physics by Walter Lewin [1,2] How to Teach Quantum Physics to Your Dog by Chad Orzel [2] Quantum Physics for Poets by Leon M. Lederman [2,3,·] How to Teach Relativity to Your Dog by Chad Orzel [3,·] The Elegant Universe by Brian Greene	

OPTIONAL SCIENCE BOOKS, GRAMMAR & DIALECTIC

[1] Magic School Bus and the Science Fair Expedition by Joanna Cole

[1] Basher Science: The Periodic Table

[1] States of Matter by Lynnette Brent

[1] The Solid Truth about States of Matter with Max Axiom, Super Scientist by Agnieszka Biskup

[1] Atoms and Molecules by Molly Aloian

[1] Lessons in Science Safety with Max Axiom, Super Scientist by Donald B. Lemke

[1] Chemical Reactions by Carol Baldwin

[1] The Dynamic World of Chemical Reactions with Max Axiom by Agnieszka Biskup

[1] Acids & Bases by Carol Baldwin

[1] Mixtures, Compounds & Solutions by Carol Baldwin

[1] Plastics and Polymers Science Fair Projects by Madeline Goodstein

[1] Vitamins and Minerals by Stephanie Watson

[1] Stories of the Discovery of Vitamins by Kun Yan

[1] Gases and Their Properties by Reagan Miller and Tom Jackson

[1] Metals by Carol Baldwin

[1] Chemical Changes by Lynnette Brent

[2,'] Simon Bloom, Gravity Keeper by Michael Reisman

[2] Physics: Why Matter Matters! by Dan Green and Simon Basher

[2] D: Physics: Investigate the Forces of Nature by Jane P. Gardner

[2] G: Forces Make Things Move by Kimberly Brubaker Bradley

[*Simon Bloom, Gravity Keeper* is fiction. It's scheduled for 2-3 chapters per week every week of the second semester for those who would like to include it.]

[2] A Crash Course in Forces and Motion with Max Axiom by Emily Sohn

[2] D: Kinetic Energy by Don Nardo

[2] Forces and Motion by Casey Rand

[2] Transforming! Chemical Energy by Emma Carlson Berne

[2] G: Magic School Bus and the Electric Field Trip by Joanna Cole

[2] G: Charged Up by Jacqui Bailey

[2] The Shocking World of Electricity with Max Axiom, by Liam O'Donnell

[2] Eyewitness Electricity

[3] The Powerful World of Energy with Max Axiom by Agnieszka Biskup

[3] The Attractive Story of Magnetism with Max Axiom, by Andrea Gianopoulos

[3] Magnetism and Electromagnets by Eve Hartman

[3] The Illuminating World of Light with Max Axiom by Emily Sohn

[3] Adventures in Sound with Max Axiom by Emily Sohn

[3] G: Up, Down, All Around by Jacqui Bailey

[3] D: Gravity, and How It Works by Peter Jedicke

[3] Insiders Flight by Von Hardesty

[3] G: How Do You Lift a Lion? by Robert E. Wells

[3] D: Simple Machines: Forces in Action by Buffy Silverman

[3] Insiders Inventions by Glenn Murphy

[3] Albert Einstein by Kathleen Krull

[3] G: Magic School Bus and the Science Fair Expedition by Joanna Cole

Notes About Books

Please feel free to skip any book on these lists. Other than the Bible, I've found no single book which is necessary for the education of Christian children. If you choose to skip a book, you can substitute another, or simply begin following the schedule when that book is complete. Below is brief commentary about the books on this list most likely to garner questions regarding the content.

LG, History Spines:
Frankly, I don't think there's a history spine out there gentle enough to cover more modern history with first and second graders. Generally speaking, I only use a spine with first and second graders when we're doing Ancient or Medieval History. We will be in Modern History the year my daughter begins first grade, and I will skip a history spine and just do the fun modern picture books, or I will do a Pathways reading list instead.

Grammar, Real Science 4 Kids:
Wayfarers has the Real Science for Kids Focus on Elementary Chemistry and Physics books scheduled for reading, but the experiments are not scheduled.

Grammar, Fizz, Bubble, and Flash:
This book has a lot of experiments in it. We find the text fun and informative even when we don't do the activity.

Dialectic, Real Science 4 Kids:
Wayfarers has Real Science 4 Kids Focus on Middle School Chemistry scheduled for part of the dialectic science reading. The experiments are scheduled as well, though of course they are completely optional. Materials for the experiments are NOT listed in Signposts, though there is a note to check the RS4K Teacher's Manual.

Dialectic, Secrets of the Universe:
The five volumes in the Secrets of the Universe collection were originally published as one volume entitled *Secrets of the Universe*. If you have or can find a used copy of it, you can use it instead. The chapters are in a different order, but to the best of my knowledge, this is the only difference.

Chapter 1 from the original book is the Introduction in each of the new books. On the schedule, the first day's reading is *Objects in Motion*, Intro. - Ch. 1. If you have *Secrets of the Universe*, you would instead read Ch. 1 - 2.

Dialectic, Heinlein Juvenile:
A Heinlein Juvenile is scheduled for 23 days in this volume of Wayfarers, but I've left the choice of books up to you. His juvenile books are numbered on Amazon, but this only refers to the order of publication. They are not actually connected to one another, so they can be read in any order.

The wonderful thing about Heinlein is that he covered serious subjects in entertaining stories—his stories are always deeper than a glance at a plot synopsis might indicate. If you are not familiar with Heinlein's juvenile books, here's a bit of information about a few of them to help you decide. *Farmer in the Sky* is about family members who become colonists on another planet and the problems that they encounter, both as colonists and as spacefarers. *Citizen of the Galaxy* deals with ideas concerning slavery and freedom. *Tunnel in the Sky* follows a group of teenagers trapped on another planet and explores how they choose to govern themselves. *Time for the Stars* deals with Einstein's theory of relativity and what it means for space travel. And one of my personal favorites, *Red Planet*, has a revolutionary flair to it, and it is the most action-packed of the books mentioned here.

Another of my personal favorites, *Have Spacesuit, Will Travel*, is scheduled in another volume of 𝔚ayfarers.

UD, Pilgrim's Progress: The original is numbered throughout, and
I scheduled according to these numbers, calling each numbered section a "part." I also scheduled a version written in modern English which includes the Bible verses instead of just referencing them. For the modern version, search for ASIN: B00Q8NFZY4.

UD and Rhetoric, Fine Arts: How to Look at and Understand
Great Art by Sharon Latchaw Hirsh is scheduled this year as an optional fine art credit. The lecture series from The Great Courses are quite expensive. However, every course goes on sale at least once a year, so I always buy a series the year before I need it.

I use this in conjunction with DK's massive book, *Art: Over 2,500 Works from Cave to Contemporary* by Andrew Graham-Dixon, though other art books, such as ones from the library, would work just as well. Each week, the student should watch one lecture, find a piece of art, and write about it. It is important to have a large selection of art from which to choose to make sure the student can find a piece of art which he can write about after seeing the lecture. For example, one lecture is on point of view, so the student would discuss the point of view in the artwork. Another lecture is on line, and the student should discuss how line is used in the artwork. I've scheduled the video on Day 2 and the writing on Day 4, though they could be done on the same day if desired.

Rhetoric, History Spines: The purpose of a history spine is to
provide an overview of the historical time period and context for the literature reading. You don't have to spend big money to accomplish this goal. I'm scheduling more expensive options because they offer a more seamless reading of history, and used books are often available. However, keep in mind that the textbooks are scheduled for only 10-20 pages per week, and you should feel free to substitute with other history books. *The Complete Idiot's Guides* and the *For Dummies* series both have inexpensive history titles including *World History*, *European History*, and *American History*.

The primary two textbooks scheduled are Spielvogel's *Western Civilization* for World History and *America: A Narrative History* for American History. These are both scheduled across the Ⓦayfarers Revolution and Modern books. You don't need to worry about any particular edition, so the least expensive one is fine.

Ⓦayfarers schedules the Brief Edition of *America: A Narrative History*, which has fewer chapters. It can be purchased in either a one-volume complete book or in two separate volumes. The Brief Edition has 34 chapters; Chapters 1-17 are scheduled in Revolution while Chapters 18-34 are scheduled in Modern.

Ⓦayfarers schedules Chapters 12-30 of Spielvogel's *Western Civilization*. I actually find Spielvogel's an interesting read, and it contains many quotes from primary sources. Spielvogel's can be purchased as either a one-volume complete book or in separate volumes; only the second volume is necessary. Chapters 12-21 are scheduled in Revolution while Chapters 22-30 are scheduled in Modern. Volume 2 includes Chapters 13-30, so if you find a good copy of it, simply skip the first few readings until the schedule gets to chapter 13.

Rhetoric, Science Spines:
My oldest son has consistently liked the For Dummies science books better than choices such as the Self-Teaching Guides, and the For Dummies books have workbooks to go along with the study. Feel free to substitute if desired. CK12.org has free high school level science textbooks for download.

I've also scheduled *Introductory Physics*, a living textbook by John Mays. One method of working through this book is to read a chapter and then work on the exercises while reading the next chapter. The last few weeks do not have assigned readings, which will give the student time to complete the exercises for the last chapter.

Introductory Physics is available in two different versions, both a Christian and a secular edition. The Christian edition is available at www.novarescienceandmath.com while the secular version is available at www.centripetalpress.com. Please be aware that in this case, "Christian" does not mean "Young Earth Creationist." Novare accepts the mainstream scientific opinion that the earth is old. You can read my review of it here: http://barefootmeandering.com/site/reviews/review-novare-science-and-math/

While the main science spine in this volume of Ⓦayfarers is *Physics I for Dummies* or *Introductory Physics*, I also have two other books scheduled: *The Manga Guide to Physics* and *The Manga Guide to Relativity*. Whether or not you should use it depends largely on your student. My oldest son says this type of cartoon introduction is not his cuppa, while my second son likes the idea of reading these books along with the more serious spine.

Rhetoric, Science Core Reading:
At the end of each book, there's a week (two science days) off which can be used as a catch-up week before the new book begins.

Rhetoric Science Lab:
A physics lab is on the schedule every third week (on Day 4), which will give you a total of twelve labs throughout the

year. Choose the labs that you'd prefer to do based on your own goals and the equipment to which you have access.

I only have one option for a physics lab manual. *Experiences in Physics* is sold by Homeschool Science Press, a family-and-homeschooler-owned company. The owners are both Christian and Creationist, but their high school lab manuals do not contain religious references except for Scripture quotes in the introduction.

Rhetoric, Les Miserables:
Les Miserables is scheduled as an option, three times per week, throughout the entire school year. I recommend the Signet Classics version. I find it much more readable than the older translations which I've seen. In addition, the paperback is unabridged, and the Kindle version has real page numbers, important since I scheduled 14 pages per day. If you choose a different edition, take the total number of pages and divide by 108. That will give you the total number of pages which need to be read on each day that it's scheduled.

Rhetoric, Martin Luther King, Jr.:
Strength to Love and *A Gift of Love* are almost identical. *A Gift of Love* is the one available for Kindle and is therefore the one our household has. One sermon, No. 10, is missing from *A Gift of Love*, and there are two additional sermons, No. 15 and 16, which are not in *Strength to Love*. The missing sermon is "How Should a Christian View Communism," which is a very interesting read. You can download a free PDF of it at www.thekinglegacy.org/giftoflove/.

Rhetoric, Geography Literature:
For rhetoric students, we schedule books that were written with adults in mind, not children. Because of this, vulgar language is frequently a problem. Our culture as a whole has embraced vulgar language to the point where it appears in books on topics that would have been completely safe even fifty years ago.

Generally speaking, I will choose a book which contains some vulgar language over a book which looks less interesting with no vulgar language. Please consider each selection carefully to make sure it is appropriate for your household.

P/K & LG Activity Supplies:

Day 1:
- Crayon sharpener
- Shavings from crayons
- Wax paper
- Paper towels
- Iron
- Construction paper
- Hole punch
- String

See examples at these sites:

www.littlebirdiesecrets.blogspot.com/2011/02/make-crayon-stained-glass-hearts-with.html

www.ramblingsfromutopia.com/2011/01/making-stained-glass-crayon-window.html

www.marthastewart.com/264114/crayon-stained-glass-heart-cards

Day 3:
- Math blocks; these can be cuisenaire rods, MUS blocks, or base-ten blocks. You can also print out pages with cuisenaire pictures such as the ones in this book: www.nurturedbylove.ca/resources/cuisenairebook.pdf

Day 4:
- Clean, empty containers with lids. Be careful of choking hazard lids! I keep a set of empty plastic spice containers on hand.

Science Experiment Supplies:

- 2 books
- 24-inch string
- Ruler
- 10 round marking pens

- Scissors
- 8-ounce paper cup
- Ruler with a center groove
- Pencil
- Marble
- Book

Eat Your Way Through the USA Supplies:

Check ingredients for dishes from Washington.

Dialectic, Real Science 4 Kids:

Experiment 1 on Day 4.

Week 25

	GRAMMAR	DIALECTIC	RHETORIC
BIBLE	Choose one of the following plans: ✟ PLAN 1: Journey Through the Bible, pp. 274-275 ✟ PLAN 2: Journey Through the Bible, pp. 256-259		
LANGUAGE ARTS	Choose appropriate level of one of the following: ❡ English Lessons Through Literature, Lesson 73 Reading Lessons Through Literature, phonogram review ❡ Rod and Staff English, Lesson 85 Copywork/Commonplace Book ❡ Your own grammar program		❡ LR: The Power in Your Hands, 1 lesson ❡ UR: WGRP, taking notes. (8 days) ❡ LR: Rod and Staff 10, L. 81
MATH	Choose appropriate level of one of the following: ✎ Math-U-See, Video and page A ✎ Miquon/Singapore Math ✎ Your own math program		✎ Math-U-See, Video and page A ✎ Your own math program
GEOGRAPHY	🌐 50 States Reading, Washington 🌐 Reading, choose one of the following: A. Hungary: The Singing Tree, 1/2 of Ch. 1 B. Texas: Holes, Ch. 43-44		🌐 Notes from a Small Island, Ch. 22
HISTORY	Choose one spine, one or more core reading selections, and optional reading as desired. ♟ Spine: SOTW, Ch. 29.1 ♟ Core reading: 1. What Was the Hindenburg, Ch. 8 2. WWII for Kids, Ch. 4 3. Albert Einstein for Kids, Ch. 3	♟ Spine: SOTW, Ch. 29.1 ♟ Core reading: 1. Trapp Family Singers, Ch. 11 2. Where the Red Fern Grows, Ch. 3	♟ Spine: Western Civ, 1/4 of Ch. 27 ♟ Core reading: 1 & 2. Les Miserables, 14 pages 1. Brave New World, Ch. 5-6 2. To Kill a Mockingbird, Ch. 21-22

Day 1

GRAMMAR	DIALECTIC	RHETORIC	
♪♪ Term 3 Composer: Choose between Shostakovich, Britten, Leon Kirchner ⧖ Timeline/Book of Centuries			ACTIVITIES
☞ Oral or written narration; LG students can draw a picture from the reading and tell about the picture. Suggested subject: history.		☞ Written narration for history or geography.	NARRATION
✠ Old Story New, Week 61 ℘ UD: Economics in One Lesson, Ch. 9		✠ LR: Cold-Case, Ch. 10 (1/2) ✠ Are Women Human? 1/2 of first essay	OTHER
📚 Literature: 1: Pinocchio, Ch. 31-32 2: Alice's Adventures in Wonderland, Ch. 7 3: The Secret Garden, Ch. 21 4: Heidi, Ch. 6	📚 Literature: 5: Little Women, Ch. 22 6: The Patchwork Girl of Oz, Ch. 19 7: The Tin Woodman of Oz, Ch. 20 8: 20,000 Leagues, Ch. 25	📚 Book of English Verse, No. 795-797 ✠ Church History: Church History in Plain Language, Ch. 32 ✠ 100 Events, A.D. 1811	LITERATURE
PRESCHOOL AND LOWER GRAMMAR			
✏ Pathways: Path 1, Day 1 A. Kindergarten Gems B. 50 Famous Stories C. 20th—"The Elves in the Shelves" D. Random House Poetry, p. 159			PATHWAYS
✏ Crayon stained-glass Use a crayon sharpener to create crayon shavings. These can all be from the same color family, or you can mix it up. Fold a long piece of wax paper in half, then spread the shavings over one-half of the wax paper, keeping the shavings away from the edges. Too many shavings will make the final product too opaque, and it's also more likely to create a big mess in the next step. Fold the edges of the was paper over. Place sheets of newspaper or paper towels underneath and over the wax paper, then iron it to melt the crayon shavings. Cut out shapes from your "stained-glass" to hang in the window. You can also sandwich between pieces of construction paper with cut-outs.			ACTIVITY

Week 25

	GRAMMAR	DIALECTIC	RHETORIC
BIBLE	Choose one of the following plans: ✠ PLAN 1: Journey Through the Bible, pp. 276-277 ✠ PLAN 2: Journey Through the Bible, pp. 260-263		
	✠ LG: TBB: A Hole in the Roof ✠ UG: Egermeier's, 2 stories	✠ LD: Hurlbut's, 1 story ✠ UD: Golden's, 3 stories	
LANGUAGE ARTS	Choose appropriate level of one of the following: ❡ Reading Lessons Through Literature, next list and story ❡ Prepared dictation from ELTL, Spelling Wisdom, or today's reading ❡ Your own grammar program		❡ UR: WGRP, outline. (2 days)
MATH	Choose appropriate level of one of the following: ✎ Math-U-See, page B ✎ Miquon/Singapore Math ✎ Your own math program		✎ Math-U-See, page B ✎ Your own math program
GEOGRAPHY	🌎 Reading, choose one of the following: A. Hungary: The Singing Tree, 1/2 of Ch. 1 B. Texas: Holes, Ch. 45-46		🌎 Geography for Dummies, 1/2 of Ch. 13
SCIENCE	Choose one spine, one or more core reading selections, and optional reading as desired.		
	⚛ Core reading: 1. RS4K Physics, Ch. 5.5-6.1 2. Thud, Ch. 1 ⚛ Spine: Quark Chronicles: Physics, Ch. 7	⚛ Core reading: 1. RS4K Physics, Ch. 7 2. Exploring the World of Physics, Ch. 13	⚛ Spine: SHSPhys, Week 6 Physics for Dummies, 1/2 of Ch. 13 Intro. Physics, pp. 233-237 ⚛ Core reading: How to Teach Relativity to Your Dog, Ch. 8

Day 2

GRAMMAR	DIALECTIC	RHETORIC	
♫ Term 3 Composer: Choose between Shostakovich, Britten, Leon Kirchner 🎨 Art Lesson: Choose appropriate level of one of the following:			ACTIVITIES
🎨 I Can Do All Things 🎨 Lamb's Book of Art I	🎨 Lamb's Book of Art II 🎨 Feed My Sheep	🎨 How Great Thou ART I or II 🎨 Book of Many Colors	
⚛ GSA The World of Light and Sound, Lesson 1		🎨 Great Art, Lecture 25	
☞ Oral or written narration; LG students can draw a picture from the reading and tell about the picture. Suggested subject: Bible.		☞ Oral or written narration for science or Bible.	NARRATION
✟ Old Story New, Week 61			OTHER
	✑ UD: The Art of Argument, Review 4 ✑ UD: Einstein Adds a New Dimension, Ch. 49	✑ UR: Classical English Rhetoric, 1/4 Ch. 13	
📚 Suggested read-aloud: The Borrowers, Ch. 11			LITERATURE
PRESCHOOL AND LOWER GRAMMAR			
✏ Pathways: Path 2 A. Little Wanderers, Ch. 25 B. Burgess Seashore Book, Ch. 27 C. Paddington Helps Out, Ch. 4 D. Random House Poetry, p. 160			PATHWAYS
🎨 Art Lesson: Choose one of the following Barry Stebbing art books for you little one to do art like the big kids: Art and the Bible for Children, Baby Lamb's Book of Art, Joseph the Canada Goose, or Little Annie's Art Book.			ACTIVITY

Week 25

	Grammar	Dialectic	Rhetoric
Bible	Choose one of the following plans: ✠ PLAN 1: Journey Through the Bible, pp. 278-279 ✠ PLAN 2: What the Bible Is All About, John		

Language Arts	Choose appropriate level of one of the following:
	
	❡ English Lessons Through Literature, Lesson 74
	    Reading Lessons Through Literature, phonogram review
	
	❡ Rod and Staff English, Lesson 86
	    Copywork/Commonplace Book
	
	❡ Your own grammar program
			❡ Essential Literary Terms, 3-4 pages
			
			❡ LR: The Power in Your Hands, 1 lesson
			
			❡ UR: WGRP, outline. (2 days)
			
			❡ LR: Rod and Staff 10, L. 82

Math	Choose appropriate level of one of the following: ✎ Math-U-See, page C ✎ Miquon/Singapore Math ✎ Your own math program		✎ Math-U-See, page C ✎ Your own math program

Geography	🌐 50 States Mapping, Washington
	
	🌐 Reading, choose one of the following:
	    A. Hungary: The Singing Tree, 1/2 of Ch. 2
	    B. Texas: Holes, Ch. 47-48
			🌐 Notes from a Small Island, Ch. 23

History	Choose one spine, one or more core reading selections, and optional reading as desired.
	
	♟ Spine: SOTW, Ch. 29.2
	
	♟ Core reading:
	    1. What Was the Hindenburg, Ch. 9
	    2. WWII for Kids, Ch. 5
	    3. Albert Einstein for Kids, Ch. 4
		♟ Spine: SOTW, Ch. 29.1
		
		♟ Core reading:
		    1. Trapp Family Singers, Ch. 12
		    2. Where the Red Fern Grows, Ch. 4
			♟ Spine:
			    America, 1/4 of Ch. 30
			
			♟ Core reading:
			    1 & 2. Les Miserables, 14 pages
			    1 & 2. Midsummer Night's Dream, 1 Scene
			    1. Brave New World, Ch. 7-8
			    2. To Kill a Mockingbird, Ch. 23-24

Day 3

	Grammar	Dialectic	Rhetoric	
♫ Term 3 Composer: Choose between Shostakovich, Britten, Leon Kirchner				ACTIVITIES
↩ Oral or written narration; could be a group project. Make a list of five questions that could be used as a quiz for your book.				NARRATION
✣ Old Story New, Week 61 ✣ UD: Simply Christian, Ch. 5		✣ LR: Cold-Case, Ch. 11 (1/2) ✣ Are Women Human? 1/2 of first essay		OTHER
📖 Literature: 1: Pinocchio, Ch. 33-34 2: Alice's Adventures in Wonderland, Ch. 8 3: The Secret Garden, Ch. 22 4: Heidi, Ch. 7	📖 Literature: 5: Little Women, Ch. 23-24 6: The Patchwork Girl of Oz, Ch. 20 7: The Tin Woodman of Oz, Ch. 21 8: 20,000 Leagues, Ch. 26		📖 Book of English Verse, No. 798-800 ✣ Church History: Church History in Plain Language, Ch. 33 ✣ 100 Events, A.D. 1812	LITERATURE

PRESCHOOL AND LOWER GRAMMAR	
✎ Pathways: Path 1, Day 2 A. Kindergarten Gems B. Among the Meadow People C. The Hundred Dresses, Ch. 5 D. Random House Poetry, p. 161	PATHWAYS
✎ Play with math blocks Play with cuisenaire rods or MUS blocks. Have your little one make pictures with blocks. You can demonstrate by making a house or a face, or use a print out such as the one mentioned in Signposts.	ACTIVITY

Week 25

	GRAMMAR	DIALECTIC	RHETORIC
BIBLE	Choose one of the following plans: ✠ PLAN 1: Journey Through the Bible, pp. 280-281 ✠ PLAN 2: The Story, Ch. 25		
	✠ LG: TBB: Jesus Calms the Storm; Two Miracles ✠ UG: Egermeier's, 2 stories	✠ LD: Hurlbut's, 1 story ✠ UD: Golden's, 3 stories	
LANGUAGE ARTS	Choose appropriate level of one of the following: ❡ Reading Lessons Through Literature, next list and story ❡ Prepared dictation from ELTL, Spelling Wisdom, or today's reading ❡ Your own grammar program		❡ UR: WGRP, first draft. (10 days)
MATH	Choose appropriate level of one of the following: ✎ Math-U-See, page D ✎ Miquon/Singapore Math ✎ Your own math program		✎ Math-U-See, page D ✎ Your own math program
GEOGRAPHY	🌎 Reading, choose one of the following: A. Hungary: The Singing Tree, 1/2 of Ch. 2 B. Texas: Holes, Ch. 49-50		
SCIENCE	Choose one spine, one or more core reading selections, and optional reading as desired.		
	⚛ Core reading: 1. RS4K Physics, Ch. 6.2-6.3 2. Thud, Ch. 2	⚛ Core reading: 1. RS4K Physics, Ch. 7 Experiment 1. Time and Space of Uncle Albert, Ch. 7 2. Exploring the World of Physics, Ch. 14	⚛ Spine: SHSPhys, Week 6 Manga Relativity, pp. 42-52 Intro. Physics, pp. 238-242 (to example) ⚛ Core reading: How to Teach Relativity to Your Dog, Ch. 9
	⚛ Optional extra reading, topic: Transferring Electrical Energy, Heat Simon Bloom, Ch. 15-16 The Powerful World of Energy with Max Axiom by Agnieszka Biskup		

Day 4

	GRAMMAR	DIALECTIC	RHETORIC	
♪♪ Term 3 Composer: Choose between Shostakovich, Britten, Leon Kirchner				ACTIVITIES
⚛ GSA *The World of Light and Sound*, Lesson 2 ⚛ *201 Awesome Experiments*, 173-174			🎨 Great Art Writing	
☞ Oral or written narration; LG students can draw a picture from the reading and tell about the picture. Suggested subject: science.			☞ Written narration for science or Bible.	NARRATION
✠ *Old Story New*, Week 61				
		ප UD: *The Art of Argument:* Write a narration on fallacies of presupposition ප UD: *Science Matters,* pp. 3-15	ප UR: *Classical English Rhetoric,* 1/4 Ch. 13	OTHER
📚 Suggested read-aloud: *The Borrowers*, Ch. 12				LITERATURE

PRESCHOOL AND LOWER GRAMMAR	
✏ Pathways: Path 3 A. *Burgess Flower Book*, Ch. 29 B. *TumTum and Nutmeg*, Ch. 12 C. *Henry Huggins*, Ch. 1 D. *Random House Poetry*, p. 162	PATHWAYS
✏ Lid game Take some empty spice containers and let your toddler play with taking the lids off and putting them back on again.	ACTIVITY

Week 25

	GRAMMAR	DIALECTIC	RHETORIC
BIBLE	Choose one of the following plans: ✠ PLAN 1: Journey Through the Bible, pp. 282-283 ✠ PLAN 2: Journey Through the Bible, pp. 264-269		

LANGUAGE ARTS	Choose appropriate level of one of the following:
	
	❡ English Lessons Through Literature, Lesson 75
	    Reading Lessons Through Literature, phonogram review
	
	❡ Rod and Staff English, Lesson 87
	    Copywork/Commonplace Book
	
	❡ Your own grammar program
			❡ A Rulebook for Arguments, Ch. 32
			
			❡ LR: The Power in Your Hands, 1 lesson
			
			❡ LR: Rod and Staff 10, L. 83

MATH	Choose appropriate level of one of the following: ✎ Math-U-See, page E ✎ Miquon/Singapore Math ✎ Your own math program		✎ Math-U-See, pages E & H ✎ Your own math program

GEOGRAPHY	🌐 Mapping: Southern Asia
	
	🌐 Reading, choose one of the following:
	    A. Hungary: The Singing Tree, 1/2 of Ch. 3
	    B. Arizona: Brighty of the Grand Canyon, Ch. 1-2
			🌐 Notes from a Small Island, Ch. 24

HISTORY	Choose one spine, one or more core reading selections, and optional reading as desired.		

	♟ Spine:
	
	♟ Core reading:
	    1. What Was the Hindenburg, Ch. 10
	    2. WWII for Kids, Ch. 6
	    3. Albert Einstein for Kids, Ch. 5
		♟ Spine:
		
		♟ Core reading:
		    1. Trapp Family Singers, Ch. 13-14
		    2. Where the Red Fern Grows, Ch. 5
			♟ Spine:
			    America, 1/4 of Ch. 30
			
			♟ Core reading:
			    1 & 2. Les Miserables, 14 pages
			    LR: 1 & 2. Philosophy Book, through Bergson
			    UR: 1 & 2. Think, Ch. 1
			    1. Brave New World, Ch. 9-10
			    2. To Kill a Mockingbird, Ch. 25-26

Day 5

Grammar	Dialectic	Rhetoric	
♪♫ Term 3 Composer: Choose between Shostakovich, Britten, Leon Kirchner 🍔 Eat Your Way Through the USA, Washington 🎨 Art Lesson: Choose appropriate level of one of the following:			**ACTIVITIES**
🎨 I Can Do All Things 🎨 Lamb's Book of Art I	🎨 Lamb's Book of Art II 🎨 Feed My Sheep	🎨 How Great Thou ART I or II 🎨 Book of Many Colors	
↪ Oral or written narration; LG students can draw a picture from the reading and tell about the picture. Suggested subject: geography.		↪ Oral or written narration for history or geography.	**NARRATION**
✝ Old Story New, Week 61			**OTHER**
📚 Suggested read-aloud: The Borrowers, Ch. 13			**LITERATURE**
📚 Literature: 1: Pinocchio, Ch. 35-36 2: Alice's Adventures in Wonderland, Ch. 9 3: The Secret Garden, Ch. 23 4: Heidi, Ch. 8	📚 Literature: 5: Little Women, Ch. 25 6: The Patchwork Girl of Oz, Ch. 21 7: The Tin Woodman of Oz, Ch. 22 8: 20,000 Leagues, Ch. 27	📚 Book of English Verse, No. 801-803 ✝ Church History: Church History in Plain Language, Ch. 34 ✝ 100 Events, A.D. 1816	

Preschool and Lower Grammar	
✏ Pathways: Path 1, Day 3 A. Kindergarten Gems B. 50 Famous Stories C. The Hundred Dresses, Ch. 6 D. Random House Poetry, p. 163	**PATHWAYS**
🎨 Art Lesson: Choose one of the following Barry Stebbing art books for you little one to do art like the big kids: Art and the Bible for Children, Baby Lamb's Book of Art, Joseph the Canada Goose, or Little Annie's Art Book.	**ACTIVITY**

Mother Teresa of Calcutta. Photo by Manfredo Ferrari.
License: CC BY-SA 4.0; via Wikimedia Commons.

History Through Art: Mother Teresa

I won't lie to you, readers—the world is not a kind place. While hopefully your needs are well taken care of, many millions of people worldwide are starving, sick, or in danger of violence. No one takes care of these people. They are mostly on their own with their dire troubles. In the 20th century, one woman became horrified at the world's indifference to their struggles and devoted herself more than any other to caring for as many people as possible. This woman was Mother Teresa, recognized around the world as one of the most caring people to ever grace this planet.

Born with the name Anjezë Gonxhe Bojaxhiu in the country of Macedonia, the young girl who would one day become Mother Teresa was fascinated by stories of missionaries in foreign lands. By the age of twelve, she was wholeheartedly determined to join them, and as soon as she was able, she joined the Sisters of Loreto, an organization which travels the world spreading Christian faith and charity. In her late twenties, she took the vows of a nun, changing her name to Teresa in honor of St. Thérèse de Lisieux, the patron saint of missionaries.

For many years, Teresa served as a teacher in the city of Calcutta, India, but she grew increasingly distressed by the poverty and misery that plagued the city. She began to wonder if she was really doing all she could do to help the poor. One fateful day on a train ride out of the city, Teresa felt she heard the voice of God telling her to leave the convent and live among the poor.

Thus began a great mission. Mother Teresa became an Indian citizen, and while at the start she was almost as needy as the people she sought to help, as time went on, her mission grew and grew as more nuns came to her aide. Under Mother Teresa they opened up a Home for the Dying; she said, "What is a beautiful death? A beautiful death is, for people who lived like animals, to die like angels—loved and wanted." People who had lived their lives in poverty and were dying on the streets, miserable and alone, were brought to the Home to live out their final hours in care and comfort. Muslims were read the Quran into their final rest. Hindus were brought sacred water from the Ganges river. Catholics had their Last Rites performed. It was a place of kindness for people who'd been shown far too little.

As the decades wore on and Mother Teresa grew older, she began to expand her reach to a global scale. When starvation struck Ethiopia, she was there. When an earthquake ravaged Armenia, she was there. When radiation from the Chernobyl disaster burned and sickened countless victims, she was there to lend a helping hand. Even after her own death, the organization she founded, the Missionaries of Charity, kept to her mission and continues even now to care for people in need worldwide. The Roman Catholic Church acknowledges Mother Teresa as the Blessed Teresa of Calcutta, a model for all Christians and human beings in general.

Alpacas

Uncle Moses rubs his hands on his black alpaca smock. Up in the windy Andes mountains, few animals can survive. It's cold. The wind stabs like a dagger. The

ground is too frosted and hard to support many plant. These mountains are just as inhospitable as the bleakest of deserts, possibly more so. Even so, there are creatures capable of surviving up there. Llamas are one such animal, surviving the cold with fine warm wool. Centuries ago, the native peoples of South America bred some llamas specifically for their wool, producing the tame animals we know today as alpacas.

A Bolivian man with his Alpaca (herd in background). Photo by Patrick Furlong from Santiago, Chile. License: CC BY 2.0; via Wikimedia Commons.

Alpacas are smaller than wild llamas, but they are fluffier. Human beings raise them in large herds high in the mountains, shearing them periodically to harvest their ultra-valuable wool. The wool of an alpacas is far softer and far warmer than the wool of a sheep, making alpacas well worth all the trouble that goes into raising them in their chilly mountainous habitats.

Cattle

Peter is saving money for a cow. Cattle are one of the many animals that mankind has domesticated, or tamed and utilized. They have become one of our most valued livestock, supplying us with meat, milk, leather, and even manure for our crops.

The very first cattle as we know them were bred from Ice Age beasts called aurochs some ten thousand years ago, and they are believed to have been one of the most ancient forms of wealth in human societies. Cattle are valuable, and the person to have the most cattle thus had the most valuable possessions. They've since developed by our sides for thousands of years and have been bred into a dazzling array of distinctive breeds specialized for particular purposes, like milk or meat production.

Goose-Bumps

Jancsi says that he has goose-pimples all over. Have you ever been so cold or so scared that you got goose bumps all over your skin? It's a sensation everyone feels every now and then. They are one of the body's many survival mechanisms which can seem strange when the true purpose isn't known.

The reason we get goose bumps in cold weather is to raise the amount of body heat we produce, keeping us warm. The muscles under each of the hairs on our skin contract, forcing the hair upwards on top of a little bump. This raises the amount of body area that's exposed to the cold, and our body becomes more heated as a result.

It's less clear why goose bumps appear when we're scared, but we're not the only creatures to do this. Cats and many other animals also have goose bumps that cause their fur to fluff out when they're frightened, making them look bigger and less vulnerable as a result. Some scientists believe human goose bumps were meant to serve the same purpose in the days before civilization.

Holes

Buried Treasure

Stanley tells Zero that he's found the treasure chest. Have you ever gone hiking out with friends or siblings in search of buried treasure, like pirates or Old West's outlaws? You're certainly not alone if you have. The image of legendary criminals burying their ill-gotten goods underground, intending to come back for them but never returning, is certainly a powerful one. Unfortunately for those who like this sort of story, however, real pirates and outlaws hardly ever buried their treasure, any more than you might hike into a forest and bury your piggy bank.

The origin of the myth appears to

Pirates burying Captain Kidd's treasure, from *Howard Pyle's Book of Pirates*. Illustration by Howard Pyle. Image is in the public domain; via Wikimedia Commons.

be with the one pirate who did bury his treasure, William Kidd. In Captain Kidd's day, the punishment for piracy was death by the hangman's noose, which Kidd understandably wished to avoid. Hoping to bribe his way out through his captor's greed, while still at large Kidd buried part of his treasure so he could trade the booty's location for his freedom at a later date. It didn't work, however, and Kidd was hanged in 1701. As far as anyone knows, his treasure is still out there, waiting for an intrepid digger to claim.

Flashlights

As Stanley is trying to get out of the hole, a bright light from a flashlight shines in his face. A flashlight, sometimes called a torch in England, is a portable light held in the hands. Most of the time, the source of the light is a small light bulb powered by batteries contained in the case. Flashlights vary in size and power, from small lights the size of a pen to large floodlights carried by hand. Some flashlights are worn on the head or as part of a helmet in order to keep the hands free for other tasks.

Flashlights could not become a viable technology until after dry cell batteries were invented in 1887. The dry cell battery used a paste instead of a liquid, and since they didn't break or spill easily and could be used even upside down, they were perfect for flashlights. In 1899, the first flashlight was patented by a British inventor named David Misell. It was a tube with a light bulb and reflector at one end and batteries in a tube behind it. The same design is essentially used today for many flashlights.

Cavemen

Stanley's camp nickname is Caveman. Have you ever been told to respect your grandfather or grandmother, or to respect elderly people in general? Our forebears, the people of ages before now, were just as smart as we are today, and sometimes wiser. With that being common knowledge, it's odd that we see our most ancient ancestors, the so-called "cavemen," as a bunch of knuckle-dragging idiots.

Our Stone Age ancestors lived in a very different world than we do today. Ice covered much of the planet. Great woolly mammoths strode in herds across the plains, and saber-toothed cats brought down bison in the warmer areas. The world was more savage back then, and what we call civilization had no place there. So our ancestors, men and women not so much different than us today, lived a more natural mode of life wherever they could find room for themselves.

Often times, they would find shelter in caves to protect themselves from the bitter cold and the vicious animals, earning for themselves the title of cavemen in the modern day. But don't think the fact that they lived in caves and not houses made them any less cultured! In many caves, we find brilliant and skillful paintings on the walls of the old habitations, depicting Ice Age animals in stunning detail. The paintings have lasted longer than our entire civilization, a message from the cavemen that they weren't the idiots they're often made out to be!

P/K & LG Activity Supplies:

Day 1:
* Pattern blocks; we like our magnetic ones with a magnetic white board or on the refrigerator, but any will do.
* Spinner or a bag to draw out random shapes.

Day 3:
* Clothes pins.
* Container or other item for the clothes pins to clip onto.

Day 4:
* Random games pieces, stones, etc. Avoid choking hazards with little ones.

Science Experiment Supplies:

* Empty, styrofoam thread spool
* Ruler
* Stiff paper (index card or cardstock)
* String
* Cellophane tape
* 2 paper clips
* Knitting needle

* Scissors
* Ruler
* String
* Book
* Duct tape
* 2 small rubber balls of equal size

Eat Your Way Through the USA Supplies:

Check ingredients for dishes from Oregon.

Dialectic, Real Science 4 Kids:

Experiment 1 on Day 4.

Week 26

	GRAMMAR	DIALECTIC	RHETORIC
BIBLE	Choose one of the following plans: ✠ PLAN 1: Journey Through the Bible, pp. 284-285 ✠ PLAN 2: Journey Through the Bible, pp. 270-275		

LANGUAGE ARTS	Choose appropriate level of one of the following:
	
	❡ English Lessons Through Literature, Lesson 76
	   Reading Lessons Through Literature, phonogram review
	
	❡ Rod and Staff English, Lesson 88
	   Copywork/Commonplace Book
	
	❡ Your own grammar program
			❡ LR: The Power in Your Hands, 1 lesson
			
			❡ UR: WGRP, first draft. (10 days)
			
			❡ LR: Rod and Staff 10, L. 84

MATH	Choose appropriate level of one of the following: ✎ Math-U-See, Video and page A ✎ Miquon/Singapore Math ✎ Your own math program		✎ Math-U-See, Video and page A ✎ Your own math program

GEOGRAPHY	🌐 50 States Reading, Oregon
	
	🌐 Reading, choose one of the following:
	   A. Hungary: The Singing Tree, 1/2 of Ch. 3
	   B. Arizona: Brighty of the Grand Canyon, Ch. 3-4
			🌐 Notes from a Small Island, Ch. 25

HISTORY	Choose one spine, one or more core reading selections, and optional reading as desired.		

	♟ Spine: SOTW, Ch. 30.1
	
	♟ Core reading:
	   1. What Was the Hindenburg, Ch. 11
	   2. WWII for Kids, Ch. 7
	   3. Albert Einstein for Kids, Ch. 6
		♟ Spine: SOTW, Ch. 30.1
		
		♟ Core reading:
		   1. Trapp Family Singers, Ch. 15
		   2. Where the Red Fern Grows, Ch. 6
			♟ Spine:
			   Western Civ, 1/4 of Ch. 27
			   World Empires, Missions, Wars, Unit 8 Week 1
			
			♟ Core reading:
			   1 & 2. Les Miserables, 14 pages
			   1. Brave New World, Ch. 11-12
			   2. To Kill a Mockingbird, Ch. 27-28

Day 1

	Grammar	Dialectic	Rhetoric	
Activities	♪♪ Term 3 Composer: Choose between Shostakovich, Britten, Leon Kirchner ⧗ Timeline/Book of Centuries			
Narration	↪ Oral or written narration; LG students can draw a picture from the reading and tell about the picture. Suggested subject: history.		↪ Written narration for history or geography.	
Other	✤ Old Story New, Week 62 ☿ UD: Economics in One Lesson, Ch. 10		✤ LR: Cold-Case, Ch. 11 (1/2) ✤ Are Women Human? 1/2 of second essay	
Literature	📚 Literature: 1: The Orange Fairy Book: The Ugly Duckling 2: Alice's Adventures in Wonderland, Ch. 10 3: The Secret Garden, Ch. 24 4: Heidi, Ch. 9	📚 Literature: 5: Little Women, Ch. 26-27 6: The Patchwork Girl of Oz, Ch. 22 7: The Tin Woodman of Oz, Ch. 23 8: 20,000 Leagues, Ch. 28	📚 Book of English Verse, No. 804-806 ✤ Church History: Church History in Plain Language, Ch. 35 ✤ 100 Events, A.D. 1817	

Preschool and Lower Grammar

Pathways	✏ Pathways: Path 1, Day 1 A. Kindergarten Gems B. Among the Meadow People C. 20th—Ten, Nine, Eight D. Random House Poetry, p. 164
Activity	✏ Pattern block game We prefer magnetic pattern blocks with a white board or refrigerator. Have your little one use the spinner, or draw a shape from a bag at random, and place the shape next to another shape to make a picture. To make the spinner, print the spinner page. Make a small slit in the center to insert the brad. Place the brad half-way through, then bend the ends and tape them to keep them in place. Slip a paper-clip over the top of the brad and give it a spin.

Week 26

	GRAMMAR	DIALECTIC	RHETORIC
BIBLE	Choose one of the following plans: ✜ PLAN 1: Journey Through the Bible, pp. 286-287 ✜ PLAN 2: Journey Through the Bible, pp. 276-281		
	✜ LG: TBB: A Fishermen's Net ✜ UG: Egermeier's, 2 stories	✜ LD: Hurlbut's, 1 story ✜ UD: Golden's, 3 stories	
LANGUAGE ARTS	Choose appropriate level of one of the following: ❡ Reading Lessons Through Literature, next list and story ❡ Prepared dictation from ELTL, Spelling Wisdom, or today's reading ❡ Rod and Staff English, Lesson 89 ❡ Your own grammar program		❡ UR: WGRP, first draft. (10 days)
MATH	Choose appropriate level of one of the following: ✎ Math-U-See, page B ✎ Miquon/Singapore Math ✎ Your own math program		✎ Math-U-See, page B ✎ Your own math program
GEOGRAPHY	🌐 Reading, choose one of the following: A. Hungary: The Singing Tree, 1/2 of Ch. 4 B. Arizona: Brighty of the Grand Canyon, Ch. 5-6		🌐 Geography for Dummies, 1/2 of Ch. 13
SCIENCE	Choose one spine, one or more core reading selections, and optional reading as desired.		
	⚛ Core reading: 1. RS4K Physics, Ch. 6.4-6.5 2. Thud, Ch. 3	⚛ Core reading: 1. RS4K Physics, Ch. 8 2. Objects in Motion, Intro. - Ch. 1	⚛ Spine: Physics for Dummies, 1/2 of Ch. 14 Intro. Physics, pp. 242-245
	⚛ Spine: Quark Chronicles: Physics, Ch. 8		⚛ Core reading: How to Teach Relativity to Your Dog, Ch. 10

Day 2

	Grammar	Dialectic	Rhetoric	
	♪♪ Term 3 Composer: Choose between Shostakovich, Britten, Leon Kirchner			**Activities**
	🎨 Art Lesson: Choose appropriate level of one of the following:			
	🎨 I Can Do All Things 🎨 Lamb's Book of Art I	🎨 Lamb's Book of Art II 🎨 Feed My Sheep	🎨 How Great Thou ART I or II 🎨 Book of Many Colors	
	⚛ GSA The World of Light and Sound, Lesson 3		🎨 Great Art, Lecture 26	
	➲ Oral or written narration; LG students can draw a picture from the reading and tell about the picture. Suggested subject: Bible.		➲ Oral or written narration for science or Bible.	**Narration**
	✠ Old Story New, Week 62			
		☙ UD: The Art of Argument, Fallacy 21 ☙ UD: Science Matters, pp. 16-30 ☙ UD: Science Matters, pp. 31-45	☙ UR: Classical English Rhetoric, 1/4 Ch. 13	**Other**
	📚 Suggested read-aloud: The Borrowers, Ch. 14			**Literature**

Preschool and Lower Grammar	
✏ Pathways: Path 2 A. Little Wanderers, Ch. 26 B. Burgess Seashore Book, Ch. 28 C. Paddington Helps Out, Ch. 5 D. Random House Poetry, p. 165	**Pathways**
🎨 Art Lesson: Choose one of the following Barry Stebbing art books for you little one to do art like the big kids: Art and the Bible for Children, Baby Lamb's Book of Art, Joseph the Canada Goose, or Little Annie's Art Book.	**Activity**

Week 26

	GRAMMAR	DIALECTIC	RHETORIC
BIBLE	Choose one of the following plans: ✛ PLAN 1: Journey Through the Bible, pp. 288-289 ✛ PLAN 2: Journey Through the Bible, pp. 282-287		

LANGUAGE ARTS	Choose appropriate level of one of the following:
	
	¶ English Lessons Through Literature, Lesson 77
	   Reading Lessons Through Literature, phonogram review
	
	¶ Rod and Staff English, Lesson 90
	   Copywork/Commonplace Book
	
	¶ Your own grammar program
			¶ Essential Literary Terms, 3-4 pages
			
			¶ LR: The Power in Your Hands, 1 lesson
			
			¶ UR: WGRP, first draft. (10 days)
			
			¶ LR: Rod and Staff 10, L. 85

MATH	Choose appropriate level of one of the following: ✎ Math-U-See, page C ✎ Miquon/Singapore Math ✎ Your own math program		✎ Math-U-See, page C ✎ Your own math program

GEOGRAPHY	🌐 50 States Mapping, Oregon
	
	🌐 Reading, choose one of the following:
	   A. Hungary: The Singing Tree, 1/2 of Ch. 4
	   B. Arizona: Brighty of the Grand Canyon, Ch. 7-8
			🌐 Notes from a Small Island, Ch. 26

HISTORY	Choose one spine, one or more core reading selections, and optional reading as desired.		
	♟ Spine: SOTW, Ch. 30.2 ♟ Core reading: 1. What Was the Hindenburg, Ch. 12 2. Grandfather Gandhi (1/2) 3. Albert Einstein for Kids, Ch. 7	♟ Spine: SOTW, Ch. 30.2 ♟ Core reading: 1. Trapp Family Singers, Ch. 16 2. Where the Red Fern Grows, Ch. 7	♟ Spine: America, 1/4 of Ch. 30 World Empires, Missions, Wars, Unit 8 Week 1 ♟ Core reading: 1 & 2. Les Miserables, 14 pages 1 & 2. Midsummer Night's Dream, 1 Scene 1. Brave New World, Ch. 13-14 2. To Kill a Mockingbird, Ch. 29-30

Day 3

GRAMMAR	DIALECTIC	RHETORIC	
♪♫ Term 3 Composer: Choose between Shostakovich, Britten, Leon Kirchner			ACTIVITIES
☞ Oral or written narration; could be a group project. Tell about how you are like, and unlike, one of the characters in your book.			NARRATION
✛ Old Story New, Week 62 ✛ UD: Simply Christian, Ch. 6		✛ LR: Cold-Case, Ch. 12 (1/2) ✛ Are Women Human? 1/2 of second essay	OTHER
📚 Literature: 1: The Orange Fairy Book: The Enchanted Wreath 2: Alice's Adventures in Wonderland, Ch. 11 3: The Secret Garden, Ch. 25 4: Heidi, Ch. 10	📚 Literature: 5: Little Women, Ch. 28 6: The Patchwork Girl of Oz, Ch. 23 7: The Tin Woodman of Oz, Ch. 24 8: 20,000 Leagues, Ch. 29	📚 Book of English Verse, No. 807-808 ✛ Church History: Church History in Plain Language, Ch. 36 ✛ 100 Events, A.D. 1830	LITERATURE
PRESCHOOL AND LOWER GRAMMAR			
✏ Pathways: Path 1, Day 2 A. Kindergarten Gems B. 50 Famous Stories C. The Hundred Dresses, Ch. 7 D. Random House Poetry, p. 166			PATHWAYS
✏ Clothes pins Have a pile of clothes pins and a container or other item that they can clip onto. Have your little one put the clothes pins on the item, and then take them off again. This exercises the handwriting muscles. You can also paint the clothes pins different colors, and paint the different colors around the container. Then the child can match the colors.			ACTIVITY

Week 26

	GRAMMAR	DIALECTIC	RHETORIC
BIBLE	Choose one of the following plans: ✚ PLAN 1: Journey Through the Bible, pp. 290-291 ✚ PLAN 2: The Story, Ch. 26		
	✚ LG: TBB: Jesus Feeds Thousands ✚ UG: Egermeier's, 2 stories	✚ LD: Hurlbut's, 1 story ✚ UD: Golden's, 3 stories	
LANGUAGE ARTS	Choose appropriate level of one of the following: ❡ Reading Lessons Through Literature, next list and story ❡ Prepared dictation from ELTL, Spelling Wisdom, or today's reading ❡ Your own grammar program		❡ UR: WGRP, first draft. (10 days)
MATH	Choose appropriate level of one of the following: ✎ Math-U-See, page D ✎ Miquon/Singapore Math ✎ Your own math program		✎ Math-U-See, page D ✎ Your own math program

GEOGRAPHY	🌐 Reading, choose one of the following:
	   A. Hungary: The Singing Tree, 1/2 of Ch. 5
	   B. Arizona: Brighty of the Grand Canyon, Ch. 9-10		

SCIENCE	Choose one spine, one or more core reading selections, and optional reading as desired.		

	⚛ Core reading:
	   1. RS4K Physics, Ch. 7.1-7.2
	   2. Thud, Ch. 4
		⚛ Core reading:
		   1. RS4K Physics, Ch. 8 Experiment
		   1. Black Holes and Uncle Albert, Ch. 1
		   2. Objects in Motion, Ch. 2
			⚛ Spine:
			   Manga Relativity, pp. 53-63
			   Intro. Physics, pp. 246-251
			
			⚛ Core reading:
			   How to Teach Relativity to Your Dog, Ch. 11

	⚛ Optional extra reading, topic: Magnetism and Types of Magnets
	   Simon Bloom, Ch. 17-18
	   The Attractive Story of Magnetism with Max Axiom, by Andrea Gianopoulos
	   Magnetism and Electromagnets by Eve Hartman		

Day 4

Grammar	Dialectic	Rhetoric	
♪♫ Term 3 Composer: Choose between Shostakovich, Britten, Leon Kirchner			Activities
⚛ GSA The World of Light and Sound, Lesson 4 ⚛ 201 Awesome Experiments, 175-176		🎨 Great Art Writing	
☞ Oral or written narration; LG students can draw a picture from the reading and tell about the picture. Suggested subject: science.		☞ Written narration for science or Bible.	Narration
✠ Old Story New, Week 62			
	☏ UD: The Art of Argument: Create an ad or an argument using this week's fallacy ☏ UD: Science Matters, pp. 46-60	☏ UR: Classical English Rhetoric, 1/4 Ch. 13	Other
📚 Suggested read-aloud: The Borrowers, Ch. 15			Literature

Preschool and Lower Grammar	
✎ Pathways: Path 3 A. Burgess Flower Book, Ch. 30 B. TumTum and Nutmeg, Ch. 13 C. Henry Huggins, Ch. 2 D. Random House Poetry, p. 167	Pathways
✎ Sorting game Have a pile of small game pieces, stones, etc. Have your little one sort them by shape or color. When the child picks small items up with his thumb and index finger, it exercises the handwriting muscles.	Activity

Week 26

	GRAMMAR	DIALECTIC	RHETORIC
BIBLE	Choose one of the following plans: ✠ PLAN 1: Journey Through the Bible, pp. 292-293 ✠ PLAN 2: Journey Through the Bible, pp. 288-293		
LANGUAGE ARTS	Choose appropriate level of one of the following: ¶ English Lessons Through Literature, Lesson 78 Reading Lessons Through Literature, phonogram review ¶ Rod and Staff English, Lesson 91 Copywork/Commonplace Book ¶ Your own grammar program		¶ A Rulebook for Arguments, Ch. 33 ¶ LR: The Power in Your Hands, 1 lesson ¶ LR: Rod and Staff 10, L. 86
MATH	Choose appropriate level of one of the following: ✏ Math-U-See, page E ✏ Miquon/Singapore Math ✏ Your own math program		✏ Math-U-See, pages E & H ✏ Your own math program
GEOGRAPHY	🌎 Mapping: Middle East		
	🌎 Reading, choose one of the following: B. Arizona: Brighty of the Grand Canyon, Ch. 11-12		🌎 Notes from a Small Island, Ch. 27
HISTORY	Choose one spine, one or more core reading selections, and optional reading as desired.		
	♟ Spine: ♟ Core reading: 1. What Was the Hindenburg, Ch. 13 2. Grandfather Gandhi (1/2) 3. Albert Einstein for Kids, Ch. 8	♟ Spine: ♟ Core reading: 1. Trapp Family Singers, Ch. 17 2. Where the Red Fern Grows, Ch. 8	♟ Spine: America, 1/4 of Ch. 30 World Empires, Missions, Wars, Unit 8 Week 1 ♟ Core reading: 1 & 2. Les Miserables, 14 pages LR: 1 & 2. Philosophy Book, through Du Bois UR: 1 & 2. Think, Ch. 2 1. Brave New World, Ch. 15-16 2. To Kill a Mockingbird, Ch. 31

Day 5

GRAMMAR	DIALECTIC	RHETORIC	
🎵 Term 3 Composer: Choose between Shostakovich, Britten, Leon Kirchner 🍔 Eat Your Way Through the USA, Oregon 🎨 Art Lesson: Choose appropriate level of one of the following:			ACTIVITIES
🎨 I Can Do All Things 🎨 Lamb's Book of Art I	🎨 Lamb's Book of Art II 🎨 Feed My Sheep	🎨 How Great Thou ART I or II 🎨 Book of Many Colors	
ᗕ Oral or written narration; LG students can draw a picture from the reading and tell about the picture. Suggested subject: geography.		ᗕ Oral or written narration for history or geography.	NARRATION
✠ Old Story New, Week 62 ☙ UD: Economics in One Lesson, Ch. 11			OTHER
📚 Suggested read-aloud: The Borrowers, Ch. 16			
📚 Literature: 1: The Orange Fairy Book: The Clever Cat 2: Alice's Adventures in Wonderland, Ch. 12 3: The Secret Garden, Ch. 26 4: Heidi, Ch. 11	📚 Literature: 5: Little Women, Ch. 29-30 6: The Patchwork Girl of Oz, Ch. 24 7: Northanger Abbey, Ch. 1 8: 20,000 Leagues, Ch. 30	📚 Book of English Verse, No. 809 ✠ Church History: Church History in Plain Language, Ch. 37 ✠ 100 Events, A.D. 1830	LITERATURE
PRESCHOOL AND LOWER GRAMMAR			
✏️ Pathways: Path 1, Day 3 A. Kindergarten Gems B. Among the Meadow People C. The Colors of Us D. Random House Poetry, pp. 168-170			PATHWAYS
🎨 Art Lesson: Choose one of the following Barry Stebbing art books for you little one to do art like the big kids: Art and the Bible for Children, Baby Lamb's Book of Art, Joseph the Canada Goose, or Little Annie's Art Book.			ACTIVITY

A baby chimp and his mother at the Baltimore zoo. Photo by Steve from Washington, DC. License: CC BY-SA 2.0; via Wikimedia Commons.

History Through Art: Dame Jane Goodall

In the history of primatology, the study of primates, three names stand out above others—Jane Goodall, Dian Fossey, and Birutė Galdikas. Each of these women was personally chosen by paleoanthropologist Louis Leakey to study primates in their natural habitats, and he called them the Trimates.

And few field researchers are as legendary as Jane Goodall. For fifty-five years, Goodall studied and taught about chimpanzee troops in the wild rainforests of Africa. Most of the information we have on this strikingly human-like species comes from either her observations or from research projects inspired by her work.

Goodall went against the grain of conventional primate research in several ways, notably by how close she got to a troop of chimpanzees. She fed the apes, gave them names like Goliath and Frodo, and was even accepted into their troop as a member at one point. Once the chimps accepted her, she was able to witness a side of chimpanzee behavior never before seen by scientists, including personal friendships between chimps, cooperative hunting, and tool use.

For the first ten years of the study, Goodall considered chimpanzees to be "rather nicer" than human beings. This ended at the Gombe Chimpanzee War, during which the troop she was monitoring split into two and waged a bitter and bloody fight for a period of four years. This was shocking, as previously human beings were the only known species to wage war. Goodall confessed in her memoir to having nightmares about the war for many years afterward. Seeing the apes, whom she had come to love and know by name, fight and kill one another profoundly disturbed her.

Regardless, Goodall continued her study and contributed a tremendous amount of knowledge about the species most similar to humans. To this day, she remains a prominent member of the primatologist community and an activist against poaching and animal cruelty.

The Singing Tree

Mandatory Military Service

Father says that everyone must do his Army service because it's the law. Every nation in every civilization requires a military to keep itself standing upright. The military could be considered the strong arm of a nation. It can be used to take what the nation wants or to defend its people and resources from other nations. At times, the military isn't strong enough to achieve a goal or protect the people, and so the government institutes what is called a draft, or conscription, to force people to join the military in either a supportive or fighting role.

Not all forms of forced military service are in the form of a temporary draft, however. In some countries, it is required that every single citizen serve the military for a few years before going about their normal lives. Those who speak in favor of such systems argue that mandatory military service makes a population stronger and smarter by virtue of military training. Those opposed to it believe that forcing citizens to join such a government organization is a violation of the inherent rights of humanity.

17th century Spanish judge in full gowns. Painting by Diego Velázquez. Image is in the public domain; via Wikimedia Commons.

Judge

The people think Judge Kormos is the best judge they've ever had. A judge is a person who presides over the activities of a court, usually in legal matters. Sometimes they will be part of a panel of several judges, but often they act alone. Across different nations and governments, the powers of a judge vary widely. The sentencing of criminals and arbitration of disputes is their chief responsibility.

In the United States, the courts are divided into multiple levels. Lower courts are responsible for trying all of the court cases in our country. In criminal cases, the judge presides over the court, but he does not decide whether a person is guilty or not guilty; that is the job of the jury. A guilty verdict from a lower court may be appealed. When this happens, higher courts hear the case again and decide whether or not the guilty verdict was justified. Cases can be appealed all the way to the Supreme Court, which is the highest court in the land. The Supreme Court consists of a panel of judges who issue verdicts on specific cases that they choose to hear. Their decisions can affect the law across the land because in many ways, the Supreme Court sits in judgement not only of the individual on trial but also on the law itself.

Iodine

Lily says that they have iodine to put on her foot at home. Iodine is one of the elements on the Periodic Table, which makes it one of the basic building blocks of all matter. It is necessary for good health in humans in small amounts and has a low toxicity. Iodine is found mainly in oceans. It is rare in soils, which has led to deficiency problems in animals and human populations without access to the oceans.

In higher animals, iodine is needed to create thyroid hormones. The hormones contain iodine and regulate many bodily functions in humans. There has been speculation that iodine deficient diets in Americans are what have led to an epidemic of thyroid problems. Foods high in iodine include fish, shellfish, and the organ meats of land animals.

Brighty of the Grand Canyon

Grand Canyon

Brighty lives in the Grand Canyon. Of the many majestic natural formations on planet Earth, the Grand Canyon is one of the most breathtaking. Two hundred and seventy-seven miles long, eighteen miles wide at some points, and over a mile deep, it is a thrilling example of what water and weather can do to the planet's surface.

The Grand Canyon was carved out by the Colorado River and its tributaries, which over a massive amount of time washed away the stone and sediments of the stream to carve a deep canyon. The geologic history can be seen within the canyon walls, and the Grand Canyon has been seen both as a holy site and as a great place to live by various Native American tribes to have inhabited Arizona in times past.

Driftwood

Old Timer throws driftwood on the fire. The ocean is a vast and ever-moving place. Things that fall into the water at one end might be swept by the currents

Ancestral Puebloan granaries high above the Colorado River at Nankoweap Creek, Grand Canyon. Photo by Drenaline. License: CC BY-SA 3.0; via Wikimedia Commons.

into a long and epic journey across the whole world before coming to the opposite shore. When trees and other wooden items are swept along in this manner, the resulting soaked pieces of wood are called driftwood.

The Vikings were one group of people with a keen fondness for driftwood. According to one version of their creation myth, Odin created the first human beings out of wet branches he found on the beach, and settling Vikings would often throw logs into the ocean and create their new settlement in the place where the driftwood met land.

Mesquite Trees

In the inner reaches of the canyon, Brighty finds the mesquite beans plentiful. If you think a desert's a harsh place for a human, imagine yourself as a tree. Unlike an animal, a tree can't get up and walk until it finds a source of water. A tree must make do with whatever water it can pull from the soil as it fends off anything that tries to eat its moist leaves.

Mesquite trees have achieved mastery of the art of desert survival. Mesquite trees have fantastically long roots that can probe deep into the soil in search of moisture, and they can produce nasty thorns to make herbivores think twice about eating them. They are perfectly adapted to hot and dry environments, so much so, in fact, that mesquites introduced to Africa and Australia are considered invasive species.

P/K & LG Activity Supplies:

Day 1:
• Cuisenaire rods or MUS blocks

Day 3:
• Stickers

Day 4:
• Board book with repetition (Brown Bear, Brown Bear, etc.)

Science Experiment Supplies:

• Scissors
• Ruler
• Typing paper
• Unopened can of soda

• 5 books
• Chair or cart with rollers

Eat Your Way Through the USA Supplies:

Check ingredients for dishes from California.

Dialectic, Real Science 4 Kids:

Experiment 1 on Day 4.

Rhetoric, Physics:

Physics lab on Day 4.

Week 27

	GRAMMAR	DIALECTIC	RHETORIC
BIBLE	Choose one of the following plans: ✠ PLAN 1: Journey Through the Bible, pp. 294-295 ✠ PLAN 2: Journey Through the Bible, pp. 294-299		

LANGUAGE ARTS	Choose appropriate level of one of the following:
	
	¶ English Lessons Through Literature, Lesson 79
	   Reading Lessons Through Literature, phonogram review
	
	¶ Rod and Staff English, Lesson 92
	   Copywork/Commonplace Book
	
	¶ Your own grammar program
			¶ LR: The Power in Your Hands, 1 lesson
			
			¶ UR: WGRP, first draft. (10 days)
			
			¶ LR: Rod and Staff 10, L. 87

MATH	Choose appropriate level of one of the following: ✎ Math-U-See, Video and page A ✎ Miquon/Singapore Math ✎ Your own math program		✎ Math-U-See, Video and page A ✎ Your own math program
GEOGRAPHY	🌍 50 States Reading, California		

	🌍 Reading, choose one of the following:
	   A. Hungary: The Singing Tree, 1/2 of Ch. 5
	   B. Arizona: Brighty of the Grand Canyon, Ch. 13-14
			🌍 Notes from a Small Island, Ch. 28

HISTORY	Choose one spine, one or more core reading selections, and optional reading as desired.		

	♟ Spine: SOTW, Ch. 31.1
	
	♟ Core reading:
	   1. What Was the Hindenburg, Ch. 14
	   2. Who Was Martin Luther King, Jr., Intro. - Ch. 1
	   3. Candy Bomber, Ch. 1
		♟ Spine: SOTW, Ch. 31.1
		
		♟ Core reading:
		   1. Trapp Family Singers, Ch. 18
		   2. Where the Red Fern Grows, Ch. 9
			♟ Spine:
			   Western Civ, 1/4 of Ch. 27
			   World Empires, Missions, Wars, Unit 8 Week 2
			
			♟ Core reading:
			   1 & 2. Les Miserables, 14 pages
			   1. Brave New World, Ch. 17-18
			   2. Strength to Love, Ch. 1

Day 1

Grammar	Dialectic	Rhetoric	
♪♪ Term 3 Composer: Choose between Shostakovich, Britten, Leon Kirchner ⧖ Timeline/Book of Centuries			Activities
☜ Oral or written narration; LG students can draw a picture from the reading and tell about the picture. Suggested subject: history.		☜ Written narration for history or geography.	Narration
✜ Old Story New, Week 63 ଓ UD: Economics in One Lesson, Ch. 12		✜ LR: Cold-Case, Ch. 12 (1/2)	Other
📖 Literature: 1: The Orange Fairy Book: The Frog and the Lion Fairy 2: Through the Looking-Glass, Ch. 1 3: The Secret Garden, Ch. 27 4: Heidi, Ch. 12	📖 Literature: 5: Little Women, Ch. 31 6: The Patchwork Girl of Oz, Ch. 25 7: Northanger Abbey, Ch. 2 8: 20,000 Leagues, Ch. 31	📖 Book of English Verse, No. 810 ✜ Church History: Church History in Plain Language, Ch. 38 ✜ 100 Events, A.D. 1833	Literature

Preschool and Lower Grammar	
✐ Pathways: Path 1, Day 1 A. Kindergarten Gems B. 50 Famous Stories C. 20th—Stellaluna D. Random House Poetry, p. 171	Pathways
✐ Play with math blocks Play with cuisenaire rods or base-10 or MUS blocks. Make a train. Start with 1 make each car one bigger. Then start with 10 and make each car one smaller. Make patterns.	Activity

Week 27

	GRAMMAR	DIALECTIC	RHETORIC
BIBLE	Choose one of the following plans: ✠ PLAN 1: Journey Through the Bible, pp. 296-297 ✠ PLAN 2: Journey Through the Bible, pp. 300-305		
	✠ LG: TBB: Jesus Walks on Water ✠ UG: Egermeier's, 2 stories	✠ LD: Hurlbut's, 1 story ✠ UD: Golden's, 3 stories	
LANGUAGE ARTS	Choose appropriate level of one of the following: ❡ Reading Lessons Through Literature, next list and story ❡ Prepared dictation from ELTL, Spelling Wisdom, or today's reading ❡ Your own grammar program		❡ UR: WGRP, first draft. (10 days) ❡ LR: Rod and Staff 10, L. 88
MATH	Choose appropriate level of one of the following:		
	✏ Math-U-See, page B ✏ Miquon/Singapore Math ✏ Your own math program		✏ Math-U-See, page B ✏ Your own math program
GEOGRAPHY	🌐 Reading, choose one of the following: A. Hungary: The Singing Tree, 1/2 of Ch. 6 B. Arizona: Brighty of the Grand Canyon, Ch. 15-16		🌐 Geography for Dummies, 1/2 of Ch. 14
SCIENCE	Choose one spine, one or more core reading selections, and optional reading as desired.		
	⚛ Core reading: 1. RS4K Physics, Ch. 7.3-7.4 2. Insiders Flight, pp. 8-13	⚛ Core reading: 1. RS4K Physics, Ch. 9 2. Objects in Motion, Ch. 3	⚛ Spine: SHSPhys, Week 7 Physics for Dummies, 1/2 of Ch. 14 Intro. Physics, pp. 252, 261-265 ⚛ Core reading: How to Teach Relativity to Your Dog, Ch. 12
	⚛ Spine: Quark Chronicles: Physics, Ch. 9		

Day 2

Grammar	Dialectic	Rhetoric	
♪ Term 3 Composer: Choose between Shostakovich, Britten, Leon Kirchner 🎨 Art Lesson: Choose appropriate level of one of the following:			Activities
🎨 I Can Do All Things 🎨 Lamb's Book of Art I	🎨 Lamb's Book of Art II 🎨 Feed My Sheep	🎨 How Great Thou ART I or II 🎨 Book of Many Colors	
⚛ GSA The World of Light and Sound, Lesson 5		🎨 Great Art, Lecture 27	
☞ Oral or written narration; LG students can draw a picture from the reading and tell about the picture. Suggested subject: Bible.		☞ Oral or written narration for science or Bible.	Narration
✠ Old Story New, Week 63			
	☙ UD: The Art of Argument, Fallacy 22 ☙ UD: Science Matters, pp. 61-75	☙ UR: Classical English Rhetoric, 1/4 Ch. 14	Other
📚 Suggested read-aloud: The Borrowers, Ch. 17			Literature

Preschool and Lower Grammar

✏ Pathways: Path 2 A. Little Wanderers, Ch. 27 B. Burgess Seashore Book, Ch. 29-30 C. Paddington Helps Out, Ch. 6 D. Random House Poetry, p. 172	Pathways
🎨 Art Lesson: Choose one of the following Barry Stebbing art books for you little one to do art like the big kids: Art and the Bible for Children, Baby Lamb's Book of Art, Joseph the Canada Goose, or Little Annie's Art Book.	Activity

Week 27

	Grammar	Dialectic	Rhetoric
Bible	Choose one of the following plans: ✠ PLAN 1: Journey Through the Bible, pp. 298-299 ✠ PLAN 2: Journey Through the Bible, pp. 306-311		
Language Arts	Choose appropriate level of one of the following: ❡ English Lessons Through Literature, Lesson 80 Reading Lessons Through Literature, phonogram review ❡ Rod and Staff English, Lesson 93 Copywork/Commonplace Book ❡ Your own grammar program		❡ Essential Literary Terms, 3-4 pages ❡ LR: The Power in Your Hands, 1 lesson ❡ UR: WGRP, first draft. (10 days) ❡ LR: Rod and Staff 10, L. 89
Math	Choose appropriate level of one of the following: ✎ Math-U-See, page C ✎ Miquon/Singapore Math ✎ Your own math program		✎ Math-U-See, page C ✎ Your own math program
Geography	🌐 50 States Mapping, California		
	🌐 Reading, choose one of the following: A. Hungary: The Singing Tree, 1/2 of Ch. 6 B. Arizona: Brighty of the Grand Canyon, Ch. 17-18		🌐 Notes from a Small Island, Ch. 29
History	Choose one spine, one or more core reading selections, and optional reading as desired.		
	♟ Spine: SOTW, Ch. 31.2 ♟ Core reading: 1. Burying the Sun, Ch. 1 2. Who Was Martin Luther King, Jr., Ch. 2 3. Candy Bomber, Ch. 2	♟ Spine: SOTW, Ch. 31.2 ♟ Core reading: 1. Trapp Family Singers, Ch. 19 2. Where the Red Fern Grows, Ch. 10	♟ Spine: America, 1/4 of Ch. 31 World Empires, Missions, Wars, Unit 8 Week 2 ♟ Core reading: 1 & 2. Les Miserables, 14 pages 1 & 2. Midsummer Night's Dream, 1 Scene 1. 1984, Book 1 Ch. 1 2. Strength to Love, Ch. 2

Day 3

GRAMMAR	DIALECTIC	RHETORIC	
♪♪ Term 3 Composer: Choose between Shostakovich, Britten, Leon Kirchner			ACTIVITIES
☞ Oral or written narration; could be a group project. Choose a quote from your book, and tell why it would or would not be a good motto to live by.			NARRATION
✠ Old Story New, Week 63 ✠ UD: Simply Christian, Ch. 7		✠ LR: Cold-Case, Ch. 13 (1/2)	OTHER
📚 Literature: 1: The Orange Fairy Book: The Princess Bella-Flor 2: Through the Looking-Glass, Ch. 2 3: The Princess and the Goblin, Ch. 1-2 4: Heidi, Ch. 13	📚 Literature: 5: Little Women, Ch. 32-33 6: The Patchwork Girl of Oz, Ch. 26 7: Northanger Abbey, Ch. 3 8: 20,000 Leagues, Ch. 32	📚 Book of English Verse, No. 811-813 ✠ Church History: Church History in Plain Language, Ch. 39 ✠ 100 Events, A.D. 1854	LITERATURE

PRESCHOOL AND LOWER GRAMMAR	
✏ Pathways: Path 1, Day 2 A. Kindergarten Gems B. Among the Meadow People C. 20th—D.W. the Picky Eater D. Random House Poetry, p. 173	PATHWAYS
✏ Stickers Decorate a page with stickers.	ACTIVITY

Week 27

	GRAMMAR	DIALECTIC	RHETORIC
BIBLE	Choose one of the following plans: ✝ PLAN 1: Journey Through the Bible, pp. 300-301 ✝ PLAN 2: The Story, Ch. 27		
	✝ LG: TBB: Jesus Heals; Money in a Fish ✝ UG: Egermeier's, 3 stories	✝ LD: Hurlbut's, 2 stories ✝ UD: Golden's, 2 stories	
LANGUAGE ARTS	Choose appropriate level of one of the following: ❡ Reading Lessons Through Literature, next list and story ❡ Prepared dictation from ELTL, Spelling Wisdom, or today's reading ❡ Your own grammar program		❡ UR: WGRP, first draft. (10 days)
MATH	Choose appropriate level of one of the following:		
	✎ Math-U-See, page D ✎ Miquon/Singapore Math ✎ Your own math program		✎ Math-U-See, page D ✎ Your own math program
GEOGRAPHY	🌐 Reading, choose one of the following: A. Hungary: The Singing Tree, 1/2 of Ch. 7 B. Arizona: Brighty of the Grand Canyon, Ch. 19-20		
SCIENCE	Choose one spine, one or more core reading selections, and optional reading as desired.		
	⚛ Core reading: 1. RS4K Physics, Ch. 8.1-8.2 2. Insiders Flight, pp. 14-19	⚛ Core reading: 1. RS4K Physics, Ch. 9 Experiment 1. Black Holes and Uncle Albert, Ch. 2 2. Objects in Motion, Ch. 4	⚛ Spine: SHSPhys, Week 7 Manga Relativity, pp. 64-74 Intro. Physics, pp. 266-270 ⚛ Core reading:
	⚛ Optional extra reading, topic: Light Energy Simon Bloom, Ch. 19-21 The Illuminating World of Light with Max Axiom by Emily Sohn		

Day 4

Grammar	Dialectic	Rhetoric	
♪♫ Term 3 Composer: Choose between Shostakovich, Britten, Leon Kirchner			Activities
⚛ GSA The World of Light and Sound, Lesson 6 ⚛ 201 Awesome Experiments, 177-178		⚛ Physics Lab 🎨 Great Art Writing	
☞ Oral or written narration; LG students can draw a picture from the reading and tell about the picture. Suggested subject: science.		☞ Written narration for science or Bible.	Narration
✟ Old Story New, Week 63			Other
	☙ UD: The Art of Argument: Create an ad or an argument using this week's fallacy ☙ UD: Science Matters, pp. 76-90	☙ UR: Classical English Rhetoric, 1/4 Ch. 14	
📚 Suggested read-aloud: The Borrowers, Ch. 18			Literature
Preschool and Lower Grammar			
✐ Pathways: Path 3 A. Burgess Flower Book, Ch. 31 B. TumTum and Nutmeg, Ch. 14 C. Henry Huggins, Ch. 3 D. Random House Poetry, p. 174			Pathways
✐ Reading in tandem Read the Bill Martin, Jr., and Eric Carle What do you see? books in tandem. My toddler "reads" the "What do you see?" page, and I read the next page. Use other favorite books with lots of repetition.			Activity

Week 27

	GRAMMAR	DIALECTIC	RHETORIC
BIBLE	Choose one of the following plans: ✚ PLAN 1: Journey Through the Bible, pp. 302-303 ✚ PLAN 2: Journey Through the Bible, pp. 312-317		
LANGUAGE ARTS	Choose appropriate level of one of the following: ❡ English Lessons Through Literature, Lesson 81 Reading Lessons Through Literature, phonogram review ❡ Rod and Staff English, Lesson 94 Copywork/Commonplace Book ❡ Your own grammar program		❡ A Rulebook for Arguments, Ch. 34 ❡ LR: The Power in Your Hands, 1 lesson ❡ LR: Rod and Staff 10, L. 90
MATH	Choose appropriate level of one of the following: ✎ Math-U-See, page E ✎ Miquon/Singapore Math ✎ Your own math program		✎ Math-U-See, pages E & H ✎ Your own math program
GEOGRAPHY	🌎 Mapping: Northern Africa 🌎 Reading, choose one of the following: A. Hungary: The Singing Tree, 1/2 of Ch. 7 B. Arizona: Brighty of the Grand Canyon, Ch. 21-22		🌎 A Walk Along the Ganges, Ch. 1
HISTORY	Choose one spine, one or more core reading selections, and optional reading as desired.		
	♟ Spine: ♟ Core reading: 1. Burying the Sun, Ch. 2 2. Who Was Martin Luther King, Jr., Ch. 3 3. Candy Bomber, Ch. 3	♟ Spine: ♟ Core reading: 1. Trapp Family Singers, Ch. 20-21 2. Where the Red Fern Grows, Ch. 11	♟ Spine: America, 1/4 of Ch. 31 World Empires, Missions, Wars, Unit 8 Week 2 ♟ Core reading: 1 & 2. Les Miserables, 14 pages LR: 1 & 2. Philosophy Book, through Ortega UR: 1 & 2. Think, 1/2 Ch. 3 1. 1984, Ch. 2 2. Strength to Love, Ch. 3

Day 5

Grammar	Dialectic	Rhetoric	
♫ Term 3 Composer: Choose between Shostakovich, Britten, Leon Kirchner			**Activities**
🍔 Eat Your Way Through the USA, California			
🎨 Art Lesson: Choose appropriate level of one of the following:			
🎨 I Can Do All Things	🎨 Lamb's Book of Art II	🎨 How Great Thou ART I or II	
🎨 Lamb's Book of Art I	🎨 Feed My Sheep	🎨 Book of Many Colors	
☞ Oral or written narration; LG students can draw a picture from the reading and tell about the picture. Suggested subject: geography.		☞ Oral or written narration for history or geography.	**Narration**
✠ Old Story New, Week 63			**Other**
📚 Suggested read-aloud: The Borrowers, Ch. 19			
📚 Literature: 1: The Orange Fairy Book: The Bird of Truth 2: Through the Looking-Glass, Ch. 3 3: The Princess and the Goblin, Ch. 3 4: Heidi, Ch. 14	📚 Literature: 5: Little Women, Ch. 34 6: The Patchwork Girl of Oz, Ch. 27 7: Northanger Abbey, Ch. 4 8: 20,000 Leagues, Ch. 33	📚 Book of English Verse, No. 814-816 ✠ Church History: Church History in Plain Language, Ch. 40 ✠ 100 Events, A.D. 1854	**Literature**
PRESCHOOL AND LOWER GRAMMAR			
✏ Pathways: Path 1, Day 3 A. Kindergarten Gems B. 50 Famous Stories C. Anno's Magic Seeds D. Random House Poetry, p. 175			**Pathways**
🎨 Art Lesson: Choose one of the following Barry Stebbing art books for you little one to do art like the big kids: Art and the Bible for Children, Baby Lamb's Book of Art, Joseph the Canada Goose, or Little Annie's Art Book.			**Activity**

Orangutan baby just born in the Munich zoo. Photo by Oliver Spalt. License: CC BY-SA 3.0; via Wikimedia Commons.

History Through Art: Birute Galdikas

In the 1950s, an anthropologist named Louis Leakey noticed a major hole in science's understanding of the natural world: the great apes. Three different genuses of large primates—gorillas, chimpanzees, and orangutans—were almost completely unknown to scientists. No one knew how they behaved or how they interacted with each other. So Leakey assembled a group of female scientists to venture into the natural habitats of these animals and learn about them from firsthand experience.

Jane Goodall was sent to study chimpanzees. Diane Fossey traveled to gorilla country to study the largest apes. The third of this little group, which would eventually be known as the Trimates, was Birute Galdikas, who would become famous for her study of orangutans in Borneo.

Orangutans were long the most mysterious out of the great apes, which is saying something. These orange apes live high in the tree tops and are thus much harder to research. Even setting aside the difficulties of finding orangutans, they live in quite the hostile environment. No sooner had Galdikas arrived than she was faced with flesh-eating bugs, blood-sucking leeches, and even dangerous poachers.

Despite the hardships, Galdikas remained in Borneo for thirty years. Her research soon developed a charitable side to it as she took in orphaned orangutans whose parents had been killed by poachers and raised them to adulthood. She both immensely furthered our knowledge of the species and saved countless of their children from suffering and death. Today, she teaches as a professor at Simon Fraser University, but she still speaks out against anything which might destroy the habitat orangutans call home.

The Singing Tree

Wheat

The family rests after a day spent in the wheat fields. Wheat is a cereal grain crop suspected to have first originated in the Middle East. It is cultivated worldwide today with a production of 713 million tons in 2013. It's the third most produced cereal crop in the world, with rice being the first and maize being the second. The earliest archaeological findings of wheat date back to southeastern Turkey in around 7,500 BC.

Early civilizations such as Babylonia emerged around the growing of wheat crops. Wheat is relatively easy to cultivate, and the harvest can be easily stored. Because of this, growing wheat helped large city-states grow in the region we now call the Fertile Crescent.

Wheat is a staple food, which means that it is eaten frequently and in large quantities in certain parts of the world. It is made into breads, cookies, cakes, breakfast cereal, noodles, pasta, and even beer. Today there is research into making biofuel to power vehicles from wheat.

Hay

Mother says that haying is hard work. A key to humanity's success has been our domestication of grazing animals like cattle, sheep, and horses. By supplying these animals with food, we ourselves gain an easily available supply of food and labor. Often times, these animals can simply be allowed to roam pastures while eating grass, but at certain times of year, there may not be enough naturally growing food available to keep the animals fed. When this happens, plants are specifically grown by humans to feed the animals. Often times this animal food is hay.

Hay is grass that has been mowed and dried so that it can be stored and used as animal fodder. Many different types of plants can be used to make hay. Some of the most common ingredients are various types of grasses, legumes like

Cover to the propaganda comic book "Is This Tomorrow" by the Catechetical Guild. Image is in the public domain; via Wikimedia Commons.

alfalfa, and clovers. It's important for hay growers to keep up with what types of plants they're growing, or else they'll cut the hay at the wrong time and wind up with dry straw instead of nutritious hay.

Propaganda

Mother says that the prisoners are just men, like their own, and that if they are well treated, perhaps the Russian men will write home to their loved ones and let them know that the Hungarians, also, are "just simple people like we are."

Propaganda is a form of communication in which a large group, often a government, speaks to an entire society by distributing posters, pamphlets, advertisements, and other pieces of media to change the way people live or think. Propaganda might take the form of a reminder not to drink and drive, or it might be a courageous depiction of the nation's army, or it could be any other image or piece of information deemed necessary for the people to see.

In war time, propaganda spreads like wildfire, as no war can be fought without the people being in support of it. A propaganda war tends to become an ugly thing—the soldiers and even the citizens of the enemy country are often depicted as ugly, inhuman monsters, encouraging people to bitterly hate the other side and lend their support to the war effort. After a war, it is interesting to view the propaganda both sides produced, and you'll often find that both sides were accusing the other of being murderous savages while depicting themselves as great heroes. The purpose is to make each side believe that the other side does *not* consist of "just simple people like we are."

Brighty of the Grand Canyon

Sourdough

Someone tosses Brighty a sourdough biscuit. Most breads are created by a partnership between bakers and tiny microbes called yeasts—fungi which produce gases which in turn produce the air pockets that make the bread rise. Sourdough breads are a particular type which involves even more microbes than usual, bacteria which ferment the dough, producing lactic-acid, before it is cooked. This results in a bread that's slightly sour for much the same reason a traditionally made pickle is.

It's impossible to find the earliest sourdough recipe as mankind has been baking breads like this since before writing down recipes became fashionable. Some of the earliest evidence of sourdough breads dates back to nearly four thousand years before the birth of Christ in Switzerland, but there's no telling how long prehistoric bakers were making it before then.

Two naturally-leavened (sourdough) loaves. Photo by Chris R. Sims (Simsc). License CC BY-SA 4.0; via Wikimedia Commons.

Painting

Brighty carries painting supplies for the painter. As members of a creative species, many humans feel the urge to depict the world around them in the form of art, including music, storytelling, sculpture, and countless other means of self-expression. Painting is a form of art that dates back thousands of years, even as far back as humans were living in caves, as the stunning paintings of mammoths and other Ice Age animals created by our ancestors can attest.

Painting can be done with many different materials, which lend themselves to different styles that have been popular in different periods of history. Oil paints are made of different kinds of plant oils and were used extensively during the Renaissance by some of the greatest painters of all time. Pastels are dry, powdery pigments that were used for portraits in early modern times. There is a universe of potential art styles to be explored with a universe of different paints, and all sorts of combinations can be found in any art gallery.

Cottonwood Trees

There are cottonwood trees near the work site. Cottonwood is one of several names applied to trees in the Populus genus, of which many species can be found across North America. Other names for species in this genus are poplar and aspen. They are useful for their wood and can be quite fast-growing, making them useful for lumber and paper.

Scientifically, the Western Basalm Poplar became the first tree to have its genetic code completely analyzed by researchers. It was chosen for having a smaller, more compact genome than other trees, making it much easier to sequence.

P/K & LG Activity Supplies:

Day 1:
• Pattern blocks

Day 3:
• Food coloring

Day 4:
• Pattern blocks

Science Experiment Supplies:

• Ruler
• 1 book
• Masking tape
• Pencil
• Walnut-size modeling clay
• Small toy car that can roll down the ruler

• Empty thread spool
• Rubber band slightly longer than the thread spool
• 2 round toothpicks
• Masking tape
• Metal washer with a diameter smaller than that of the spool

Eat Your Way Through the USA Supplies:

Check ingredients for dishes from Alaska.

Dialectic, Real Science 4 Kids:

Experiment 1 on Day 4.

Week 28

	GRAMMAR	DIALECTIC	RHETORIC
BIBLE	Choose one of the following plans: ✠ PLAN 1: Journey Through the Bible, pp. 304-305 ✠ PLAN 2: Journey Through the Bible, pp. 318-323		
LANGUAGE ARTS	Choose appropriate level of one of the following: ❡ English Lessons Through Literature, Lesson 82 Reading Lessons Through Literature, phonogram review ❡ Rod and Staff English, Lesson 95 Copywork/Commonplace Book ❡ Your own grammar program		❡ LR: The Power in Your Hands, 1 lesson ❡ UR: WGRP, first draft. (10 days) ❡ LR: Rod and Staff 10, L. 91
MATH	Choose appropriate level of one of the following: ✎ Math-U-See, Video and page A ✎ Miquon/Singapore Math ✎ Your own math program		✎ Math-U-See, Video and page A ✎ Your own math program
GEOGRAPHY	🌐 50 States Reading, Alaska 🌐 Reading, choose one of the following: A. Hungary: The Singing Tree, 1/2 of Ch. 8 B. Arizona: Brighty of the Grand Canyon, Ch. 23-24		🌐 A Walk Along the Ganges, Ch. 2
HISTORY	Choose one spine, one or more core reading selections, and optional reading as desired.		
	♟ Spine: SOTW, Ch. 32.1 ♟ Core reading: 1. Burying the Sun, Ch. 3 2. Who Was Martin Luther King, Jr., Ch. 4 3. Candy Bomber, Ch. 4	♟ Spine: SOTW, Ch. 32.1 ♟ Core reading: 1. Hiroshima, pp. 1-15 (Kindle edition, 12 pages) 2. Where the Red Fern Grows, Ch. 12	♟ Spine: Western Civ, 1/4 of Ch. 27 World Empires, Missions, Wars, Unit 8 Week 3 ♟ Core reading: 1 & 2. Les Miserables, 14 pages 1. 1984, Ch. 3 2. Strength to Love, Ch. 4

Day 1

GRAMMAR	DIALECTIC	RHETORIC	
♪♪ Term 3 Composer: Choose between Shostakovich, Britten, Leon Kirchner ⧗ Timeline/Book of Centuries			ACTIVITIES
☞ Oral or written narration; LG students can draw a picture from the reading and tell about the picture. Suggested subject: history.		☞ Written narration for history or geography.	NARRATION
✛ Old Story New, Week 64 ℭ UD: Economics in One Lesson, Ch. 13		✛ LR: Cold-Case, Ch. 13 (1/2)	OTHER
📚 Literature: 1: The Orange Fairy Book: The White Slipper 2: Through the Looking-Glass, Ch. 4 3: The Princess and the Goblin, Ch. 4 4: Heidi, Ch. 15	📚 Literature: 5: Little Women, Ch. 35-36 6: The Patchwork Girl of Oz, Ch. 28 7: Northanger Abbey, Ch. 5 8: 20,000 Leagues, Ch. 34	📚 Book of English Verse, No. 817-818 ✛ Church History: Church History in Plain Language, Ch. 41 ✛ 100 Events, A.D. 1855	LITERATURE

PRESCHOOL AND LOWER GRAMMAR	
✎ Pathways: Path 1, Day 1 A. Kindergarten Gems B. Among the Meadow People C. 20th—Petunia D. Random House Poetry, p. 176	PATHWAYS
✎ Pattern block patterns Make patterns with the blocks, and have your little one tell you which block comes next. For example: Keep the pattern very simple for the youngest ones, and get more complicated for older children.	ACTIVITY

Week 28

	GRAMMAR	DIALECTIC	RHETORIC
BIBLE	Choose one of the following plans: ✜ PLAN 1: Journey Through the Bible, pp. 306-307 ✜ PLAN 2: Journey Through the Bible, pp. 324-327		
	✜ LG: TBB: The Good Samaritan ✜ UG: Egermeier's, 2 stories	✜ LD: Hurlbut's, 1 story ✜ UD: Golden's, 3 stories	
LANGUAGE ARTS	Choose appropriate level of one of the following: ❡ Reading Lessons Through Literature, next list and story ❡ Prepared dictation from ELTL, Spelling Wisdom, or today's reading ❡ Rod and Staff English, Lesson 96 ❡ Your own grammar program		
MATH	Choose appropriate level of one of the following:		
	✎ Math-U-See, page B ✎ Miquon/Singapore Math ✎ Your own math program		✎ Math-U-See, page B ✎ Your own math program
GEOGRAPHY	🌎 Reading, choose one of the following: A. Hungary: The Singing Tree, 1/2 of Ch. 8 B. Arizona: Brighty of the Grand Canyon, Ch. 25-26		🌎 Geography for Dummies, 1/2 of Ch. 14
SCIENCE	Choose one spine, one or more core reading selections, and optional reading as desired.		
	⚛ Core reading: 1. RS4K Physics, Ch. 8.3-8.4 2. Insiders Flight, pp. 20-25	⚛ Core reading: 1. RS4K Physics, Ch. 10 2. Objects in Motion, Ch. 5	⚛ Spine: SHSPhys, Week 8 Physics for Dummies, 1/2 of Ch. 15 Intro. Physics, pp. 270-273 (to last paragraph)
	⚛ Spine: Quark Chronicles: Physics, Ch. 10		⚛ Core reading:

Day 2

Grammar	Dialectic	Rhetoric	
♪ Term 3 Composer: Choose between Shostakovich, Britten, Leon Kirchner			Activities
🎨 Art Lesson: Choose appropriate level of one of the following:			
🎨 I Can Do All Things	🎨 Lamb's Book of Art II	🎨 How Great Thou ART I or II	
🎨 Lamb's Book of Art I	🎨 Feed My Sheep	🎨 Book of Many Colors	
⚛ GSA The World of Light and Sound, Lesson 7		🎨 Great Art, Lecture 28	
☛ Oral or written narration; LG students can draw a picture from the reading and tell about the picture. Suggested subject: Bible.		☛ Oral or written narration for science or Bible.	Narration
✟ Old Story New, Week 64			Other
	ങ UD: The Art of Argument, Fallacy 23	ങ UR: Classical English Rhetoric, 1/4 Ch. 14	
	ങ UD: Science Matters, pp. 91-105		
📚 Suggested read-aloud: The Borrowers, Ch. 20			Literature

Preschool and Lower Grammar	
✐ Pathways: Path 2 A. Little Wanderers, Ch. 28 B. Burgess Seashore Book, Ch. 31 C. Paddington Helps Out, Ch. 7 D. Random House Poetry, p. 177	Pathways
🎨 Art Lesson: Choose one of the following Barry Stebbing art books for you little one to do art like the big kids: Art and the Bible for Children, Baby Lamb's Book of Art, Joseph the Canada Goose, or Little Annie's Art Book.	Activity

Week 28

	GRAMMAR	DIALECTIC	RHETORIC
BIBLE	Choose one of the following plans: ✜ PLAN 1: Journey Through the Bible, pp. 308-309 ✜ PLAN 2: Journey Through the Bible, pp. 328-333		

LANGUAGE ARTS	Choose appropriate level of one of the following:
	
	❡ English Lessons Through Literature, Lesson 83
	    Reading Lessons Through Literature, phonogram review
	
	❡ Rod and Staff English, Lesson 97
	    Copywork/Commonplace Book
	
	❡ Your own grammar program
			❡ Essential Literary Terms, 3-4 pages
			
			❡ LR: The Power in Your Hands, 1 lesson
			
			❡ UR: WGRP, additional sources. (4 days)
			
			❡ LR: Rod and Staff 10, L. 92

MATH	Choose appropriate level of one of the following: ✎ Math-U-See, page C ✎ Miquon/Singapore Math ✎ Your own math program		✎ Math-U-See, page C ✎ Your own math program

GEOGRAPHY	🌐 50 States Mapping, Alaska
	
	🌐 Reading, choose one of the following:
	    A. Hungary: The Singing Tree, 1/2 of Ch. 9
	    B. Arizona: Brighty of the Grand Canyon, Ch. 27-28
			🌐 A Walk Along the Ganges, Ch. 3

HISTORY	Choose one spine, one or more core reading selections, and optional reading as desired.
	
	♟ Spine: SOTW, Ch. 32.2
	
	♟ Core reading:
	    1. Burying the Sun, Ch. 4
	    2. Who Was Martin Luther King, Jr., Ch. 5
	    3. Candy Bomber, Ch. 5
		♟ Spine: SOTW, Ch. 32.2
		
		♟ Core reading:
		    1. Hiroshima, pp. 16-30 (Kindle edition, 12 pages)
		    2. Where the Red Fern Grows, Ch. 13
			♟ Spine:
			    America, 1/4 of Ch. 31
			    World Empires, Missions, Wars, Unit 8 Week 3
			
			♟ Core reading:
			    1 & 2. Les Miserables, 14 pages
			    1. 1984, Ch. 4
			    2. Strength to Love, Ch. 5

Day 3

Grammar	Dialectic	Rhetoric	
♪♫ Term 3 Composer: Choose between Shostakovich, Britten, Leon Kirchner			Activities
☞ Oral or written narration; could be a group project. If you were going to join the characters in your book, what would you pack?			Narration
✚ Old Story New, Week 64 ✚ UD: Simply Christian, Ch. 8		✚ LR: Cold-Case, Ch. 14	Other
📖 Literature: 1: The Velveteen Rabbit 2: Through the Looking-Glass, Ch. 5 3: The Princess and the Goblin, Ch. 5 4: Heidi, Ch. 16	📖 Literature: 5: Little Women, Ch. 37 6: Otto of the Silver Hand, Ch. 1 7: Northanger Abbey, Ch. 6 8: 20,000 Leagues, Ch. 35	📖 Book of English Verse, No. 819-821 ✚ Church History: Church History in Plain Language, Ch. 42 ✚ 100 Events, A.D. 1857	Literature

Preschool and Lower Grammar	
✏ Pathways: Path 1, Day 2 A. Kindergarten Gems B. 50 Famous Stories C. JH—Moses the Kitten D. Random House Poetry, p. 178	Pathways
✏ Primary, secondary, and tertiary colors Explore colors with food coloring. Start with clear containers with water in them. Add primary colors of food coloring to each: read, blue, and yellow. To make secondary colors, combine two primary colors. And to make tertiary colors, add one primary color to one secondary color.	Activity

Week 28

	GRAMMAR	DIALECTIC	RHETORIC
BIBLE	Choose one of the following plans: ✠ PLAN 1: Journey Through the Bible, pp. 310-311 ✠ PLAN 2: Journey Through the Bible, pp. 334-339		
	✠ LG: TBB: Mary and Martha ✠ UG: Egermeier's, 2 stories	✠ LD: Hurlbut's, 1 story ✠ UD: Golden's, 3 stories	
LANGUAGE ARTS	Choose appropriate level of one of the following: ❡ Reading Lessons Through Literature, next list and story ❡ Prepared dictation from ELTL, Spelling Wisdom, or today's reading ❡ Your own grammar program		❡ UR: WGRP, additional sources. (4 days)
MATH	Choose appropriate level of one of the following:		
	✎ Math-U-See, page D ✎ Miquon/Singapore Math ✎ Your own math program		✎ Math-U-See, page D ✎ Your own math program
GEOGRAPHY	🌐 Reading, choose one of the following: A. Hungary: The Singing Tree, 1/2 of Ch. 9 B. Arizona: Brighty of the Grand Canyon, Ch. 29-30		
SCIENCE	Choose one spine, one or more core reading selections, and optional reading as desired.		
	⚛ Core reading: 1. RS4K Physics, Ch. 9.1-9.2 2. Insiders Flight, pp. 26-31	⚛ Core reading: 1. RS4K Physics, Ch. 10 Experiment 1. Black Holes and Uncle Albert, Ch. 3 2. Liquids and Gases, Ch. 1	⚛ Spine: SHSPhys, Week 8 Manga Relativity, pp. 75-85 Intro. Physics, pp. 273-276 ⚛ Core reading: The Elegant Universe, Ch. 1
	⚛ Optional extra reading, topic: Sound Energy Simon Bloom, Ch. 22-23 Adventures in Sound with Max Axiom by Emily Sohn		

Day 4

GRAMMAR	DIALECTIC	RHETORIC	
♪♫ Term 3 Composer: Choose between Shostakovich, Britten, Leon Kirchner			ACTIVITIES
⚛ GSA The World of Light and Sound, Lesson 8 ⚛ 201 Awesome Experiments, 179-180		🎨 Great Art Writing	
↩ Oral or written narration; LG students can draw a picture from the reading and tell about the picture. Suggested subject: science.		↩ Written narration for science or Bible.	NARRATION
✢ Old Story New, Week 64			OTHER
	ℭℬ UD: The Art of Argument: Create an ad or an argument using this week's fallacy ℭℬ UD: Science Matters, pp. 106-120	ℭℬ UR: Classical English Rhetoric, 1/4 Ch. 14	
📚 Suggested read-aloud: The Neverending Story, Ch. 1			LITERATURE
PRESCHOOL AND LOWER GRAMMAR			
✏ Pathways: Path 3 A. Burgess Flower Book, Ch. 32 B. TumTum and Nutmeg, Ch. 15 C. Henry Huggins, Ch. 4 D. Random House Poetry, p. 179			PATHWAYS
✏ Pattern block sides and corners Teach the terms side and corner. A side is the straight part, and a corner is the point where two sides meet. Have the child count the sides and corners of each shape.			ACTIVITY

Week 28

	GRAMMAR	DIALECTIC	RHETORIC
BIBLE	Choose one of the following plans: ✛ PLAN 1: Journey Through the Bible, pp. 312-313 ✛ PLAN 2: Journey Through the Bible, pp. 340-343		

LANGUAGE ARTS	Choose appropriate level of one of the following:
	
	❡ English Lessons Through Literature, Lesson 84
	   Reading Lessons Through Literature, phonogram review
	
	❡ Rod and Staff English, Lesson 98
	   Copywork/Commonplace Book
	
	❡ Your own grammar program
			❡ A Rulebook for Arguments, Ch. 35-36
			
			❡ LR: The Power in Your Hands, 1 lesson
			
			❡ LR: Rod and Staff 10, L. 93

MATH	Choose appropriate level of one of the following: ✎ Math-U-See, page E ✎ Miquon/Singapore Math ✎ Your own math program		✎ Math-U-See, pages E & H ✎ Your own math program
GEOGRAPHY	🌏 Mapping: Western Africa 🌏 Reading, choose one of the following: B. Arizona: Brighty of the Grand Canyon, Ch. 31-32		🌏 A Walk Along the Ganges, Ch. 4

HISTORY	Choose one spine, one or more core reading selections, and optional reading as desired.
	
	♟ Spine:
	
	♟ Core reading:
	   1. Burying the Sun, Ch. 5
	   2. Who Was Martin Luther King, Jr., Ch. 6
	   3. Candy Bomber, Ch. 6
		♟ Spine:
		
		♟ Core reading:
		   1. Hiroshima, pp. 31-45 (Kindle edition, 12 pages)
		   2. Where the Red Fern Grows, Ch. 14
			♟ Spine:
			   America, 1/4 of Ch. 31
			   World Empires, Missions, Wars, Unit 8 Week 3
			
			♟ Core reading:
			   1 & 2. Les Miserables, 14 pages
			   LR: 1 & 2. Philosophy Book, through Wittgenstein
			   UR: 1 & 2. Think, 1/2 Ch. 3
			   1. 1984, Ch. 5
			   2. Strength to Love, Ch. 6

Day 5

Grammar	Dialectic	Rhetoric	
♪♪ Term 3 Composer: Choose between Shostakovich, Britten, Leon Kirchner 🍔 Eat Your Way Through the USA, Alaska 🎨 Art Lesson: Choose appropriate level of one of the following:			ACTIVITIES
🎨 I Can Do All Things 🎨 Lamb's Book of Art I	🎨 Lamb's Book of Art II 🎨 Feed My Sheep	🎨 How Great Thou ART I or II 🎨 Book of Many Colors	
👉 Oral or written narration; LG students can draw a picture from the reading and tell about the picture. Suggested subject: geography.		👉 Oral or written narration for history or geography.	NARRATION
✠ Old Story New, Week 64 ෴ UD: Economics in One Lesson, Ch. 14			OTHER
📚 Suggested read-aloud: The Neverending Story, Ch. 2			LITERATURE
📚 Literature: 1: Five Little Peppers and How They Grew, Ch. 1 2: Through the Looking-Glass, Ch. 6 3: The Princess and the Goblin, Ch. 6 4: Heidi, Ch. 17	📚 Literature: 5: Little Women, Ch. 38-39 6: Otto of the Silver Hand, Ch. 2 7: Northanger Abbey, Ch. 7 8: 20,000 Leagues, Ch. 36	📚 Book of English Verse, No. 822-824 ✠ Church History: Church History in Plain Language, Ch. 43 ✠ 100 Events, A.D. 1865	

Preschool and Lower Grammar	
✏ Pathways: Path 1, Day 3 A. Kindergarten Gems B. Among the Meadow People C. JH—Only One Woof D. Random House Poetry, p. 180	PATHWAYS
🎨 Art Lesson: Choose one of the following Barry Stebbing art books for you little one to do art like the big kids: Art and the Bible for Children, Baby Lamb's Book of Art, Joseph the Canada Goose, or Little Annie's Art Book.	ACTIVITY

Moka, a fifteen year old female western lowland gorilla at the Pittsburgh Zoo, with her new baby, a male born on February 8 or 9). The baby gorilla's father is a twenty year old silverback named Mrithi. Photo by Sage Ross. License: CC BY-SA 3.0; via Wikimedia Commons.

History Through Art: Diane Fossey

Long before the Western world knew that gorillas existed, stories existed about them, stories of the terrifying "pongo" which lived in the darkest jungles of Africa, intent on killing and devouring any human who ventured too close. For a time, they were a myth. Even when they were finally discovered to be fact, they were still thought of as near-legendary monsters, not as animals fit for study. In particular, the mountain gorilla, rarest of all gorillas, was barely known at all.

Then came Dian Fossey. One of the foremost primatologists in the entire world, Fossey traveled to the remote country of Rwanda to live in the high jungles to study mountain gorillas in their natural habitats. Her research took an unconventional form. Instead of tracking the gorillas from a distance or studying the remains of dead animals, she crawled into forest clearings with them, imitating their grunts and even eating the same plants that they ate. She eventually became accepted by a group of the large apes, and the true bulk of her research could take place.

Through Fossey's research, the world learned what gorillas truly are: largely peaceful herbivores which roam the mountains in closely bonded groups. They care for their young, and while the big males can be a tad threatening if they feel their families are in danger, they are generally not overly aggressive and would certainly never eat a human being!

Unfortunately, humans proved to be the more dangerous of the two species in regards to the other. Poachers would constantly capture infant gorillas to sell to zoos. Since the other gorillas of the group wouldn't allow this without a fight, these expeditions often ended in dozens of gorillas being shot and left to die in the forest. Dian Fossey fiercely opposed the activities of poachers and argued against keeping the animals in zoos on the grounds that keeping such intelligent creatures locked away against their will was tantamount to slavery.

The struggle eventually claimed Fossey's life when a poacher found her in her remote research outpost. She was found murdered in a case that has never been solved, killed for her passion and courage.

The Singing Tree

Spiders

Peter calls Uncle Moses "the old spider." Have you ever stumbled through a spider web, finding yourself scrambling to pull the sticky bits of thread off of you before the eight-legged creature within touches your skin? I certainly have. While it's unpleasant, I suppose I should consider myself lucky—a bug that flies into a spider web is in for a much worse time!

Out of the many different types of spiders, only some of them spin webs. The ones that do are masters of capturing insects while barely having to move or work for themselves. The ones that don't are like tiny wolves or panthers, stalking along the ground to ambush bugs and bring them down with a swift venomous bite. One thing all spiders have in common, besides their eight legs, is the fact that every single one of them is a predator for all bugs to fear.

The Metric System

Mother's parents live over fifty kilometers away. A fathom is 2 yards. A yard is 3 feet. A foot has 12 inches. And a mile is 5,280 feet, or 1,760 yards. And that's just for measuring length. For measuring volume, a gallon is 128 ounces or 16 cups or 8 pints or 4 quarts. For measuring mass, we have the pound, which is 16 ounces. A stone is 14 pounds. A hundredweight is (are you ready for this?) 112 pounds; I was really expecting 100 pounds to a hundredweight. And a ton is 2,240 pounds. And did you notice that ounces can be used to measure both volume and mass?

If you find this confusing, you're not the only one.

Consider instead a system which has base units for different types of measurements—the meter for length, the kilogram for mass, and the liter for volume. And to keep it simple, consider a system of prefixes that we can add to these basic measurements. *Kilo* means thousand, so a kilometer is 1,000 meters. *Centi* means 1/100th and *milli* means 1/1,000th, so a meter has 100 centimeters and 1,000 millimeters. And these prefixes also work with grams and liters! With this system, called the metric system, learning just a few basic facts such as these helps us with all measurements, and it makes the math of measurements simpler, too.

The metric system is based off of a French system which dates back to 1799. Over the years, the meter and kilogram have been refined as units of measurements, and more units have been added. Today, the metric system is an internationally agreed upon decimal system of measurement. Although the metric system was officially sanctioned in the United States in 1866, it is still not in common usage. Most other industrialized nations have adopted it at least for official purposes.

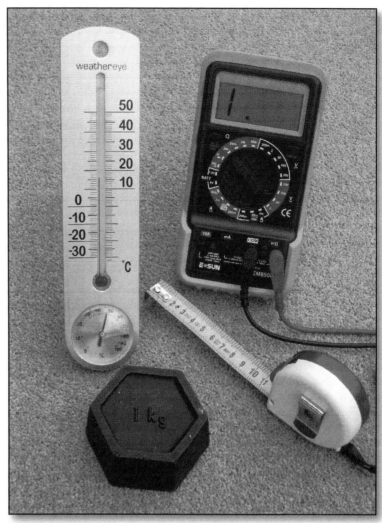

Four metric measuring devices - a tape measure, a thermometer, a one kilogram weight and an electrical multimeter. These instruments were selected to show some of the units of measure that part of the metric system (or more correctly) SI - centimetres, kilograms, degrees Celsius, amperes, volts and ohms. Photo by Martinvl. License: CC BY-SA 3.0; via Wikimedia Commons.

The old system of fathoms, feet, and yards is called the imperial system of measure. It's not only inconsistent but impractical for scientific and industrial purposes. There is an estimated cost for using the imperial system in the United States when many instruments and tools are based on the metric system. For example, car mechanics must maintain two sets of tools for cars that are produced overseas but also in the United States. More and more, the metric system is being taught in schools and it is suspected that eventually the imperial system will simply be phased out.

Amnesia

One man in the hospital has amnesia. Amnesia is memory loss which can be caused by brain damage, sedatives or other drugs, or even psychological trauma. Two main types of amnesia have been identified. The first, retrograde amnesia, prevents the sufferer from retrieving information before a certain point in time, such as the date of an accident which caused the amnesia. Anterograde amnesia prevents the sufferer from acquiring new memories.

Many types of amnesia will heal over time, and the sufferer can expect most if not all memories to return. Occupational therapy has also made great strides in developing methods to help amnesiacs use the memory skills they still have in order to organize information or improve quality of life. Today's technology also provides many small digital devices which can be used to keep track of day-to-day tasks. Amnesia, while still frightening and poorly understood, is not as devastating as it was in previous decades.

Brighty of the Grand Canyon

Tracking

Irons had dreamed that law enforcement had tracked his footprints and found him. Tracking is the art of looking at animal tracks and other signs of their passing in order to learn about their habits, their trails, and their presence. It has been a premier skill for hunters from the earliest times because in order to successfully hunt an animal, you first have to find it. Tracking was really the first ecological science, next to the anatomical exercise of butchering an animal for food.

A skilled tracker learns the habits of the animals in their environments and studies their behavior intensively. For instance, if the tracker follows deer in a forest, he will learn where the deer go in order to safely sleep, or what they like to eat and where they go for water. They learn the size of the deer herds and even how many adult males or females are present. They can even judge the number of young deer, called fawns, present in the herd by the size of the tracks.

Tracking is still used by hunters, but is also by scientists who study animals in the wild. Sometimes skilled trackers are called into help locate lost people in the wilderness or escaped criminals. With a little skill and practice, tracking can be done in your backyard or a park as easily as in the forests or deserts.

Mountain Lions

Homer and Jake hear the sound of a mountain lion. Powerful and mysterious, the mountain lion is one of the most successful predators in the Americas. It is a huge cat, big enough to bring down deer and elk as easily as lions bring down antelopes on the African plains. Despite its size, however, it is more closely related to purring house cats than it is to roaring lions!

The true measure of the mountain lion's success is its range. The mountain lion is the only predator to inhabit every environment from the frigid forests of Alaska, down through the arid western United States, straight through the Amazon rainforest, and all the way to the Andes mountains at the southernmost tip of South America. It is found everywhere, and has earned quite a few names over the whole of its range. Cougar, puma, catamount, and panther are all proper titles for this remarkable feline.

Lumberjacks

Home had been offered a job as a lumberjack. Lumberjacks are people who work to cut down trees. The lumberjacks cut down the trees and ship them to other locations for use in wood products. The romanticism of the lumberjack comes from the previous century in the United States when hand tools were used and lumberjacking was a hazardous profession for hardy men in the wilderness. The term is part of popular American culture and is often used to describe robust, bearded men in the forests. The work was hard and dangerous for little pay, and the men lived in primitive conditions. Their work was centered around the Pacific Northwest and up into the Canadian wilderness.

A woman who works in the timber industry is sometimes called a "lumberjill." The term originated in Britain during World War II. More common today is the term logger to describe woodcutters of either sex.

Logging scene, near Bellingham, WA, from a c. 1910 postcard published by Sprouse & Son, Importers & Publishers, Tacoma, Washington. Image is in the public domain; via Wikimedia Commons.

P/K & LG Activity Supplies:

Day 1:
• Address labels

Day 3:
• Pattern blocks
• Pattern block pictures, if desired. This site has some incredible pattern block designs, including some more complicated designs for older children. Don't miss the links at the bottom of the screen! There are three pages total. There are also PDFs which have all the images in black and white instead of color:

www.raebear.net/goodies/patternblocks/

This site has games and other activities for grades K-2:

catalog.mathlearningcenter.org/files/pdfs/PBLCCSSK2-0412w.pdf

Day 4:
• Address labels
• Cardstock

Science Experiment Supplies:

• 1-gallon paint can, never opened
• 6 marbles
• 3 heavy books

• Modeling clay
• 12 round toothpicks
• 2 pencils

Eat Your Way Through the USA Supplies:

Check ingredients for dishes from Hawaii.

LR, Cold-Case Christianity: This week, you'll read the Postscript of *Cold-Case Christianity*, in which J. Warner Wallace describes the "Two Decision Christian," a concept not mentioned in the Bible. The Bible does explain what happens when someone seems to accept Christ, only to then reject Him. In the parable of the sower, Jesus covers four possibilities for what happens when someone hears the word. The parable is found in Matthew 13:3-9, 18-23:

> And He spoke many things to them in parables, saying, "Behold, the sower went out to sow; and as he sowed, some seeds fell beside the road, and the

birds came and ate them up. Others fell on the rocky places, where they did not have much soil; and immediately they sprang up, because they had no depth of soil. But when the sun had risen, they were scorched; and because they had no root, they withered away. Others fell among the thorns, and the thorns came up and choked them out. And others fell on the good soil and yielded a crop, some a hundredfold, some sixty, and some thirty. He who has ears, let him hear."...

"Hear then the parable of the sower. When anyone hears the word of the kingdom and does not understand it, the evil one comes and snatches away what has been sown in his heart. This is the one on whom seed was sown beside the road. The one on whom seed was sown on the rocky places, this is the man who hears the word and immediately receives it with joy; yet he has no firm root in himself, but is only temporary, and when affliction or persecution arises because of the word, immediately he falls away. And the one on whom seed was sown among the thorns, this is the man who hears the word, and the worry of the world and the deceitfulness of wealth choke the word, and it becomes unfruitful. And the one on whom seed was sown on the good soil, this is the man who hears the word and understands it; who indeed bears fruit and brings forth, some a hundredfold, some sixty, and some thirty."

Week 29

	Grammar	Dialectic	Rhetoric
Bible	Choose one of the following plans: ✠ PLAN 1: Journey Through the Bible, pp. 314-315 ✠ PLAN 2: What the Bible Is All About, Acts (1/2)		

Language Arts	Choose appropriate level of one of the following:
	
	¶ English Lessons Through Literature, Lesson 85
	    Reading Lessons Through Literature, phonogram review
	
	¶ Rod and Staff English, Lesson 99
	    Copywork/Commonplace Book
	
	¶ Your own grammar program
			¶ LR: The Power in Your Hands, 1 lesson
			
			¶ UR: WGRP, additional sources. (4 days)
			
			¶ LR: Rod and Staff 10, L. 94

Math	Choose appropriate level of one of the following: ✎ Math-U-See, Video and page A ✎ Miquon/Singapore Math ✎ Your own math program		✎ Math-U-See, Video and page A ✎ Your own math program

Geography	🌐 50 States Reading, Hawaii
	
	🌐 Reading, choose one of the following:
	    A. Hungary: The Singing Tree, 1/2 of Ch. 10
	    B. Arizona: Brighty of the Grand Canyon, Ch. 33-34
			🌐 A Walk Along the Ganges, Ch. 5

History	Choose one spine, one or more core reading selections, and optional reading as desired.		

	♟ Spine: SOTW, Ch. 33.1
	
	♟ Core reading:
	    1. Burying the Sun, Ch. 6
	    2. Who Was Martin Luther King, Jr., Ch. 7
	    3. Who Was Gandhi, Intro. - Ch. 1
		♟ Spine: SOTW, Ch. 33.1
		
		♟ Core reading:
		    1. Hiroshima, pp. 46-60 (Kindle edition, 12 pages)
		    2. Where the Red Fern Grows, Ch. 15
			♟ Spine:
			    Western Civ, 1/4 of Ch. 28
			    World Empires, Missions, Wars, Unit 8 Week 4
			
			♟ Core reading:
			    1 & 2. Les Miserables, 14 pages
			    1. 1984, Ch. 6
			    2. Strength to Love, Ch. 7

Day 1

Grammar	Dialectic	Rhetoric	
♪♪ Term 3 Composer: Choose between Shostakovich, Britten, Leon Kirchner ⧗ Timeline/Book of Centuries			Activities
☞ Oral or written narration; LG students can draw a picture from the reading and tell about the picture. Suggested subject: history.		☞ Written narration for history or geography.	Narration
✛ Old Story New, Week 65 ଓ UD: Economics in One Lesson, Ch. 15		✛ LR: Cold-Case, Postscript	Other
📚 Literature: 1: Five Little Peppers and How They Grew, Ch. 2 2: Through the Looking-Glass, Ch. 7 3: The Princess and the Goblin, Ch. 7 4: Heidi, Ch. 18	📚 Literature: 5: Little Women, Ch. 40 6: Otto of the Silver Hand, Ch. 3 7: Northanger Abbey, Ch. 8 8: 20,000 Leagues, Ch. 37	📚 Book of English Verse, No. 825-827 ✛ Church History: Church History in Plain Language, Ch. 44 ✛ 100 Events, A.D. 1870	Literature
Preschool and Lower Grammar			
✏ Pathways: Path 1, Day 1 A. Kindergarten Gems B. 50 Famous Stories C. 20th—First Tomato D. Random House Poetry, p. 181			Pathways
✏ Address label stickers Have your child create his own stickers with address labels, then decorate a page with them. He can draw pictures on each sticker individually, or draw a large picture that covers the whole page.			Activity

Week 29

	GRAMMAR	DIALECTIC	RHETORIC
BIBLE	Choose one of the following plans: ✠ PLAN 1: Journey Through the Bible, pp. 316-317 ✠ PLAN 2: What the Bible Is All About, Acts (1/2)		
	✠ LG: TBB: The Lost Sheep ✠ UG: Egermeier's, 2 stories	✠ LD: Hurlbut's, 1 story ✠ UD: Golden's, 3 stories	
LANGUAGE ARTS	Choose appropriate level of one of the following: ❡ Reading Lessons Through Literature, next list and story ❡ Prepared dictation from ELTL, Spelling Wisdom, or today's reading ❡ Your own grammar program		❡ UR: WGRP, additional sources. (4 days)
MATH	Choose appropriate level of one of the following:		
	✎ Math-U-See, page B ✎ Miquon/Singapore Math ✎ Your own math program		✎ Math-U-See, page B ✎ Your own math program
GEOGRAPHY	🌐 Reading, choose one of the following: A. Hungary: The Singing Tree, 1/2 of Ch. 10 B. Arizona: Brighty of the Grand Canyon, Ch. 35-36		🌐 Geography for Dummies, 1/2 of Ch. 15
SCIENCE	Choose one spine, one or more core reading selections, and optional reading as desired.		
	⚛ Core reading: 1. RS4K Physics, Ch. 9.3-9.4 2. Insiders Flight, pp. 32-37	⚛ Core reading: 1. Black Holes and Uncle Albert, Ch. 4 2. Liquids and Gases, Ch. 2	⚛ Spine: SHSPhys, Week 9 Physics for Dummies, 1/2 of Ch. 15 Intro. Physics, pp. 279-284 ⚛ Core reading: The Elegant Universe, Ch. 2
	⚛ Spine: Quark Chronicles: Physics, Ch. 11		

Day 2

Grammar	Dialectic	Rhetoric	
♪ Term 3 Composer: Choose between Shostakovich, Britten, Leon Kirchner 🎨 Art Lesson: Choose appropriate level of one of the following:			**ACTIVITIES**
🎨 I Can Do All Things 🎨 Lamb's Book of Art I	🎨 Lamb's Book of Art II 🎨 Feed My Sheep	🎨 How Great Thou ART I or II 🎨 Book of Many Colors	
⚛ GSA The World of Light and Sound, Lesson 9		🎨 Great Art, Lecture 29	
↪ Oral or written narration; LG students can draw a picture from the reading and tell about the picture. Suggested subject: Bible.		↪ Oral or written narration for science or Bible.	**NARRATION**
✠ Old Story New, Week 65			**OTHER**
	✿ UD: The Art of Argument, Fallacy 24 ✿ UD: Science Matters, pp. 121-135	✿ UR: Classical English Rhetoric, 1/4 Ch. 15	
📚 Suggested read-aloud: The Neverending Story, Ch. 3			**LITERATURE**
PRESCHOOL AND LOWER GRAMMAR			
✏ Pathways: Path 2 A. Little Wanderers, Ch. 29 B. Burgess Seashore Book, Ch. 32 C. Paddington Helps Out, Ch. 8 D. Random House Poetry, p. 182			**PATHWAYS**
🎨 Art Lesson: Choose one of the following Barry Stebbing art books for you little one to do art like the big kids: Art and the Bible for Children, Baby Lamb's Book of Art, Joseph the Canada Goose, or Little Annie's Art Book.			**ACTIVITY**

Week 29

	GRAMMAR	DIALECTIC	RHETORIC
BIBLE	Choose one of the following plans: ✛ PLAN 1: Journey Through the Bible, pp. 318-319 ✛ PLAN 2: The Story, Ch. 28		

LANGUAGE ARTS	Choose appropriate level of one of the following:
	
	❡ English Lessons Through Literature, Lesson 86
	    Reading Lessons Through Literature, phonogram review
	
	❡ Rod and Staff English, Lesson 100
	    Copywork/Commonplace Book
	
	❡ Your own grammar program
			❡ Essential Literary Terms, 3-4 pages
			
			❡ LR: The Power in Your Hands, 1 lesson
			
			❡ UR: WGRP, int. sources. (3 days)
			
			❡ LR: Rod and Staff 10, L. 95

MATH	Choose appropriate level of one of the following: ✎ Math-U-See, page C ✎ Miquon/Singapore Math ✎ Your own math program		✎ Math-U-See, page C ✎ Your own math program
GEOGRAPHY	🌐 50 States Mapping, Hawaii		

	🌐 Reading, choose one of the following:
	    A. Hungary: The Singing Tree, 1/2 of Ch. 11
	    B. Montana: Smoky the Cowhorse, Ch. 1
			🌐 A Walk Along the Ganges, Ch. 6

HISTORY	Choose one spine, one or more core reading selections, and optional reading as desired.		

	♟ Spine: SOTW, Ch. 33.2
	
	♟ Core reading:
	    1. Burying the Sun, Ch. 7
	    2. Who Was Martin Luther King, Jr., Ch. 8
	    3. Who Was Gandhi, Ch. 2
		♟ Spine: SOTW, Ch. 33.2
		
		♟ Core reading:
		    1. Hiroshima, pp. 61-75 (Kindle edition, 12 pages)
		    2. Where the Red Fern Grows, Ch. 16
			♟ Spine:
			    Western Civ, 1/4 of Ch. 28
			    America, 1/4 of Ch. 32
			    World Empires, Missions, Wars, Unit 8 Week 4
			
			♟ Core reading:
			    1 & 2. Les Miserables, 14 pages
			    1. 1984, Ch. 7
			    2. Strength to Love, Ch. 8

Day 3

Grammar	Dialectic	Rhetoric	
♪♪ Term 3 Composer: Choose between Shostakovich, Britten, Leon Kirchner			ACTIVITIES
✆ Oral or written narration; could be a group project. Create a newspaper for your book. Have brief articles to summarize the plot and tell about the main character. Have a section telling about the weather, and include ads for the clothing of the time.			NARRATION
✛ Old Story New, Week 65 ✛ UD: Simply Christian, Ch. 9			OTHER
📚 Literature: 1: Five Little Peppers and How They Grew, Ch. 3 2: Through the Looking-Glass, Ch. 8 3: The Princess and the Goblin, Ch. 8 4: Heidi, Ch. 19	📚 Literature: 5: Little Women, Ch. 41-42 6: Otto of the Silver Hand, Ch. 4 7: Northanger Abbey, Ch. 9 8: 20,000 Leagues, Ch. 38	📚 Book of English Verse, No. 828-830 ✛ Church History: Church History in Plain Language, Ch. 45 ✛ 100 Events, A.D. 1886	LITERATURE

Preschool and Lower Grammar	
✐ Pathways: Path 1, Day 2 A. Kindergarten Gems B. Among the Meadow People C. JH—The Christmas Day Kitten D. Random House Poetry, p. 183	PATHWAYS
✐ Pattern block pictures Use pattern blocks to make pictures. You can find lots of designs online by searching "pattern block designs." These can be printed, and the child can fill the picture in with blocks.	ACTIVITY

Week 29

	GRAMMAR	DIALECTIC	RHETORIC
BIBLE	Choose one of the following plans: ✠ PLAN 1: Journey Through the Bible, pp. 320-321 ✠ PLAN 2: Journey Through the Bible, pp. 344-349		
	✠ LG: TBB: The Lost Son; Ten Lepers ✠ UG: Egermeier's, 2 stories	✠ LD: Hurlbut's, 1 story ✠ UD: Golden's, 3 stories	
LANGUAGE ARTS	Choose appropriate level of one of the following: ❡ Reading Lessons Through Literature, next list and story ❡ Prepared dictation from ELTL, Spelling Wisdom, or today's reading ❡ Your own grammar program		❡ UR: WGRP, int. sources. (3 days)
MATH	Choose appropriate level of one of the following: ✎ Math-U-See, page D ✎ Miquon/Singapore Math ✎ Your own math program		✎ Math-U-See, page D ✎ Your own math program
GEOGRAPHY	🌍 Reading, choose one of the following: A. Hungary: The Singing Tree, 1/2 of Ch. 11 B. Montana: Smoky the Cowhorse, Ch. 2		
SCIENCE	Choose one spine, one or more core reading selections, and optional reading as desired.		
	⚛ Core reading: 1. RS4K Physics, Ch. 10.1-10.2 2. Insiders Flight, pp. 38-43	⚛ Core reading: 1. Black Holes and Uncle Albert, Ch. 5 2. Liquids and Gases, Ch. 3	⚛ Spine: SHSPhys, Week 9 Manga Relativity, pp. 86-96 Intro. Physics, pp. 284-287 ⚛ Core reading: The Elegant Universe, Ch. 3
	⚛ Optional extra reading, topic: Law of Conservation of Energy Simon Bloom, Ch. 24-25		

Day 4

Grammar	Dialectic	Rhetoric	
♪♪ Term 3 Composer: Choose between Shostakovich, Britten, Leon Kirchner			ACTIVITIES
⚛ GSA The World of Light and Sound, Lesson 10 ⚛ 201 Awesome Experiments, 181-182		🎨 Great Art Writing	ACTIVITIES
↪ Oral or written narration; LG students can draw a picture from the reading and tell about the picture. Suggested subject: science.		↪ Written narration for science or Bible.	NARRATION
✛ Old Story New, Week 65			OTHER
	☙ UD: The Art of Argument: Create an ad or an argument using this week's fallacy ☙ UD: Science Matters, pp. 136-150	☙ UR: Classical English Rhetoric, 1/4 Ch. 15	OTHER
📚 Suggested read-aloud: The Neverending Story, Ch. 4			LITERATURE

Preschool and Lower Grammar

✏ Pathways: Path 3 A. Burgess Flower Book, Ch. 33 B. Gooney Bird Greene, Ch. 1 C. Henry Huggins, Ch. 5 D. Random House Poetry, pp. 184-185	PATHWAYS
✏ Address label puzzle Have your child make a large picture on a sheet of address labels. Then, place the labels on a piece of cardstock. Cut the labels apart, and enjoy your puzzle.	ACTIVITY

Week 29

	GRAMMAR	DIALECTIC	RHETORIC
BIBLE	Choose one of the following plans: ✛ PLAN 1: Journey Through the Bible, pp. 322-323 ✛ PLAN 2: Journey Through the Bible, pp. 350-355		

LANGUAGE ARTS	Choose appropriate level of one of the following:
	
	❡ English Lessons Through Literature, Lesson 87
	   Reading Lessons Through Literature, phonogram review
	
	❡ Rod and Staff English, Lesson 101
	   Copywork/Commonplace Book
	
	❡ Your own grammar program
			❡ A Rulebook for Arguments, Ch. 37-38
			
			❡ LR: The Power in Your Hands, 1 lesson
			
			❡ LR: Rod and Staff 10, L. 96

MATH	Choose appropriate level of one of the following: ✏ Math-U-See, page E ✏ Miquon/Singapore Math ✏ Your own math program		✏ Math-U-See, pages E & H ✏ Your own math program
GEOGRAPHY	🌍 Mapping: Central Africa 🌍 Reading, choose one of the following: B. Montana: Smoky the Cowhorse, Ch. 3		🌍 A Walk Along the Ganges, Ch. 7
HISTORY	Choose one spine, one or more core reading selections, and optional reading as desired.		

	♟ Spine: SOTW, Ch. 34.1
	
	♟ Core reading:
	   1. Burying the Sun, Ch. 8
	   2. Who Was Martin Luther King, Jr., Ch. 9
	   3. Who Was Gandhi, Ch. 3
		♟ Spine: SOTW, Ch. 34.1
		
		♟ Core reading:
		   1. Hiroshima, pp. 76-90 (Kindle edition, 12 pages)
		   2. Where the Red Fern Grows, Ch. 17
			♟ Spine:
			   America, 1/4 of Ch. 32
			   World Empires, Missions, Wars, Unit 8 Week 4
			
			♟ Core reading:
			   1 & 2. Les Miserables, 14 pages
			   LR: 1 & 2. Philosophy Book, through Marcuse
			   UR: 1 & 2. Think, Ch. 4
			   1. 1984, Ch. 8
			   2. Strength to Love, Ch. 9

Day 5

Grammar	Dialectic	Rhetoric	
♪ Term 3 Composer: Choose between Shostakovich, Britten, Leon Kirchner			Activities
🍔 Eat Your Way Through the USA, Hawaii			
🎨 Art Lesson: Choose appropriate level of one of the following:			
🎨 I Can Do All Things	🎨 Lamb's Book of Art II	🎨 How Great Thou ART I or II	
🎨 Lamb's Book of Art I	🎨 Feed My Sheep	🎨 Book of Many Colors	
☞ Oral or written narration; LG students can draw a picture from the reading and tell about the picture. Suggested subject: geography.		☞ Oral or written narration for history or geography.	Narration
✚ Old Story New, Week 65			Other
📚 Suggested read-aloud: The Neverending Story, Ch. 5			
📚 Literature: 1: Five Little Peppers and How They Grew, Ch. 4 2: Through the Looking-Glass, Ch. 9 3: The Princess and the Goblin, Ch. 9 4: Heidi, Ch. 20	📚 Literature: 5: Little Women, Ch. 43 6: Otto of the Silver Hand, Ch. 5 7: Northanger Abbey, Ch. 10 8: 20,000 Leagues, Ch. 39	📚 Book of English Verse, No. 831-833 ✚ Church History: Church History in Plain Language, Ch. 46 ✚ 100 Events, A.D. 1906	Literature

Preschool and Lower Grammar	
🖊 Pathways: Path 1, Day 3 A. Kindergarten Gems B. 50 Famous Stories C. JH—Bonny's Big Day D. Random House Poetry, p. 186	Pathways
🎨 Art Lesson: Choose one of the following Barry Stebbing art books for you little one to do art like the big kids: Art and the Bible for Children, Baby Lamb's Book of Art, Joseph the Canada Goose, or Little Annie's Art Book.	Activity

Alex the Parrot. © Copyright 2015 Alex Foundation (www.alexfoundation.org).
Used by permission.

History Through Art: Alex the Parrot

Parrots are one of the only creatures on this planet gifted with the power of speech, with humankind itself being the only other notable example. While parrots can mimic human voices with startling precision, they generally don't fully comprehend what they are saying, just like you could repeat a sentence in a foreign language without understanding the meaning of the words. Or so people thought. One study conducted with a parrot named Alex suggests that some parrots may be a lot more clever than they let on.

Alex was a normal African gray parrot purchased at a pet store by animal psychologist Irene Pepperberg, who wished to find out just how much a parrot was capable of understanding. The name Alex was an acronym for Avian Language EXperiment, and that's just what Alex's education would be: an experiment to discover whether or not birds like the African gray parrot could understand language.

The experiment certainly revealed a lot! The testing was simple in the beginning. They taught Alex the names of colors and numbers. Afterward, they asked him to tell them things about blocks that they put in front of him. Alex learned to correctly say how many blocks were put in front of him and what color each was, proving that he was aware of the meaning of the words which he'd been taught. Later on, Alex figured out how to use our language for his own purposes. For instance, he learned to say, "Sorry," if he thought the researchers were irritated with him. When he was first given an apple, a type of fruit he'd never seen before, he didn't know what to call it. So he combined the names of two fruits he did know about, cherries and bananas, and called the new fruit a banerry!

According to Dr. Pepperberg, Alex the parrot was roughly equal in intelligence to a five year-old human child when he died suddenly at the age of thirty-one. The last words he said to the woman who taught him language were the same words he spoke every night: "You be good. See you tomorrow. I love you." Alex was an ordinary parrot who proved extraordinary things for our understanding of animal intelligence. His legacy lives on as the Alex Foundation continues to support research to better understand the intelligence of these birds. Some of the goals of the Alex Foundation include the promotion of responsible ownership of parrots as well as conservation and preservation of them in the wild. You can see videos of Alex and other African grays on YouTube.com.

The Singing Tree

Handkerchiefs

Marie and Pauline have no handkerchiefs. Human beings are drippy creatures. We drool, shed tears, and drip from our noses to a degree seen as unacceptable by most civilized cultures. Thus, we invented special squares of fabric called handkerchiefs to discreetly wipe ourselves when in polite company.

In the odd way that only humans can do, however, what started as a way to not drip mucus all over oneself became a way for humans to show how much better they were than other people. In many old-fashioned societies, handkerchiefs became a mark of how wealthy one was, depending on whether they were made of cotton or a more pricey fabric like silk or linen. This got so ridiculous that some ladies and gentlemen would wear ornamental handkerchiefs they'd never dream of actually blowing their noses on! In fact, many men's business suits still have a place for a decorative pocket handkerchief.

You might find it interesting to note that there are two spellings of the word mucus. The noun is **mucus** while the adjective is **mucous**. Now you know which way to spell it when your mother says, "Quit saying snot."

Apple Trees

Mother says that when the apple tree is showing white, it's time to thin out the tomato seedlings. An apple is the fruit of the tree *Malus domestica*, or apple tree. It is a deciduous tree, meaning that it sheds its leaves each year, and it is in the same family as roses. The apple tree originated in Central Asia, and its wild ancestor is still there today. Apples have been grown for thousands of years in both Asia and Europe. It came to North America on the very first ships carrying European colonists.

Apples have religious significance in many cultures throughout history, such as Iðunn, a Norse goddess of apples and youth—specifically, of an orchard of magic apples that granted eternal youth to anyone who ate of them. She is spoken of in a work of Norse poetry that describes how Loki once tricked her into leaving the orchard, causing the apples there to wither and decay. The rest of the gods began to grow old without her apples to keep them young, and they forced Loki to bring her back so that they could be immortal and young again.

Brita as Iduna. Painting by Carl Larsson. Image is in the public domain; via Wikimedia Commons.

Tomatoes

Tomatoes are North American plants in the nightshade family, notable for the bright red fruits they produce that humans love to eat. The word tomato comes from the Aztec word for the plant, *tomatl*, which should give you an idea of how long this plant has been grown and used by humanity.

Tomatoes can be used for an astonishing variety of dishes. You can eat them raw, cook them, mix them in with stews, or even make sauces out of them to pour over pasta. They are one of the most useful fruits to cook with, though somewhat confusingly, they are often referred to as a vegetable. As tomatoes have seeds in them, this is not an accurate description.

In fact, tomatoes are not only a fruit, they are actually in the same category of fruit as berries. But the tomato's status as a fruit came on trial in the late 1800s, quite literally, in the case of Nix vs. Hedden. The Tariff Act of 1883 required a tax be paid on imported vegetables but not on fruit! Edward Hedden, the Collector of the Port of New York, had charged the tax on imported tomatoes, and the Nix family sued to get their money back, arguing that botanically, tomatoes are fruits. But, alas for the Nix family, the court insisted that the tax applied to tomatoes, using the "common" meanings of the words **fruit** and **vegetable** rather than the strict botanical meaning.

Smoky the Cowhorse

Livestock Branding

Smoky is branded with the Rocking R brand. In many societies, keeping up with livestock can be quite the chore. Grazing animals tend to wander and mix together, so figuring out which livestock belong to whom can be pretty difficult. In addition, if thieves were to steal a valuable bull and were later caught, it could be difficult to prove to whom the bull originally belonged.

For these reasons, livestock branding was invented. From ancient times all the way up to the present, a hot iron has been used to burn a symbol into the hide of an animal, to emblazon the animal with a permanent mark of ownership, rather like writing your name on a belonging. In modern times, freeze branding sometimes takes the place of hot iron branding, and it is a less painful and more humane way of marking animals. However, it does have some issues. In some place, it is not considered a legally recognized way of branding animals. It is also a more expensive and less predictable method of branding, and it does not work on some animals such as pigs.

The ancient Romans combined the ownership mark with a spell believed to have the power to keep livestock healthy. In the American southwest, cattle branding evolved into a complex visual language that's still used to this day.

Predators

The mountain lion has a big rock that serves as his game hunting perch. In any ecosystem, there are some living things that can only live by damaging or killing other living things. This is called predation, and it takes many forms. Every sheep that eats a blade of grass is engaging in predation, as is every hawk that snatches up a field mouse. Every animal is a predator in some way, even the herbivores.

However, when naturalists refer to predators, they generally refer to **carnivores**—animals which eat meat. These predators are huge in number and incredible in diversity. Predators come in every shape and size imaginable, from microscopic amoebas to extinct monsters like the Tyrannosaurus rex. Few things can be said about every single predator, but they all have some form of adaptation that allows them to beat their prey in the game of life, whether its superb camouflage, sharp fangs, or a venomous bite.

Constellations

The narrator says that the braves are chasing the buffalo plum around the Big Dipper in the night sky. Have you ever had fun finding patterns in something random, like leaves falling on the ground or clouds in the sky? Cultures have done the same for many thousands of years, but most random patterns in nature are gone in a day. Men have spotted some patterns, however, that are as close to eternal as the human mind can comprehend: the constellations.

A constellation is a pattern of stars in the night sky that looks like a shape when looked at the right way. For instance, Ursa Major is said by many to look like a bear. Orion looks like an ancient Greek hero raising his sword. Scorpius resembles a scorpion. These constellations are meaningless except in name alone, as none of the stars within a constellation are close to each other in space or otherwise related. But it's a fun way of looking at the heavens, and constellations represent the unique way of viewing the world that humans seem to possess.

While constellations are frivolous things on their own, ancient constellations are nowadays used as the basis for serious astronomy. Visible stars are often named for the constellation in which they appear. For instance, Alpha Centauri is the brightest star in the system Centaurus. In addition, the entire night sky has been divided into eighty-eight distinct constellations, so any object in the sky can be said to belong to a constellation.

Illustration of the Orion constellation. Illustration by Johannes Hevelius. Image is in the public domain; via Wikimedia Commons.

P/K & LG Activity Supplies:

Day 1:
* Plastic lids, one per child, from a sour cream or yogurt container
* Glue
* Food coloring
* Hole punch

Day 3:
* Shoe box
* Natural objects such as twigs, leaves, plants, small stones
* Glue
* Paint or food coloring

Day 4:
* Sand
* Shadow box frame or short plastic bin
* Magnetic items
* Magnetic wand

Science Experiment Supplies:

* Piece of cardboard
* Pencil

* Large screw

Rhetoric: This week: Find an example of a literary technique from Essential Literary Terms and discuss it. How did the author use this technique? Why do you think the author used it? Write a paper, complete with introduction and conclusion.

Rhetoric, Physics:

Physics lab on Day 4.

Week 30

	GRAMMAR	DIALECTIC	RHETORIC
BIBLE	Choose one of the following plans: ✠ PLAN 1: Journey Through the Bible, pp. 324-325 ✠ PLAN 2: The Story, Ch. 29		
LANGUAGE ARTS	Choose appropriate level of one of the following: ¶ English Lessons Through Literature, Lesson 88 Reading Lessons Through Literature, phonogram review ¶ Rod and Staff English, Lesson 102 Copywork/Commonplace Book ¶ Your own grammar program		¶ LR: The Power in Your Hands, 1 lesson ¶ UR: WGRP, int. sources. (3 days) ¶ LR: Rod and Staff 10, L. 97
MATH	Choose appropriate level of one of the following: ✏ Math-U-See, Video and page A ✏ Miquon/Singapore Math ✏ Your own math program		✏ Math-U-See, Video and page A ✏ Your own math program
GEOGRAPHY	🌐 50 States, The Oregon Trail		
	🌐 Reading, choose one of the following: A. United States: Moccasin Trail, Ch. 1 B. Montana: Smoky the Cowhorse, Ch. 4		🌐 A Walk Along the Ganges, Ch. 8
HISTORY	Choose one spine, one or more core reading selections, and optional reading as desired.		
	♟ Spine: SOTW, Ch. 34.2 ♟ Core reading: 1. Burying the Sun, Ch. 9 2. Who Was Martin Luther King, Jr., Ch. 10 3. Who Was Gandhi, Ch. 4	♟ Spine: SOTW, Ch. 34.2 ♟ Core reading: 1. Hiroshima, pp. 91-105 (Kindle edition, 12 pages) 2. Where the Red Fern Grows, Ch. 18	♟ Spine: Western Civ, 1/4 of Ch. 28 ♟ Core reading: 1 & 2. Les Miserables, 14 pages 1. 1984, Book 2 Ch. 1 2. Strength to Love, Ch. 10

Day 1

	Grammar	Dialectic	Rhetoric	
Activities	♪♪ Term 3 Composer: Choose between Shostakovich, Britten, Leon Kirchner ⧖ Timeline/Book of Centuries			
Narration	☞ Oral or written narration; LG students can draw a picture from the reading and tell about the picture. Suggested subject: history.		☞ Written narration for history or geography.	
Other	✛ Old Story New, Week 66 ෬ UD: Economics in One Lesson, Ch. 16		✛ Great Divorce, Ch. 1	
Literature	📚 Literature: 1: Five Little Peppers and How They Grew, Ch. 5 2: Through the Looking-Glass, Ch. 10-12 3: The Princess and the Goblin, Ch. 10 4: Heidi, Ch. 21	📚 Literature: 5: Little Women, Ch. 44-45 6: Otto of the Silver Hand, Ch. 6 7: Northanger Abbey, Ch. 11 8: 20,000 Leagues, Ch. 40	📚 Book of English Verse, No. 834-836 ✛ Church History: Church History in Plain Language, Ch. 47 ✛ 100 Events, A.D. 1910	

Preschool and Lower Grammar

Pathways	✏ Pathways: Path 1, Day 1 A. Kindergarten Gems B. Among the Meadow People C. 20th—Amelia Bedelia D. Random House Poetry, p. 187
Activity	✏ White glue sun-catcher See examples at: www.babbledabbledo.com/art-for-kids-cosmic-suncatchers/ Take a plastic lid (e.g. from a sour cream or yogurt container) and apply a liberal amount of glue to the inside of the lid, enough to cover the entire inside of the lid. Place a drop or two of each color of food coloring in the glue at random spots. Take a toothpick and swirl the color around through the glue. Be careful not to over mix the colors. Allow to dry for several days, and then the glue will easily peel out of the lid. Punch a hole and use string to hang it in a sunny spot.

Week 30

	GRAMMAR	DIALECTIC	RHETORIC
BIBLE	Choose one of the following plans: ✠ PLAN 1: Journey Through the Bible, pp. 326-327 ✠ PLAN 2: What the Bible Is All About, 1 Thessalonians		
	✠ LG: TBB: Jesus and the Children ✠ UG: Egermeier's, 2 stories	✠ LD: Hurlbut's, 1 story ✠ UD: Golden's, 3 stories	
LANGUAGE ARTS	Choose appropriate level of one of the following: ℊ Reading Lessons Through Literature, next list and story ℊ Prepared dictation from ELTL, Spelling Wisdom, or today's reading ℊ Rod and Staff English, Lesson 103 ℊ Your own grammar program		ℊ Essential Literary Terms This week: Find an example of a literary technique from Essential Literary Terms and discuss it. ℊ UR: WGRP, internal documentation. (2 days) ℊ LR: Rod and Staff 10, L. 98
MATH	Choose appropriate level of one of the following: ✎ Math-U-See, page B ✎ Miquon/Singapore Math ✎ Your own math program		✎ Math-U-See, page B ✎ Your own math program
GEOGRAPHY	🌐 Reading, choose one of the following: A. United States: Moccasin Trail, Ch. 2 B. Montana: Smoky the Cowhorse, Ch. 5		🌐 Geography for Dummies, 1/2 of Ch. 15
SCIENCE	Choose one spine, one or more core reading selections, and optional reading as desired.		
	⚛ Core reading: 1. RS4K Physics, Ch. 10.3 2. Insiders Flight, pp. 44-49	⚛ Core reading: 1. Black Holes and Uncle Albert, Ch. 6 2. Liquids and Gases, Ch. 4	⚛ Spine: Physics for Dummies, 1/2 of Ch. 16 Intro. Physics, pp. 288-292 ⚛ Core reading: The Elegant Universe, Ch. 4
	⚛ Spine: Quark Chronicles: Physics, Ch. 12		

Day 2

Grammar	Dialectic	Rhetoric	
♪ Term 3 Composer: Choose between Shostakovich, Britten, Leon Kirchner 🎨 Art Lesson: Choose appropriate level of one of the following:			ACTIVITIES
🎨 I Can Do All Things 🎨 Lamb's Book of Art I	🎨 Lamb's Book of Art II 🎨 Feed My Sheep	🎨 How Great Thou ART I or II 🎨 Book of Many Colors	
⚛ GSA The World of Light and Sound, Lesson 11		🎨 Great Art, Lecture 30	
☞ Oral or written narration; LG students can draw a picture from the reading and tell about the picture. Suggested subject: Bible.		☞ Oral or written narration for science or Bible.	Narration
✠ Old Story New, Week 66			
	෬ UD: The Art of Argument, Fallacy 25 ෬ UD: Science Matters, pp. 151-165	෬ UR: Classical English Rhetoric, 1/4 Ch. 15	Other
📚 Suggested read-aloud: The Neverending Story, Ch. 6			Literature

Preschool and Lower Grammar

✏ Pathways: Path 2 A. Little Wanderers, Ch. 30 B. Burgess Seashore Book, Ch. 33 C. Paddington Helps Out, Ch. 9 D. Random House Poetry, pp. 188-190	Pathways
🎨 Art Lesson: Choose one of the following Barry Stebbing art books for you little one to do art like the big kids: Art and the Bible for Children, Baby Lamb's Book of Art, Joseph the Canada Goose, or Little Annie's Art Book.	Activity

Week 30

	GRAMMAR	DIALECTIC	RHETORIC
BIBLE	Choose one of the following plans: ✠ PLAN 1: Journey Through the Bible, pp. 328-329 ✠ PLAN 2: What the Bible Is All About, 2 Thessalonians		

LANGUAGE ARTS	Choose appropriate level of one of the following:
	
	¶ English Lessons Through Literature, Lesson 89
	    Reading Lessons Through Literature, phonogram review
	
	¶ Rod and Staff English, Lesson 104
	    Copywork/Commonplace Book
	
	¶ Your own grammar program
			¶ Essential Literary Terms, 3-4 pages
			
			¶ LR: The Power in Your Hands, 1 lesson
			
			¶ UR: WGRP, internal documentation. (2 days)
			
			¶ LR: Rod and Staff 10, L. 99

MATH	Choose appropriate level of one of the following: ✎ Math-U-See, page C ✎ Miquon/Singapore Math ✎ Your own math program		✎ Math-U-See, page C ✎ Your own math program

GEOGRAPHY	🌐 Reading, choose one of the following:
	    A. United States: Moccasin Trail, Ch. 3
	    B. Montana: Smoky the Cowhorse, Ch. 6
			🌐 A Walk Along the Ganges, Ch. 9

HISTORY	Choose one spine, one or more core reading selections, and optional reading as desired.
	
	♟ Spine: SOTW, Ch. 35.1
	
	♟ Core reading:
	    1. Burying the Sun, Ch. 10
	    2. Who Was Martin Luther King, Jr., Ch. 11
	    3. Who Was Gandhi, Ch. 5
		♟ Spine: SOTW, Ch. 35.1
		
		♟ Core reading:
		    1. Hiroshima, pp. 106-120 (Kindle edition, 12 pages)
		    2. Where the Red Fern Grows, Ch. 19
			♟ Spine:
			    Western Civ, 1/4 of Ch. 28
			    America, 1/4 of Ch. 32
			
			♟ Core reading:
			    1 & 2. Les Miserables, 14 pages
			    1. 1984, Ch. 2
			    2. Strength to Love, Ch. 11

Day 3

Grammar	Dialectic	Rhetoric	
♪♪ Term 3 Composer: Choose between Shostakovich, Britten, Leon Kirchner			ACTIVITIES
☞ Oral or written narration; could be a group project. Create a lost or deleted scene from your book. This can be completely original, or it could be an event which was mentioned in passing, but was not actually shown in detail.			NARRATION
✛ Old Story New, Week 66 ✛ UD: Simply Christian, Ch. 10		✛ Great Divorce, Ch. 2	OTHER
📚 Literature: 1: Five Little Peppers and How They Grew, Ch. 6 2: 3: The Princess and the Goblin, Ch. 11 4: Heidi, Ch. 22	📚 Literature: 5: Little Women, Ch. 46-47 6: Otto of the Silver Hand, Ch. 7 7: Northanger Abbey, Ch. 12 8: 20,000 Leagues, Ch. 41	📚 Book of English Verse, No. 837-839 ✛ Church History: Church History in Plain Language, Ch. 48 ✛ 100 Events, A.D. 1919	LITERATURE

Preschool and Lower Grammar

✎ Pathways: Path 1, Day 2 A. Kindergarten Gems B. 50 Famous Stories C. JH—Blossom Comes Home D. Random House Poetry, p. 191	PATHWAYS
✎ Shadow boxes See examples at: www.teachpreschool.org/2011/11/our-nature-shadow-boxes-in-preschool/ Collect a variety of natural objects: twigs, leaves, plants, small stones, etc. Cover the bottom of a shoe box lid with glue and arrange items in the glue. Sprinkle paint or drops of food coloring to add color.	ACTIVITY

Week 30

	GRAMMAR	DIALECTIC	RHETORIC
BIBLE	Choose one of the following plans: ✠ PLAN 1: Journey Through the Bible, pp. 330-331 ✠ PLAN 2: Journey Through the Bible, pp. 356-361		
	✠ LG: TBB: A Short Man ✠ UG: Egermeier's, 3 stories	✠ LD: Hurlbut's, 2 stories ✠ UD: Golden's, 2 stories	
LANGUAGE ARTS	Choose appropriate level of one of the following: ❡ Reading Lessons Through Literature, next list and story ❡ Prepared dictation from ELTL, Spelling Wisdom, or today's reading ❡ Your own grammar program		❡ UR: WGRP, Works Cited. (1 day)
MATH	Choose appropriate level of one of the following: ✎ Math-U-See, page D ✎ Miquon/Singapore Math ✎ Your own math program		✎ Math-U-See, page D ✎ Your own math program
GEOGRAPHY	🌎 Reading, choose one of the following: 　A. United States: Moccasin Trail, Ch. 4 　B. Montana: Smoky the Cowhorse, Ch. 7		
SCIENCE	Choose one spine, one or more core reading selections, and optional reading as desired.		
	⚛ Core reading: 　1. RS4K Physics, Ch. 10.4-10.5 　2. Insiders Flight, pp. 50-55	⚛ Core reading: 　1. Black Holes and Uncle Albert, Ch. 7 　2. Matter and Energy, Ch. 1	⚛ Spine: Manga Relativity, pp. 97-107 Intro. Physics, pp. 292-296 ⚛ Core reading: 　The Elegant Universe, Ch. 5
	⚛ Optional extra reading, topic: Gravity Simon Bloom, Ch. 26-28 G: Up, Down, All Around by Jacqui Bailey D: Gravity, and How It Works by Peter Jedicke Insiders Flight by Von Hardesty		

Day 4

GRAMMAR	DIALECTIC	RHETORIC	
♪♪ Term 3 Composer: Choose between Shostakovich, Britten, Leon Kirchner			ACTIVITIES
⚛ GSA The World of Light and Sound, Lesson 12 ⚛ 201 Awesome Experiments, 183-184	⚛ Physics Lab 🎨 Great Art Writing		
➪ Oral or written narration; LG students can draw a picture from the reading and tell about the picture. Suggested subject: science.		➪ Written narration for science or Bible.	NARRATION
✜ Old Story New, Week 66			
	♋ UD: The Art of Argument: Create an ad or an argument using this week's fallacy ♋ UD: Science Matters, pp. 166-180	♋ UR: Classical English Rhetoric, 1/4 Ch. 15	OTHER
📚 Suggested read-aloud: The Neverending Story, Ch. 7			LITERATURE

PRESCHOOL AND LOWER GRAMMAR	
✎ Pathways: Path 3 A. Burgess Flower Book, Ch. 34-35 B. Gooney Bird Greene, Ch. 2 C. Henry Huggins, Ch. 6 D. Random House Poetry, p. 192	PATHWAYS
✎ Magnetic sand box Add a small amount of fine sand to a shadow box frame or a short plastic bin. Add magnetic items to the sand. Use the magnetic wand to move the items around. This can be from underneath with the plastic bin or from on top with the shadow box frame. The shadow box frame would be more contained, and therefore less messy. The plastic bin would allow playing in the sand.	ACTIVITY

Week 30

	GRAMMAR	DIALECTIC	RHETORIC
BIBLE	Choose one of the following plans: ✠ PLAN 1: Journey Through the Bible, pp. 332-333 ✠ PLAN 2: What the Bible Is All About, 1 Corinthians		

LANGUAGE ARTS	Choose appropriate level of one of the following:
	
	𝄞 English Lessons Through Literature, Lesson 90
	    Reading Lessons Through Literature, phonogram review
	
	𝄞 Rod and Staff English, Lesson 105
	    Copywork/Commonplace Book
	
	𝄞 Your own grammar program
			𝄞 A Rulebook for Arguments, Ch. 39
			
			𝄞 LR: The Power in Your Hands, 1 lesson
			
			𝄞 LR: Rod and Staff 10, L. 100

MATH	Choose appropriate level of one of the following: ✏ Math-U-See, page E ✏ Miquon/Singapore Math ✏ Your own math program		✏ Math-U-See, pages E & H ✏ Your own math program

GEOGRAPHY	🌍 Mapping: Eastern Africa
	
	🌍 Reading, choose one of the following:
	    A. United States: Moccasin Trail, Ch. 5
	    B. Montana: Smoky the Cowhorse, Ch. 8
			🌍 A Walk Along the Ganges, Ch. 10

HISTORY	Choose one spine, one or more core reading selections, and optional reading as desired.		

	♟ Spine: SOTW, Ch. 35.2
	
	♟ Core reading:
	    1. Burying the Sun, Ch. 11
	    2. Neil Armstrong, Ch. 1
	    3. Who Was Gandhi, Ch. 6
		♟ Spine: SOTW, Ch. 35.2
		
		♟ Core reading:
		    1. Hiroshima, pp. 121-135 (Kindle edition, 12 pages)
		    2. Where the Red Fern Grows, Ch. 20
			♟ Spine:
			    America, 1/4 of Ch. 32
			
			♟ Core reading:
			    1 & 2. Les Miserables, 14 pages
			    LR: 1 & 2. Philosophy Book, through Adorno
			    UR: 1 & 2. Think, 1/2 Ch. 5
			    1. 1984, Ch. 3
			    2. Strength to Love, Ch. 12

Day 5

	Grammar	Dialectic	Rhetoric	
♪♪ Term 3 Composer: Choose between Shostakovich, Britten, Leon Kirchner				Activities
🎨 Art Lesson: Choose appropriate level of one of the following:				
🎨 I Can Do All Things 🎨 Lamb's Book of Art I	🎨 Lamb's Book of Art II 🎨 Feed My Sheep	🎨 How Great Thou ART I or II 🎨 Book of Many Colors		
☞ Oral or written narration; LG students can draw a picture from the reading and tell about the picture. Suggested subject: geography.		☞ Oral or written narration for history or geography.		Narration
✠ Old Story New, Week 66 ଔ UD: Economics in One Lesson, Ch. 17				Other
📚 Suggested read-aloud: The Neverending Story, Ch. 8				Literature
📚 Literature: 1: Five Little Peppers and How They Grew, Ch. 7 2: 3: The Princess and the Goblin, Ch. 12-13 4: Heidi, Ch. 23	📚 Literature: 5: Around the World in 80 Days, Ch. 1-2 6: Otto of the Silver Hand, Ch. 8 7: Northanger Abbey, Ch. 13 8: 20,000 Leagues, Ch. 42	📚 Book of English Verse, No. 840-842 ✠ Church History: Church History in Plain Language, Ch. 49 ✠ 100 Events, A.D. 1921		
Preschool and Lower Grammar				
✏ Pathways: Path 1, Day 3 A. Kindergarten Gems B. Among the Meadow People C. JH—The Market Square Dog D. Random House Poetry, p. 193				Pathways
🎨 Art Lesson: Choose one of the following Barry Stebbing art books for you little one to do art like the big kids: Art and the Bible for Children, Baby Lamb's Book of Art, Joseph the Canada Goose, or Little Annie's Art Book.				Activity

First successful flight of the Wright Flyer, by the Wright brothers. This is described as "the first sustained and controlled heavier-than-air, powered flight" by the Fédération Aéronautique Internationale, but is not listed by the FAI as an official record. Photo by John T. Daniels. Image in the public domain; via Wikimedia Commons.

History Through Art: The Wright Brothers

Sometimes the most world-changing inventions come from unlikely sources. For instance, the airplane, the mechanism by which humanity learned to conquer the skies, was invented by a couple of brothers in America during the early 1900s. They were not the heads of inventing companies like Thomas Edison or employed by the government. They were humble bicycle repairmen.

For many years, there had been a worldwide race to solve "the flying problem." Humans had figured out how to get into the air—zeppelins and hot air balloons were easy. Just fill a balloon with something that rises above normal air, and you rise up off the ground like a rubber duck floating in a bathtub. What we wanted, however, was heavier-than-air flight like birds, bats, and insects have. There was a race to discover a method for building a heavy metal machine capable of propelling itself across the sky.

Orville and Wilbur Wright were two self-taught engineers with an interest in all things related to aircraft. They read as much as they could about the attempts of less successful inventors, learning from their mistakes. They built their wind tunnel for testing ideas and started building prototypes.

In 1903 above a beach in North Carolina, the Wright Brothers successfully tested the first heavier-than-air flying machine. Within ten years, the military was using the spectacular design of the airplane for fighting, spying, and, eventually, transporting letters. Nowadays the design they started has led to commercial jet liners capable of carrying countless people across the country and the world every year. The Wright brothers are a striking example of how anyone with the interest and the drive to follow his passions can wind up changing the world.

Moccasin Trail

Buckskins

Jim is wearing buckskins, the clothing of a white trapper. When the settlers first colonized the wild frontiers of North America, they found themselves in a world totally without shopping malls. It's true! The wilderness was vast and seemingly without end, but nowhere within those ancient forests and prairies was anything like a clothing factory, much less a clothing store. For civilized settlers, going naked was hardly an option, so they resorted to wearing the skins of local animals, called buckskins.

Based on the attire of certain Native American tribes, buckskins are a form of stylized deerskin clothing meant to provide full coverage of the body and protection from the elements. Buckskin is a soft leather that's relatively easy to make and wear, so it became an instant favorite among the frontiersmen as they headed west. In the modern age of malls and thrift marts, they have lost a great deal of their necessity, but buckskins are still worn by some as a rugged fashion choice, a nostalgic reminder of the days when America was still wild.

Salmon

There had been trading for smoked salmon between the Indians and the wagons. Salmon is the name for several species of fish in the family Salmonidae. Included in that same family are trout, whitefish, and graylings. They're native to the rivers and tributaries which empty into the North Atlantic and Pacific Oceans. Many other species of salmon have been put into the Great Lakes of North America. They are produced in great number through aquaculture all around the world.

Usually salmon are born in fresh water, far up rivers where they reproduce and lay their eggs. Folklore always told of how the salmon would return to the exact spot they were born in order to lay their eggs, and recent studies using tracking devices have shown that the folklore has more truth to it than not. A small percentage of the salmon will go off course and lay their eggs elsewhere, but the majority will return to the same spot.

Salmon are nutritious and a major source of food for humans who live in the areas where they spawn or "run." Bears consume many pounds of salmon during these rounds in order to prepare themselves for winter hibernation. Salmon contains many fats and large amounts of protein.

Grizzly Bears

Jim is wearing a grizzly cloak. When the Lewis and Clark expedition ventured across the west of North America, they had many fearsome encounters with one of the most frightening predators on the continent. The predator was bigger than any bear they'd seen before, frequently vicious, and could run for miles even after being shot in the lungs or heart. The animal they encountered was the grizzly bear, even now one of the most feared animals in all North America.

The word **grizzly** refers to the coat of the animal—many of a grizzly's hairs end with a grey or golden tip, giving the bear a "grizzled" appearance. Scientists generally frown on the name, instead calling this animal the North American brown bear. In addition to the brown bear, North America is also home to black

Bear cub with salmon. Photo by Jitze Couperus.
License: CC BY 2.0; via Wikimedia Commons.

bears, which are smaller and less fearsome but no less of a nuisance in regions in which they're common.

Although bears are the largest carnivores in the Americas, they're only half carnivorous. Most bears are **omnivores**, partaking in both meat and vegetable food sources where available. Don't think that lessens the grizzly's prowess as a predator, though. The brown bear has been known to feed on just about every animal in North America, including bison, elk, and moose!

Smoky the Cowhorse

Chaps

Clint wears a pair of chaps. Chaps are coverings, usually made of leather, for the legs. They are normally worn buckled over trousers and have no seat or crotch. They are typically meant to provide protection for a horse's rider when going through brush and low timber where thorns or sharp branches might pierce the rider's legs. They are associated with the cowboy culture of the American southwest though they originated in Spain and Mexico. The American Indians also had versions which predate even their usage of horses.

Aside from the horseman aspect of chaps, other professions wear varieties of these protective leggings as well. Lumberjacks wear them to protect the legs while working in the forests and brush, and hunters sometimes wear them to protect themselves from snakebites.

Trapping

The wolves circle well away from a carcass because they fear a trap. Trapping is the use of a device to remotely catch an animal. People trap animals for many reasons, ranging from food to fur to the removal of pests. Historically, it is one of the oldest skills as it was safer and more reliable than other forms of hunting. A trapper can put out traps in multiple locations and have them effectively gathering animals around the clock. A hunter can be in only one place at a time and for only limited periods.

Chaps traditionally were worn by cow herding cowboys to avoid rope burns or damage to their clothing while working on horseback, and are today mostly worn at the rodeo as protection from the trampling of a bull and to add design or flair to the sport. Davie Rodeo, Davie, Fl., USA. Photo by Emilio Labrador; cropped and color isolated by Themightyquill. License: CC BY 2.0; via Wikimedia Commons.

Neolithic hunters were using traps as early as 5,500 BC. Some traps captured the animal intact while others killed or wounded it so that it was easier to bring down when the hunters would arrive. In modern times, steel-jawed traps made trapping so efficient that in some parts of the country, the wild game were nearly eliminated. In much of the United States now, there are laws against trapping which either prevent it altogether outside of specific times of year or limit how much trapping can be done or what kind of traps can be used.

Bats

Clint's chaps are in a style called bat-wing. After rodents, bats are the largest group of mammals on the planet, with over 1, 200 species across most of the earth's continents. There are two main varieties of bats: megabats and microbats. Megabats are the larger variety, and are called fruit bats for their herbivorous nature. Microbats are small and agile fliers that use a method called echolocation to hunt insects. When echolocating, a microbat releases bursts of high-frequency sound into its surroundings. When the sounds bounce off of objects—creating echoes—the bat can trace the echo back to its source to catch juicy bugs.

Bats are often threatened by human activities. Not as charismatic as the enormous elephants and rhinos that conservation groups rally behind, bats are often ignored when their habitats are destroyed, threatening many species with extinction. In addition, many are deliberately persecuted by humanity, killed for their reputation as disease-carriers. And in Africa, they are often hunted for their reputation as delicious bushmeat.

P/K & LG Activity Supplies:

Day 1:
• Pinecone
• Vegetable shortening or peanut butter
• Birdseed
• String

Day 3:
• Shoe box or plastic container
• Sand

Day 4:
• Items to trace such as lids, bowls, board books, shapes cut for card board

Science Experiment Supplies:

• Scissors
• Ruler
• Sheet of paper
• Pencil
• Cellophane tape

• Scissors
• Ruler
• Typing paper

Week 31

	GRAMMAR	DIALECTIC	RHETORIC
BIBLE	Choose one of the following plans: ✛ PLAN 1: Journey Through the Bible, pp. 334-335 ✛ PLAN 2: What the Bible Is All About, 2 Corinthians		

LANGUAGE ARTS	Choose appropriate level of one of the following:
	
	ℊ English Lessons Through Literature, Lesson 91
	   Reading Lessons Through Literature, phonogram review
	
	ℊ Rod and Staff English, Lesson 106
	   Copywork/Commonplace Book
	
	ℊ Your own grammar program
			ℊ LR: The Power in Your Hands, 1 lesson
			
			ℊ UR: WGRP, front and end matter. (2 days)
			
			ℊ LR: Rod and Staff 10, L. 101

MATH	Choose appropriate level of one of the following: ✎ Math-U-See, Video and page A ✎ Miquon/Singapore Math ✎ Your own math program		✎ Math-U-See, Video and page A ✎ Your own math program

GEOGRAPHY	🌎 50 States, Review New England
	
	🌎 Reading, choose one of the following:
	   A. United States: Moccasin Trail, Ch. 6
	   B. Montana: Smoky the Cowhorse, Ch. 9
			🌏 A Walk Along the Ganges, Ch. 11

HISTORY	Choose one spine, one or more core reading selections, and optional reading as desired.		

	♟ Spine: SOTW, Ch. 36.1
	
	♟ Core reading:
	   1. Burying the Sun, Ch. 12
	   2. Neil Armstrong, Ch. 2
	   3. Who Was Gandhi, Ch. 7
		♟ Spine: SOTW, Ch. 36.1
		
		♟ Core reading:
		   1. Hiroshima, pp. 136-end (Kindle edition, 12 pages)
		   2. Warriors Don't Cry, Ch. 1
			♟ Spine:
			   Western Civ, 1/4 of Ch. 29
			   World Empires, Missions, Wars, Unit 9 Week 1
			
			♟ Core reading:
			   1 & 2. Les Miserables, 14 pages
			   1. 1984, Ch. 4
			   2. Strength to Love, Ch. 13

Day 1

	Grammar	Dialectic	Rhetoric	
	♫ Term 3 Composer: Choose between Shostakovich, Britten, Leon Kirchner ⧗ Timeline/Book of Centuries			ACTIVITIES
	↻ Oral or written narration; LG students can draw a picture from the reading and tell about the picture. Suggested subject: history.		↻ Written narration for history or geography.	NARRATION
	✠ Old Story New, Week 67 ಐ UD: Economics in One Lesson, Ch. 18		✠ Great Divorce, Ch. 3	OTHER
	📚 Suggested read-aloud:			
	📚 Literature: 1: Five Little Peppers and How They Grew, Ch. 8 2: This Week: A Wonder-Book for Girls and Boys: The Gorgon's Head 3: The Princess and the Goblin, Ch. 14 4: This Week: Tanglewood Tales, The Minotaur	📚 Literature: 5: Around the World in 80 Days, Ch. 3-4 6: Otto of the Silver Hand, Ch. 9 7: Northanger Abbey, Ch. 14 8: 20,000 Leagues, Ch. 43	📚 Book of English Verse, No. 843-845 ✠ Church History: Church History in Plain Language, Epilogue ✠ 100 Events, A.D. 1934	LITERATURE
	✎ Pathways: Path 1, Day 1 A. Kindergarten Gems B. 50 Famous Stories C. 20th—I Am a Bunny D. Random House Poetry, p. 194			PATHWAYS
	✎ Pinecone bird feeder Coat a pinecone in vegetable shortening or peanut butter. Roll in birdseed. Add a string and hang outside.			ACTIVITY

Week 31

	GRAMMAR	DIALECTIC	RHETORIC
BIBLE	Choose one of the following plans: ✠ PLAN 1: Journey Through the Bible, pp. 336-337 ✠ PLAN 2: Journey Through the Bible, pp. 362-367		
	✠ LG: TBB: Lazarus Lives Again ✠ UG: Egermeier's, 2 stories	✠ LD: Hurlbut's, 1 story ✠ UD: Golden's, 3 stories	
LANGUAGE ARTS	Choose appropriate level of one of the following: ❡ Reading Lessons Through Literature, next list and story ❡ Prepared dictation from ELTL, Spelling Wisdom, or today's reading ❡ Your own grammar program		❡ UR: WGRP, front and end matter. (2 days)
MATH	Choose appropriate level of one of the following:		
	✎ Math-U-See, page B ✎ Miquon/Singapore Math ✎ Your own math program		✎ Math-U-See, page B ✎ Your own math program
GEOGRAPHY	🌐 Reading, choose one of the following: A. United States: Moccasin Trail, Ch. 7 B. Montana: Smoky the Cowhorse, Ch. 10		🌐 Geography for Dummies, 1/2 of Ch. 16
SCIENCE	Choose one spine, one or more core reading selections, and optional reading as desired.		
	⚛ Core reading: 1. Isaac Newton for Kids, Ch. 1 2. Insiders Flight, pp. 56-61 ⚛ Spine: Quark Chronicles: Physics, Ch. 13	⚛ Core reading: 1. Black Holes and Uncle Albert, Ch. 8 2. Matter and Energy, Ch. 2	⚛ Spine: SHSPhys, Week 10 Physics for Dummies, 1/2 of Ch. 16 Intro. Physics, pp. 296-301 ⚛ Core reading: The Elegant Universe, Ch. 6

Day 2

GRAMMAR	DIALECTIC	RHETORIC	
♪♪ Term 3 Composer: Choose between Shostakovich, Britten, Leon Kirchner 🎨 Art Lesson: Choose appropriate level of one of the following:			ACTIVITIES
🎨 I Can Do All Things 🎨 Lamb's Book of Art I	🎨 Lamb's Book of Art II 🎨 Feed My Sheep	🎨 How Great Thou ART I or II 🎨 Book of Many Colors	
⚛ GSA The World of Light and Sound, Lesson 13		🎨 Great Art, Lecture 31	
👁‍🗨 Oral or written narration; LG students can draw a picture from the reading and tell about the picture. Suggested subject: Bible.		👁‍🗨 Oral or written narration for science or Bible.	NARRATION
✛ Old Story New, Week 67			
	☙ UD: The Art of Argument, Review 5 ☙ UD: Science Matters, pp. 181-195	☙ UR: Classical English Rhetoric, 1/4 Ch. 16	OTHER
📚 Suggested read-aloud: The Neverending Story, Ch. 9			LITERATURE

PRESCHOOL AND LOWER GRAMMAR	
✎ Pathways: Path 2 A. Little Wanderers, Ch. 31 B. Burgess Seashore Book, Ch. 34 C. Paddington Helps Out, Ch. 10 D. Random House Poetry, p. 195	PATHWAYS
🎨 Art Lesson: Choose one of the following Barry Stebbing art books for you little one to do art like the big kids: Art and the Bible for Children, Baby Lamb's Book of Art, Joseph the Canada Goose, or Little Annie's Art Book.	ACTIVITY

Week 31

	GRAMMAR	DIALECTIC	RHETORIC
BIBLE	Choose one of the following plans: ✚ PLAN 1: Journey Through the Bible, pp. 338-339 ✚ PLAN 2: What the Bible Is All About, Galatians		
LANGUAGE ARTS	Choose appropriate level of one of the following: ❡ English Lessons Through Literature, Lesson 92 Reading Lessons Through Literature, phonogram review ❡ Rod and Staff English, Lesson 107 Copywork/Commonplace Book ❡ Your own grammar program		❡ Essential Literary Terms, 3-4 pages ❡ LR: The Power in Your Hands, 1 lesson ❡ UR: WGRP, editing. (6 days) ❡ LR: Rod and Staff 10, L. 102
MATH	Choose appropriate level of one of the following:		
	✎ Math-U-See, page C ✎ Miquon/Singapore Math ✎ Your own math program		✎ Math-U-See, page C ✎ Your own math program
GEOGRAPHY	🌐 Reading, choose one of the following: A. United States: Moccasin Trail, Ch. 8 B. Montana: Smoky the Cowhorse, Ch. 11		🌐 A Walk Along the Ganges, Ch. 12
HISTORY	Choose one spine, one or more core reading selections, and optional reading as desired.		
	♟ Spine: SOTW, Ch. 36.2 ♟ Core reading: 1. Burying the Sun, Ch. 13 2. Neil Armstrong, Ch. 3 3. Who Was Gandhi, Ch. 8	♟ Spine: SOTW, Ch. 36.2 ♟ Core reading: 1. Red Scarf Girl, Ch. 1 2. Warriors Don't Cry, Ch. 2	♟ Spine: America, 1/4 of Ch. 33 World Empires, Missions, Wars, Unit 9 Week 1 ♟ Core reading: 1 & 2. Les Miserables, 14 pages 1. 1984, Ch. 5 2. Strength to Love, Ch. 14

Day 3

GRAMMAR	DIALECTIC	RHETORIC	
♪♫ Term 3 Composer: Choose between Shostakovich, Britten, Leon Kirchner			ACTIVITIES
☞ Oral or written narration; could be a group project. Make a picture book version of your book for a young child. Artists can focus on the art, and writers can focus on the text of the book.			NARRATION
✠ Old Story New, Week 67 ✠ UD: Simply Christian, Ch. 11		✠ Great Divorce, Ch. 4	OTHER
📚 Literature: 1: Five Little Peppers and How They Grew, Ch. 9 2: This Week: A Wonder-Book for Girls and Boys: The Gorgon's Head 3: The Princess and the Goblin, Ch. 15 4: This Week: Tanglewood Tales, The Minotaur	📚 Literature: 5: Around the World in 80 Days, Ch. 5-6 6: Otto of the Silver Hand, Ch. 10 7: Northanger Abbey, Ch. 15 8: 20,000 Leagues, Ch. 44	📚 Book of English Verse, No. 846-848 ✠ Church History: Book of Common Prayer Biography, pp. 6-15 ✠ 100 Events, A.D. 1945	LITERATURE

PRESCHOOL AND LOWER GRAMMAR

✏ Pathways: Path 1, Day 2 A. Kindergarten Gems B. Among the Meadow People C. 20th—Harry the Dirty Dog D. Random House Poetry, p. 196	PATHWAYS
✏ Multi-sensory bin Add sand to a shoebox size plastic container. Use tiny cups for pouring sand, spoons for shovels, and forks for rakes.	ACTIVITY

Week 31

	GRAMMAR	DIALECTIC	RHETORIC
BIBLE	Choose one of the following plans: ✠ PLAN 1: Journey Through the Bible, pp. 340-341 ✠ PLAN 2: What the Bible Is All About, Romans		
	✠ LG: TBB: A Gift for Jesus; The True King ✠ UG: Egermeier's, 2 stories	✠ LD: Hurlbut's, 1 story ✠ UD: Golden's, 3 stories	
LANGUAGE ARTS	Choose appropriate level of one of the following: ❡ Reading Lessons Through Literature, next list and story ❡ Prepared dictation from ELTL, Spelling Wisdom, or today's reading ❡ Your own grammar program		❡ UR: WGRP, editing. (6 days)
MATH	Choose appropriate level of one of the following: ✎ Math-U-See, page D ✎ Miquon/Singapore Math ✎ Your own math program		✎ Math-U-See, page D ✎ Your own math program
GEOGRAPHY	🌏 Reading, choose one of the following: A. United States: Moccasin Trail, Ch. 9 B. Montana: Smoky the Cowhorse, Ch. 12		
SCIENCE	Choose one spine, one or more core reading selections, and optional reading as desired.		
	⚛ Core reading: 1. Isaac Newton for Kids, Ch. 2 2. Insiders Inventions, pp. 8-13	⚛ Core reading: 1. Uncle Albert and the Quantum Quest, Ch. 1 2. Matter and Energy, Ch. 3	⚛ Spine: SHSPhys, Week 10 Manga Relativity, pp. 108-118 ⚛ Core reading: The Elegant Universe, Ch. 7
	⚛ Optional extra reading, topic: Friction Simon Bloom, Ch. 29-30		

Day 4

Grammar	Dialectic	Rhetoric	
♪♪ Term 3 Composer: Choose between Shostakovich, Britten, Leon Kirchner			Activities
⊛ GSA The World of Light and Sound, Lesson 14 ⊛ 201 Awesome Experiments, 185-186		🎨 Great Art Writing	
⟿ Oral or written narration; LG students can draw a picture from the reading and tell about the picture. Suggested subject: science.		⟿ Written narration for science or Bible.	Narration
✠ Old Story New, Week 67			
	ೞ UD: The Art of Argument: Write a narration on fallacies of induction ೞ UD: Science Matters, pp. 196-210	ೞ UR: Classical English Rhetoric, 1/4 Ch. 16	Other
📚 Suggested read-aloud: The Neverending Story, Ch. 10			Literature
Preschool and Lower Grammar			
✎ Pathways: Path 3 A. Burgess Flower Book, Ch. 36 B. Gooney Bird Greene, Ch. 3 C. The Magic School Bus Explores the Senses D. Random House Poetry, p. 197			Pathways
✎ Trace shapes Trace lids, plates, bowls, board books. Cut out other shapes from cardboard and trace those.			Activity

Week 31

	GRAMMAR	DIALECTIC	RHETORIC
BIBLE	Choose one of the following plans: ✚ PLAN 1: Journey Through the Bible, pp. 342-343 ✚ PLAN 2: The Story, Ch. 30		
LANGUAGE ARTS	Choose appropriate level of one of the following: ❡ English Lessons Through Literature, Lesson 93 Reading Lessons Through Literature, phonogram review ❡ Rod and Staff English, Lesson 108 Copywork/Commonplace Book ❡ Your own grammar program		❡ A Rulebook for Arguments, Ch. 40 ❡ LR: The Power in Your Hands, 1 lesson ❡ LR: Rod and Staff 10, L. 103
MATH	Choose appropriate level of one of the following: ✏ Math-U-See, page E ✏ Miquon/Singapore Math ✏ Your own math program		✏ Math-U-See, pages E & H ✏ Your own math program
GEOGRAPHY	🌎 Mapping: Southern Africa 🌎 Reading, choose one of the following: B. Montana: Smoky the Cowhorse, Ch. 13		🌎 A Walk Along the Ganges, Ch. 13
HISTORY	Choose one spine, one or more core reading selections, and optional reading as desired. ♟ Spine: ♟ Core reading: 1. Who Was Nelson Mandela, Intro. - Ch. 1 2. Neil Armstrong, Ch. 4 3. Who Was Gandhi, Ch. 9	♟ Spine: ♟ Core reading: 1. Red Scarf Girl, Ch. 2 2. Warriors Don't Cry, Ch. 3	♟ Spine: America, 1/4 of Ch. 33 World Empires, Missions, Wars, Unit 9 Week 1 ♟ Core reading: 1 & 2. Les Miserables, 14 pages LR: 1 & 2. Philosophy Book, through Merleau-Ponty UR: 1 & 2. Think, 1/2 Ch. 5 1. 1984, Ch. 6 2. Strength to Love, Ch. 15

Day 5

Grammar	Dialectic	Rhetoric	
♪♪ Term 3 Composer: Choose between Shostakovich, Britten, Leon Kirchner			ACTIVITIES
🎨 Art Lesson: Choose appropriate level of one of the following:			
🎨 I Can Do All Things	🎨 Lamb's Book of Art II	🎨 How Great Thou ART I or II	
🎨 Lamb's Book of Art I	🎨 Feed My Sheep	🎨 Book of Many Colors	
☞ Oral or written narration; LG students can draw a picture from the reading and tell about the picture. Suggested subject: geography.		☞ Oral or written narration for history or geography.	NARRATION
✛ Old Story New, Week 67			OTHER
📖 Suggested read-aloud: The Neverending Story, Ch. 11			
📚 Literature: 1: Five Little Peppers and How They Grew, Ch. 10 2: This Week: A Wonder-Book for Girls and Boys: The Gorgon's Head 3: The Princess and the Goblin, Ch. 16 4: This Week: Tanglewood Tales, The Minotaur	📚 Literature: 5: Around the World in 80 Days, Ch. 7-8 6: Otto of the Silver Hand, Ch. 11 7: Northanger Abbey, Ch. 16 8: 20,000 Leagues, Ch. 45	📚 Book of English Verse, No. 849-851 ✛ Church History: Book of Common Prayer Biography, pp. 15-24 ✛ 100 Events, A.D. 1948	LITERATURE

Preschool and Lower Grammar

✏ Pathways: Path 1, Day 3 A. Kindergarten Gems B. 50 Famous Stories C. JH—Oscar, Cat-About-Town D. Random House Poetry, pp. 198-200	PATHWAYS
🎨 Art Lesson: Choose one of the following Barry Stebbing art books for you little one to do art like the big kids: Art and the Bible for Children, Baby Lamb's Book of Art, Joseph the Canada Goose, or Little Annie's Art Book.	ACTIVITY

Amelia Earhart, circa 1928. Image in the public domain; via Wikimedia Commons.

History Through Art: Amelia Earhart

During the early age of planes and flying, countless pilots sought to make names for themselves by being the first to make historic flights across the Earth. In this time, even women, a class of humanity quite subjected at the time, had the opportunity to achieve everlasting fame through the power of flight. Amelia Earhart was one such woman.

As a little girl Amelia already showed signs of an adventurous spirit. Countless biographers have noted her love of climbing trees and sledding down hills. According to some accounts, she got up breathless from one particularly spirited sled trip exclaiming, "It's just like flying!"

As a grown woman, Earhart worked hard to become an aviator, and she found many opportunities for adventurous flights. In 1928, she was part of a flight across the huge Atlantic Ocean, the first woman to do so. However, she did little of the flying on this trip and yearned to try it on her own. She got her chance in 1932 when she became the first woman to fly across the Atlantic with nothing but her plane and her skill for company.

Though world-famous for her exploit, Earhart was still dedicated to pushing flight as far as it would go, and in 1937, she decided to attempt a hazardous trip around the whole planet in her plane. This was an undertaking which would not have a happy ending. Along with her navigator, Fred Noonan, Earhart and her plane vanished partway through their trip, never to be seen again. The untamed skies and seas of Earth had claimed another victim, but no one was forgotten. Earhart lives on as a legend for her devotion to flight.

Moccasin Trail

Panthers

Sally had refused to eat panther meat. Being compared to a panther is undoubtedly a favorable description. The name evokes a series of thoughts and adjectives, all of which lend themselves towards visualizing a swift, powerful, exotic, and cunning creature. Who wouldn't want to be compared to such a beast? But while the word **panther** is useful in simile, it's a tad more complicated when used for zoology.

The word panther can refer to several large cats in the world. The leopard of Africa and Asia is often called by this name, as is the cougar of North America. The jaguar of South America usually isn't, but when all-black jaguars are born they are called black panthers along with leopards born with the same genetic trait. While these three cats are the only ones commonly called panthers, any member of the subfamily Pantherinae can technically be called such; this group encompasses most big cats except for cheetahs and cougars. In this respect, then, the word panther can refer to any of the feline apex predators of the world.

Are you beginning to find this definition confusing? You've seen nothing yet; artists and scholars in Europe's Middle Ages had often never seen a big cat in person, and thus began using the word panther to describe all number of strange mythical beasts. One account describing a beast called a panther describes the animal as a large predator that sleeps in caves. Every three days the so-called panther will wake up and breathe out a sweet smell that lures prey animals to their doom. No such animal exists, let alone in the cat family—but even that mythical panther is closer to reality than the horned and hooved dragons inexplicably called panthers in some medieval heraldry. All things considered, the word panther is best used for similes—the word should probably be avoided in zoology unless you make it perfectly clear what animal you're talking about.

Surveying

The surveyor leaves after he has measured and staked the Rutledges' land. Surveying is the process of locating the three dimensional position of points and the distances between them. This is usually done in regards to land, property, and territory. Those who practice this profession are known as surveyors. They use special skills and tools to establish maps and boundaries.

In surveying, the skills of mathematics, geometry, physics, and engineering all come into play. Modern surveying may use global positioning systems, radios, computers, and specialized software, but ancient surveying used little more than string and rocks. As a skill, surveying has been around since early in human civilization. Almost all forms of construction require some degree of planning and surveying. Even the Egyptian pyramids had to be planned and surveyed.

Elk

Jim cuts elk meat into strips. Elk are the second largest members of the deer family, second only to moose, and are among the largest hoofed herbivores in North America. Their numbers have diminished over the years due to human expansion and hunting, a shame as the elk is a surviving relic of the far-off Ice Age.

Modern elk live in the north west of North America and in the far east of Siberia. They are descended from huge herds that used to live in Beringia, an

Elks, Cervus canadensis, at the Opal terrace at Mammoth Hot Springs, Yellowstone National Park, Montana, United States. Photo by Brocken Inaglory. License: CC BY-SA 3.0; via Wikimedia Commons.

expanse of frigid tundra that once lay between Asia and Alaska. Though Beringia has long since sunk into the sea, elk are still found on either side of it, lending evidence to its existence with their presence in parts of the world no longer connected to each other.

One of the most distinctive traits of an elk stag are its magnificent antlers, used to attract mates and fight away rival males. Rutting season is a spectacular time to watch elk as they will lock antlers in a ritualized combat to determine which males will win the right to mate.

Smoky the Cowhorse

Names of Livestock

When a steer breaks out, Old Tom goes after him. Often livestock will have different names based on the different stages of their development, their sex, or changes made to them. A female bovine is called a cow while a male bovine is called a bull. A baby bovine is referred to as a calf or sometimes, more specific to its sex, a bull calf for males or a heifer for females. A female bovine who is young or who has not yet had a calf of her own is called a heifer. Young goats are called kids. A female goat is a doe while the male is a buck. Rabbits also are divided into does and bucks. Even cats are sometimes divided into male and female variants. A female cat is called a queen while a male is a tom.

This differentiation is important in cultures which evolved around livestock. If a man wishes to trade another man an animal, he will want to know whether it will be a male or a female, and these specific names help smooth trade and conversation. They also have become part of the vernacular of farming and herding communities. These sorts of terms may seem confusing to outsiders, but their inclusion in speech helps to establish cultural ties and set boundaries.

Thermometers

After the blizzard, the thermometer goes down. A thermometer is a device specifically made to measure temperature or temperature changes. The most common type of thermometer works by the expansion of a small bulb filled with mercury. As the temperature rises, the mercury expands up a small tube. Measurements alongside the tube indicate the temperature corresponding to the current level of mercury expansion.

The creation of the thermometer has been credited to many different people though it did not come about as a single invention. Various individuals knew of the principles of expansion that drive the mercury and demonstrated this by placing liquids in water of various temperatures. In the 16th and 17th centuries, these principles had been used to create devices used to measure the temperature of the air. Galileo is said to have invented the thermometer, but it wasn't until much later that scales or markings were added to the device to actually keep track of the temperature.

Telegraphs

All around the town of Gramah, big posters are tacked on the telegraph poles. Early telegraphing is the long-distance sending of messages without using a physical object to carry it. For instance, using signal fires or smoke to send a message is telegraphy, but a letter sent in the mail is not. In order for telegraphy to work, people on both the sending side and the receiving side have to have a code or agreed upon method for interpreting the signals. Boats and navies have used a complicated system with flags while aboriginal tribes around the world have used drums or smoke from fires to signal others over long distances.

In the 19th century, electricity enabled the invention of electrical telegraphy, which we generally just call "the telegraph". Through wires strung up across miles and miles, an electrical signal could be sent which would be decrypted on each end. The method of encryption used was known as "Morse code" after the man who invented it. Radio would advance the technology even further, allowing Morse code to be broadcast without wires within the long-distances allowed by radio waves.

Replica of Claude Chappe's optical telegraph on the Litermont near Nalbach, Germany. Photo by Lokilech. License: CC BY-SA 3.0; via Wikimedia Commons.

In modern times, the Internet has allowed us to send telegraphic messages all around the world almost instantly with email and instant messaging.

P/K & LG Activity Supplies:

Day 1:
- Photo of each child, one which can be cut in half
- Cardstock

Day 3:
- Paint chips

Day 4:
- Pattern blocks

Science Experiment Supplies:

- Drinking straw
- Bottle of soda

- 1 cup uncooked rice
- Sock
- Pencil

Week 32

	GRAMMAR	DIALECTIC	RHETORIC
BIBLE	Choose one of the following plans: ✛ PLAN 1: Journey Through the Bible, pp. 344-345 ✛ PLAN 2: What the Bible Is All About, Ephesians		

LANGUAGE ARTS	Choose appropriate level of one of the following:
	
	¶ English Lessons Through Literature, Lesson 94
	  Reading Lessons Through Literature, phonogram review
	
	¶ Rod and Staff English, Lesson 109
	  Copywork/Commonplace Book
	
	¶ Your own grammar program
			¶ LR: The Power in Your Hands, 1 lesson
			
			¶ UR: WGRP, editing. (6 days)
			
			¶ LR: Rod and Staff 10, L. 104

MATH	Choose appropriate level of one of the following: ✎ Math-U-See, Video and page A ✎ Miquon/Singapore Math ✎ Your own math program		✎ Math-U-See, Video and page A ✎ Your own math program

GEOGRAPHY	🌐 50 States, Review Mid-Atlantic
	
	🌐 Reading, choose one of the following:
	  A. United States: Moccasin Trail, Ch. 10
	  B. Montana: Smoky the Cowhorse, Ch. 14
			🌐 A Walk Along the Ganges, Ch. 14

HISTORY	Choose one spine, one or more core reading selections, and optional reading as desired. ♟ Spine: SOTW, Ch. 37.1 ♟ Core reading: 1. Who Was Nelson Mandela, Ch. 2 2. Neil Armstrong, Ch. 5 3. Journey to Jo'burg, Ch. 1	♟ Spine: SOTW, Ch. 37.1 ♟ Core reading: 1. Red Scarf Girl, Ch. 3 2. Warriors Don't Cry, Ch. 4	♟ Spine: Western Civ, 1/4 of Ch. 29 World Empires, Missions, Wars, Unit 9 Week 2 ♟ Core reading: 1 & 2. Les Miserables, 14 pages 1. 1984, Ch. 7 2. Ender's Game, Ch. 1

Day 1

GRAMMAR	DIALECTIC	RHETORIC	
♪♪ Term 3 Composer: Choose between Shostakovich, Britten, Leon Kirchner ⧖ Timeline/Book of Centuries			ACTIVITIES
↪ Oral or written narration; LG students can draw a picture from the reading and tell about the picture. Suggested subject: history.		↪ Written narration for history or geography.	NARRATION
✠ Old Story New, Week 68 ℅ UD: Economics in One Lesson, Ch. 19		✠ Great Divorce, Ch. 5	OTHER
📚 Literature: 1: Five Little Peppers and How They Grew, Ch. 11 2: This Week: A Wonder-Book for Girls and Boys: The Golden Touch 3: The Princess and the Goblin, Ch. 17 4: This Week: Tanglewood Tales, The Pygmies	📚 Literature: 5: Around the World in 80 Days, Ch. 9-10 6: Otto of the Silver Hand, Ch. 12 7: Northanger Abbey, Ch. 17 8: 20,000 Leagues, Ch. 46	📚 Book of English Verse, No. 852-854 ✠ Church History: Book of Common Prayer Biography, pp. 24-34 ✠ 100 Events, A.D. 1949	LITERATURE

PRESCHOOL AND LOWER GRAMMAR

✐ Pathways: Path 1, Day 1 A. Kindergarten Gems B. Among the Meadow People C. 20th—Whose Mouse Are You? D. Random House Poetry, p. 201	PATHWAYS
✐ Self-portrait Take a "mug-shot" picture of each child. Cut it in half and glue half of it on a card. Have the child draw the other half of his face.	ACTIVITY

Week 32

	GRAMMAR	DIALECTIC	RHETORIC
BIBLE	Choose one of the following plans: ✣ PLAN 1: Journey Through the Bible, pp. 346-347 ✣ PLAN 2: What the Bible Is All About, Philippians		
	✣ LG: TBB: A Poor Widow's Gift ✣ UG: Egermeier's, 2 stories	✣ LD: Hurlbut's, 1 story ✣ UD: Golden's, 3 stories	
LANGUAGE ARTS	Choose appropriate level of one of the following: ❡ Reading Lessons Through Literature, next list and story ❡ Prepared dictation from ELTL, Spelling Wisdom, or today's reading ❡ Rod and Staff English, Lesson 110 ❡ Your own grammar program		
MATH	Choose appropriate level of one of the following: ✎ Math-U-See, page B ✎ Miquon/Singapore Math ✎ Your own math program		✎ Math-U-See, page B ✎ Your own math program
GEOGRAPHY	🌎 Reading, choose one of the following: A. United States: Moccasin Trail, Ch. 11 B. Nevada: Mustang: Wild Spirit of the West, Ch. 1		🌎 Geography for Dummies, 1/2 of Ch. 16
SCIENCE	Choose one spine, one or more core reading selections, and optional reading as desired.		
	⚛ Core reading: 1. Isaac Newton for Kids, Ch. 3 2. Insiders Inventions, pp. 14-19	⚛ Core reading: 1. Uncle Albert and the Quantum Quest, Ch. 2 2. Matter and Energy, Ch. 4	⚛ Spine: SHSPhys, Week 11 Physics for Dummies, 1/2 of Ch. 17 ⚛ Core reading: The Elegant Universe, Ch. 8
	⚛ Spine: Quark Chronicles: Physics, Ch. 14		

Day 2

GRAMMAR	DIALECTIC	RHETORIC	
♪ Term 3 Composer: Choose between Shostakovich, Britten, Leon Kirchner 🎨 Art Lesson: Choose appropriate level of one of the following:			ACTIVITIES
🎨 I Can Do All Things 🎨 Lamb's Book of Art I	🎨 Lamb's Book of Art II 🎨 Feed My Sheep	🎨 How Great Thou ART I or II 🎨 Book of Many Colors	
⚛ GSA The World of Light and Sound, Lesson 15		🎨 Great Art, Lecture 32	
👉 Oral or written narration; LG students can draw a picture from the reading and tell about the picture. Suggested subject: Bible.		👉 Oral or written narration for science or Bible.	NARRATION
✚ Old Story New, Week 68			
	❦ UD: The Art of Argument, Intro. to Clarity ❦ UD: Science Matters, pp. 211-225	❦ UR: Classical English Rhetoric, 1/4 Ch. 16	OTHER
📚 Suggested read-aloud: The Neverending Story, Ch. 12			LITERATURE
PRESCHOOL AND LOWER GRAMMAR			
🖌 Pathways: Path 2 A. Little Wanderers, Ch. 32 B. Burgess Seashore Book, Ch. 35 C. Paddington Helps Out, Ch. 11 D. Random House Poetry, p. 202			PATHWAYS
🎨 Art Lesson: Choose one of the following Barry Stebbing art books for you little one to do art like the big kids: Art and the Bible for Children, Baby Lamb's Book of Art, Joseph the Canada Goose, or Little Annie's Art Book.			ACTIVITY

Week 32

	GRAMMAR	DIALECTIC	RHETORIC
BIBLE	Choose one of the following plans: ✚ PLAN 1: Journey Through the Bible, pp. 348-349 ✚ PLAN 2: What the Bible Is All About, Quick Look at Matthew to Philippians (not in all versions)		

LANGUAGE ARTS	Choose appropriate level of one of the following:
	
	❡ English Lessons Through Literature, Lesson 95
	    Reading Lessons Through Literature, phonogram review
	
	❡ Rod and Staff English, Lesson 111
	    Copywork/Commonplace Book
	
	❡ Your own grammar program
			❡ Essential Literary Terms, 3-4 pages
			
			❡ LR: The Power in Your Hands, 1 lesson
			
			❡ UR: WGRP, editing. (6 days)
			
			❡ LR: Rod and Staff 10, L. 105

MATH	Choose appropriate level of one of the following: ✎ Math-U-See, page C ✎ Miquon/Singapore Math ✎ Your own math program		✎ Math-U-See, page C ✎ Your own math program

GEOGRAPHY	🌐 Reading, choose one of the following:
	    A. United States: Moccasin Trail, Ch. 12
	    B. Nevada: Mustang: Wild Spirit of the West, Ch. 2
			🌐 Kilimanjaro Diaries, Ch. 1-2

HISTORY	Choose one spine, one or more core reading selections, and optional reading as desired.		
	♟ Spine: SOTW, Ch. 37.2 ♟ Core reading: 1. Who Was Nelson Mandela, Ch. 3 2. Neil Armstrong, Ch. 6 3. Journey to Jo'burg, Ch. 2	♟ Spine: SOTW, Ch. 37.2 ♟ Core reading: 1. Red Scarf Girl, Ch. 4 2. Warriors Don't Cry, Ch. 5	♟ Spine: America, 1/4 of Ch. 33 World Empires, Missions, Wars, Unit 9 Week 2 ♟ Core reading: 1 & 2. Les Miserables, 14 pages 1. 1984, Ch. 8 2. Ender's Game, Ch. 2

Day 3

Grammar	Dialectic	Rhetoric	
♪♪ Term 3 Composer: Choose between Shostakovich, Britten, Leon Kirchner			Activities
☞ Oral or written narration; could be a group project. Hollywood is making a movie of your book. Which actors should be cast for each character? Tell why each actor be a good choice for each character.			Narration
✤ Old Story New, Week 68 ✤ UD: Simply Christian, Ch. 12		✤ Great Divorce, Ch. 6	Other
📚 Literature: 1: Five Little Peppers and How They Grew, Ch. 12 2: This Week: A Wonder-Book for Girls and Boys: The Golden Touch 3: The Princess and the Goblin, Ch. 18 4: This Week: Tanglewood Tales, The Pygmies	📚 Literature: 5: Around the World in 80 Days, Ch. 11-12 6: Otto of the Silver Hand, Ch. 13 7: Northanger Abbey, Ch. 18 8: A Double Story, Ch. 1	📚 Book of English Verse, No. 855-857 ✤ Church History: Book of Common Prayer Biography, pp. 34-44 ✤ 100 Events, A.D. 1960	Literature
Preschool and Lower Grammar			
✎ Pathways: Path 1, Day 2 A. Kindergarten Gems B. 50 Famous Stories C. JH—Smudge, the Little Lost Lamb D. Random House Poetry, p. 203			Pathways
✎ Colors, lightest to darkest Cut apart paint chip cards. Have child arrange the paint chips from lightest to darkest or darkest to lightest.			Activity

Week 32

	GRAMMAR	DIALECTIC	RHETORIC
BIBLE	Choose one of the following plans: ✠ PLAN 1: Journey Through the Bible, pp. 350-351 ✠ PLAN 2: Journey Through the Bible, pp. 368-373		
	✠ LG: TBB: Washing the Disciples' Feet ✠ UG: Egermeier's, 2 stories	✠ LD: Hurlbut's, 1 story ✠ UD: Golden's, 3 stories	
LANGUAGE ARTS	Choose appropriate level of one of the following: ❡ Reading Lessons Through Literature, next list and story ❡ Prepared dictation from ELTL, Spelling Wisdom, or today's reading ❡ Your own grammar program		❡ UR: WGRP, editing. (6 days)
MATH	Choose appropriate level of one of the following:		
	✎ Math-U-See, page D ✎ Miquon/Singapore Math ✎ Your own math program		✎ Math-U-See, page D ✎ Your own math program
GEOGRAPHY	🌐 Reading, choose one of the following: A. United States: Moccasin Trail, Ch. 13 B. Nevada: Mustang: Wild Spirit of the West, Ch. 3		
SCIENCE	Choose one spine, one or more core reading selections, and optional reading as desired.		
	⚛ Core reading: 1. Isaac Newton for Kids, Ch. 4 2. Insiders Inventions, pp. 20-25	⚛ Core reading: 1. Uncle Albert and the Quantum Quest, Ch. 3 2. Matter and Energy, Ch. 5	⚛ Spine: SHSPhys, Week 11 Manga Relativity, pp. 119-129 ⚛ Core reading: The Elegant Universe, Ch. 9
	⚛ Optional extra reading, topic: Simple Machines Simon Bloom, Ch. 31-32 G: How Do You Lift a Lion? by Robert E. Wells D: Simple Machines: Forces in Action by Buffy Silverman Insiders Inventions by Glenn Murphy		

Day 4

GRAMMAR	DIALECTIC	RHETORIC	
♪♪ Term 3 Composer: Choose between Shostakovich, Britten, Leon Kirchner			ACTIVITIES
⊛ GSA The World of Light and Sound, Lesson 16 ⊛ 201 Awesome Experiments, 187-188		🎨 Great Art Writing	
☞ Oral or written narration; LG students can draw a picture from the reading and tell about the picture. Suggested subject: science.		☞ Written narration for science or Bible.	NARRATION
✛ Old Story New, Week 68			
	✇ UD: The Art of Argument, Fallacy 26; Create an ad or an argument using this week's fallacy ✇ UD: Science Matters, pp. 226-240	✇ UR: Classical English Rhetoric, 1/4 Ch. 16	OTHER
📚 Suggested read-aloud: The Neverending Story, Ch. 13			LITERATURE

PRESCHOOL AND LOWER GRAMMAR

✎ Pathways: Path 3 A. Burgess Flower Book, Ch. 37 B. Gooney Bird Greene, Ch. 4 C. The Magic School Bus Inside a Beehive D. Random House Poetry, p. 204	PATHWAYS

✎ Pattern block shapes

Use the three-period lesson to learn the names and/or colors of the shapes.

yellow hexagon   orange square   blue rhombus

red trapezoid   green triangle   white rhombus

Week 32

	GRAMMAR	DIALECTIC	RHETORIC
BIBLE	Choose one of the following plans: ✠ PLAN 1: Journey Through the Bible, pp. 352-353 ✠ PLAN 2: What the Bible Is All About, Colossians		

LANGUAGE ARTS	Choose appropriate level of one of the following:
	
	¶ English Lessons Through Literature, Lesson 96
	    Reading Lessons Through Literature, phonogram review
	
	¶ Rod and Staff English, Lesson 112
	    Copywork/Commonplace Book
	
	¶ Your own grammar program
			¶ A Rulebook for Arguments, Ch. 41-42
			
			¶ LR: The Power in Your Hands, 1 lesson
			
			¶ LR: Rod and Staff 10, L. 106

MATH	Choose appropriate level of one of the following: ✎ Math-U-See, page E ✎ Miquon/Singapore Math ✎ Your own math program		✎ Math-U-See, pages E & H ✎ Your own math program
GEOGRAPHY	🌍 Mapping: Northern Europe 🌍 Reading, choose one of the following: B. Nevada: Mustang: Wild Spirit of the West, Ch. 4		🌍 Kilimanjaro Diaries, Ch. 3-4

HISTORY	Choose one spine, one or more core reading selections, and optional reading as desired.
	
	♟ Spine:
	
	♟ Core reading:
	    1. Who Was Nelson Mandela, Ch. 4
	    2. Neil Armstrong, Ch. 7
	    3. Journey to Jo'burg, Ch. 3
		♟ Spine:
		
		♟ Core reading:
		    1. Red Scarf Girl, Ch. 5
		    2. Warriors Don't Cry, Ch. 6
			♟ Spine:
			    America, 1/4 of Ch. 33
			    World Empires, Missions, Wars, Unit 9 Week 2
			
			♟ Core reading:
			    1 & 2. Les Miserables, 14 pages
			    LR: 1 & 2. Philosophy Book, through Camus
			    UR: 1 & 2. Think, 1/2 Ch. 6
			    1. 1984, Ch. 9
			    2. Ender's Game, Ch. 3

Day 5

	Grammar	Dialectic	Rhetoric	
♪♪ Term 3 Composer: Choose between Shostakovich, Britten, Leon Kirchner				Activities
🎨 Art Lesson: Choose appropriate level of one of the following:				
🎨 I Can Do All Things	🎨 Lamb's Book of Art II	🎨 How Great Thou ART I or II	
🎨 Lamb's Book of Art I	🎨 Feed My Sheep	🎨 Book of Many Colors	
☞ Oral or written narration; LG students can draw a picture from the reading and tell about the picture. Suggested subject: geography.		☞ Oral or written narration for history or geography.	Narration
✠ Old Story New, Week 68 ଔ UD: Economics in One Lesson, Ch. 20			Other
📚 Suggested read-aloud: The Neverending Story, Ch. 14			Literature
📚 Literature: 1: Five Little Peppers and How They Grew, Ch. 13 2: This Week: A Wonder-Book for Girls and Boys: The Golden Touch 3: The Princess and the Goblin, Ch. 19 4: This Week: Tanglewood Tales, The Pygmies	📚 Literature: 5: Around the World in 80 Days, Ch. 13-14 6: Otto of the Silver Hand, Ch. 14 7: Northanger Abbey, Ch. 19 8: A Double Story, Ch. 2	📚 Book of English Verse, No. 858-860 ✠ Church History: Book of Common Prayer Biography, pp. 44-52 ✠ 100 Events, A.D. 1962	

Preschool and Lower Grammar

✎ Pathways: Path 1, Day 3 A. Kindergarten Gems B. Among the Meadow People C. A Year at Maple Hill Farm D. Random House Poetry, p. 205	Pathways
🎨 Art Lesson: Choose one of the following Barry Stebbing art books for you little one to do art like the big kids: Art and the Bible for Children, Baby Lamb's Book of Art, Joseph the Canada Goose, or Little Annie's Art Book.	Activity

Charles Lindbergh, with Spirit of St. Louis in background. Restored by Wikipedia user Crisco 1492 who removed dust, scratches, including black spots on the wings which may or may not have been there in the original. Image in the public domain; via Wikimedia Commons.

History Through Art: Charles Lindbergh

The airplane opened up a new world of possibilities for the human race—or rather, it opened up the world in which we were already living to new exploration and adventures. The early 20th century was filled with flying firsts as adventurous folk raced to become the first people to make historic flights. One of the most remarkable of these flyers was Charles Lindbergh, also known as Lucky Lindy.

During the 1920s, many tried and failed to collect a prize of $25, 000 for making a non-stop airplane flight across the Atlantic Ocean, from New York City to Paris, France. No one had ever done it. The greatest flying aces of the day constantly failed when they tried; some failed with disastrous consequences.

Charles Lindbergh worked in Air Mail, using a plane to carry packages and other supplies across the land. Essentially an airborne mailman, he was the last person anyone expected to see collecting the coveted prize and outdoing the great flyers of the world. Nonetheless, Lindbergh got it in his head to make a try, and scraping together what funds he could, he acquired a plane called the Spirit of St. Louis and made his attempt.

He almost failed like everyone else had. The distance was incredible, and the skies were rough. His plane had to skip off the tops of storm clouds and press for miles and miles through dense fog. But by pressing on and applying some clever maneuvering, Linbergh managed to successfully cross the ocean and land in France—and in every aeronautical history written since.

Moccasin Trail

Hail

Dan'l says he feels like he's been in a hailstorm. Do you remember what figure of speech this is? It's a simile because it uses *like* or *as*.

Everyone knows that water freezes when cold enough, forming ice. Everyone also knows that water can fall from the sky in the form of rain. When these two facts come together, we get the phenomenon of hail.

Hailstones are formed in the hearts of cold storms and can be anything from tiny specks to lumps of ice the size of golf balls. The largest hailstone ever recorded was eight inches in diameter—the size of a small bowling ball! Hail can be dangerous and damaging, and it can make travel in icy weather quite unpleasant.

Rawhide

They use a rawhide rope for a halter. Rawhide is animal skin that has not been tanned. It is tougher and lighter in color than leather. To create rawhide, all fur, meat, and fat is removed, and the hide is usually stretched over a frame to dry. The result is very hard, and it will be shaped and worked by rewetting and forming. It is often made pliable by bending it repeatedly in multiple directions or rubbing it against a tree or post. Traditionally, it was made pliable by chewing.

Worked rawhide is often used for lamp shades, the heads of drums, or whips. Very durable, it is often used in making horse saddles, and it shrinks as it dries, which can make the saddle even stronger by tightly holding the wooden structure intact. Rawhide has often been used in making wooden bows as it takes some of the stress out of the wood when the bow is fired.

Ferns

Jim rounds a clump of ferns. Many of the world's plants follow a basic and successful strategy: they produce flowers, which are then pollinated by the wind or by helpful insects, and the flowers then wilt and become packages for seeds that will grow into new plants. It is a timeless and brilliant way to ensure that the world is always covered in trees and grasses and flowers without count.

Ferns are a stubborn group of plants that insist on doing things very differently. Easily recognized by their distinctive, perfectly symmetrical leaves, ferns do not produce flowers or produce seeds. Instead, they produce microscopic counterparts to seeds called spores, much like mushrooms and other fungi. Spores are smaller than any speck of dust you've ever seen, and once they are produced, they easily blow away on the winds far away from the original fern that gave them birth. When

Athyrium filix-femina at Cambridge Botanic Garden. Photo by Rror. License: CC BY-SA 3.0; via Wikimedia Commons.

they reach a place of suitable soil, they sprout and slowly grow into full-sized ferns, which then produce more spores and start the cycle all over again.

Mustang: Wild Spirit of the West

Mesas

The first time Annie remembers seeing a band of wild mustangs, they were running across a mesa. Standing tall in arid and windy areas around the world are mesas, also known as table hills or table mountains. Mesas are tall pieces of land with flat tops, which is why they're so often referred to as table mountains. They are formed when earthquakes thrust a piece of rock higher than the surrounding land, and the wind and the water—but mostly the wind—of an arid countryside wears away its top, making a smooth, table-like surface.

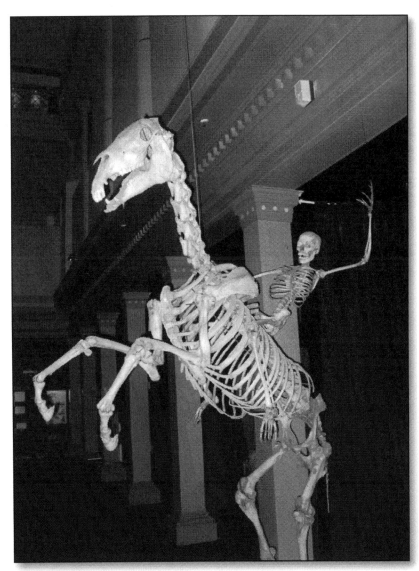

Particularly small mesas, or mesas that have been worn down to a particularly small size, are called buttes. On the other end of the scale, very large mesas are called plateaus and can have quite vast tracts of land at their tops. One particularly spectacular plateau is in Tibet and, with its great height and proximity to the mighty Himalaya Mountains, has been known through history as "the roof of the world."

Skeletons

Annie's Pa has high cheekbones, which are part of the skull. The brain controls the body. The heart controls the blood. The muscles are vital to our movement. But without our skeletons, we'd dissolve into piles of jelly on the pavement. The body of a vertebrate—a creature with a backbone—is a squishy pile of highly specialized organs that depend on an internal skeleton to support it and keep it in shape.

Bones are perfectly designed for supporting our weight as we go about our day-to-day lives, and they are jointed to allow us to move and

A composite of the skeletons of a Human and a Horse arranged into a lifelike pose, at an exhibit in the Australian Museum, Sydney, Australia. Photo by Hibernian. Image is in the public domain; via Wikimedia Commons.

put ourselves in different positions. Bones are rock hard and filled with squishy marrow which plays an important role in the body by producing blood cells.

All vertebrates have skeletons that are perfectly suited for what the vertebrate needs to do. For instance, birds have hollow skeletons that are lightweight to make it easier for them to fly. Even animals that aren't vertebrates often have other structures to support their bodies, like the outer body armor called an exoskeleton that insects employ.

Polio

Annie gets a crippling disease called polio. Polio is the common name for poliomyelitis. It is an infectious disease caused by a virus, and it has been common since ancient times. Egyptian wall art depicted people afflicted by polio. Many people fully recover from polio, but some people will develop a muscle weakness resulting in paralysis. This weakness often manifests in the legs, but it can also involve the head, neck, or chest. In a small percentage of children and adults, death may occur.

The most common way in which polio spreads is by the ingestion of infected feces, usually from touching surfaces and then the mouth or from eating contaminated food. In the 19th century, major polio outbreaks were occurring in the United States, potentially due to the overcrowding of the cities and mass immigration. By the 20th century, it was one of the most common childhood diseases. A vaccine was developed by Jonas Salk in the 1950s, and a massive undertaking worldwide attempted to eradicate the disease altogether. For several decades it was believed that humanity had won ant that polio was beaten, but in 2013, there were new cases in Syria, and the World Health Organization declared it a public health emergency as outbreaks continued to spread the disease in Asia, Africa, and the Middle East.

P/K & LG Activity Supplies:

Day 1:
- Small items such as felt balls
- Ice cube tray

Day 3:
- Pipe cleaners
- Colander

Day 4:
- Zipper board

Science Experiment Supplies:

- Card table
- 2 books of equal thickness
- 2 jar lids, the same size
- 1 large roll of masking tape
- Marble
- Masking tape

- 2 sheets typing paper
- Pencil
- Compass
- Ruler
- Scissors
- Cellophane tape

Rhetoric, Physics:

Physics lab on Day 4.

Week 33

	GRAMMAR	DIALECTIC	RHETORIC
BIBLE	Choose one of the following plans: ✚ PLAN 1: Journey Through the Bible, pp. 354-356 ✚ PLAN 2: What the Bible Is All About, Philemon		

LANGUAGE ARTS	Choose appropriate level of one of the following:
	
	❡ English Lessons Through Literature, Lesson 97
	   Reading Lessons Through Literature, phonogram review
	
	❡ Rod and Staff English, Lesson 113
	   Copywork/Commonplace Book
	
	❡ Your own grammar program
			❡ LR: The Power in Your Hands, 1 lesson
			
			❡ UR: WGRP, editing. (6 days)
			
			❡ LR: Rod and Staff 10, L. 107

MATH	Choose appropriate level of one of the following: ✎ Math-U-See, Video and page A ✎ Miquon/Singapore Math ✎ Your own math program		✎ Math-U-See, Video and page A ✎ Your own math program

GEOGRAPHY	🌐 50 States, Review Midwest
	
	🌍 Reading, choose one of the following:
	   A. United States: Moccasin Trail, Ch. 14
	   B. Nevada: Mustang: Wild Spirit of the West, Ch. 5
			🌍 Kilimanjaro Diaries, Ch. 5-6

HISTORY	Choose one spine, one or more core reading selections, and optional reading as desired.		
	♟ Spine: SOTW, Ch. 38.1 ♟ Core reading: 1. Who Was Nelson Mandela, Ch. 5 2. Neil Armstrong, Ch. 8 3. Journey to Jo'burg, Ch. 4	♟ Spine: SOTW, Ch. 38.1 ♟ Core reading: 1. Red Scarf Girl, Ch. 6 2. Warriors Don't Cry, Ch. 7	♟ Spine: Western Civ, 1/4 of Ch. 29 World Empires, Missions, Wars, Unit 9 Week 3 ♟ Core reading: 1 & 2. Les Miserables, 14 pages 1. 1984, Ch. 10 2. Ender's Game, Ch. 4

Day 1

GRAMMAR	DIALECTIC	RHETORIC	
♪♪ Term 3 Composer: Choose between Shostakovich, Britten, Leon Kirchner ⧖ Timeline/Book of Centuries			ACTIVITIES
↪ Oral or written narration; LG students can draw a picture from the reading and tell about the picture. Suggested subject: history.		↪ Written narration for history or geography.	NARRATION
✝ Old Story New, Week 69 ✿ UD: Economics in One Lesson, Ch. 21		✝ Great Divorce, Ch. 7	OTHER
📚 Literature: 1: Five Little Peppers and How They Grew, Ch. 14 2: This Week: A Wonder-Book for Girls and Boys: The Paradise of Children 3: The Princess and the Goblin, Ch. 20 4: This Week: Tanglewood Tales, The Dragon's Teeth	📚 Literature: 5: Around the World in 80 Days, Ch. 15-16 6: The Adventures of Sherlock Holmes, Ch. 1 7: Northanger Abbey, Ch. 20 8: A Double Story, Ch. 3	📚 Book of English Verse, No. 861-863 ✝ Church History: Book of Common Prayer Biography, pp. 52-60 ✝ 100 Events, A.D. 1963 ✝ Science and Religion Lecture 1	LITERATURE

PRESCHOOL AND LOWER GRAMMAR

✎ Pathways: Path 1, Day 1
A. Kindergarten Gems
B. 50 Famous Stories
C. 20th—Owen
D. Random House Poetry, p. 206

PATHWAYS

✎ Separate

Have your little one separate items such as felt balls into ice-cube trays.

ACTIVITY

Week 33

	GRAMMAR	DIALECTIC	RHETORIC
BIBLE	Choose one of the following plans: ✛ PLAN 1: Journey Through the Bible, pp. 357-359 ✛ PLAN 2: Journey Through the Bible, pp. 374-379		
	✛ LG: TBB: The Last Supper ✛ UG: Egermeier's, 2 stories	✛ LD: Hurlbut's, 1 story ✛ UD: Golden's, 3 stories	
LANGUAGE ARTS	Choose appropriate level of one of the following: ❡ Reading Lessons Through Literature, next list and story ❡ Prepared dictation from ELTL, Spelling Wisdom, or today's reading ❡ Your own grammar program		❡ UR: WGRP, keyboarding. (3 days)
MATH	Choose appropriate level of one of the following:		
	✎ Math-U-See, page B ✎ Miquon/Singapore Math ✎ Your own math program		✎ Math-U-See, page B ✎ Your own math program
GEOGRAPHY	🌎 Reading, choose one of the following: A. United States: Moccasin Trail, Ch. 15 B. Nevada: Mustang: Wild Spirit of the West, Ch. 6		🌎 Geography for Dummies, 1/2 of Ch. 17
SCIENCE	Choose one spine, one or more core reading selections, and optional reading as desired.		
	⚛ Core reading: 1. Isaac Newton for Kids, Ch. 5 2. Insiders Inventions, pp. 26-31	⚛ Core reading: 1. Uncle Albert and the Quantum Quest, Ch. 4 2. Waves, Ch. 1	⚛ Spine: SHSPhys, Week 12 Physics for Dummies, 1/2 of Ch. 17 ⚛ Core reading: The Elegant Universe, Ch. 10
	⚛ Spine: Quark Chronicles: Physics, Ch. 15		

Day 2

	GRAMMAR	DIALECTIC	RHETORIC	
♫ Term 3 Composer: Choose between Shostakovich, Britten, Leon Kirchner 🎨 Art Lesson: Choose appropriate level of one of the following:				ACTIVITIES
🎨 I Can Do All Things 🎨 Lamb's Book of Art I	🎨 Lamb's Book of Art II 🎨 Feed My Sheep	🎨 How Great Thou ART I or II 🎨 Book of Many Colors		
⚛ GSA The World of Light and Sound, Lesson 17		🎨 Great Art, Lecture 33		
☞ Oral or written narration; LG students can draw a picture from the reading and tell about the picture. Suggested subject: Bible.		☞ Oral or written narration for science or Bible.		NARRATION
✛ Old Story New, Week 69				
	❧ UD: The Art of Argument, Fallacy 27 ❧ UD: Science Matters, pp. 241-255	❧ UR: Classical English Rhetoric, 1/4 Ch. 17		OTHER
📚 Suggested read-aloud: The Neverending Story, Ch. 15				LITERATURE
PRESCHOOL AND LOWER GRAMMAR				
✐ Pathways: Path 2 A. Little Wanderers, Ch. 33 B. Burgess Seashore Book, Ch. 36 C. D. Random House Poetry, p. 207				PATHWAYS
🎨 Art Lesson: Choose one of the following Barry Stebbing art books for you little one to do art like the big kids: Art and the Bible for Children, Baby Lamb's Book of Art, Joseph the Canada Goose, or Little Annie's Art Book.				ACTIVITY

Week 33

	GRAMMAR	DIALECTIC	RHETORIC
BIBLE	Choose one of the following plans: ✙ PLAN 1: Journey Through the Bible, pp. 360-361 ✙ PLAN 2: What the Bible Is All About, 1 Timothy		

LANGUAGE ARTS	Choose appropriate level of one of the following:
	
	℘ English Lessons Through Literature, Lesson 98
	   Reading Lessons Through Literature, phonogram review
	
	℘ Rod and Staff English, Lesson 114
	   Copywork/Commonplace Book
	
	℘ Your own grammar program
			℘ Essential Literary Terms, 3-4 pages
			
			℘ LR: The Power in Your Hands, 1 lesson
			
			℘ UR: WGRP, keyboarding. (3 days)
			
			℘ LR: Rod and Staff 10, L. 108

MATH	Choose appropriate level of one of the following: ✎ Math-U-See, page C ✎ Miquon/Singapore Math ✎ Your own math program		✎ Math-U-See, page C ✎ Your own math program

GEOGRAPHY	🌐 Reading, choose one of the following:
	  A. United States: Moccasin Trail, Ch. 16
	  B. Nevada: Mustang: Wild Spirit of the West, Ch. 7
			🌐 Kilimanjaro Diaries, Ch. 7-8

HISTORY	Choose one spine, one or more core reading selections, and optional reading as desired.		

	♟ Spine: SOTW, Ch. 38.2
	
	♟ Core reading:
	  1. Who Was Nelson Mandela, Ch. 6
	  2. Neil Armstrong, Ch. 9
	  3. Journey to Jo'burg, Ch. 5
		♟ Spine: SOTW, Ch. 38.2
		
		♟ Core reading:
		  1. Red Scarf Girl, Ch. 7
		  2. Warriors Don't Cry, Ch. 8
			♟ Spine:
			  America, 1/4 of Ch. 34
			  World Empires, Missions, Wars, Unit 9 Week 3
			
			♟ Core reading:
			  1 & 2. Les Miserables, 14 pages
			  1. 1984, Book 3 Ch. 1
			  2. Ender's Game, Ch. 5

Day 3

	Grammar	Dialectic	Rhetoric	
♪♪ Term 3 Composer: Choose between Shostakovich, Britten, Leon Kirchner				Activities
☞ Oral or written narration; could be a group project. Retell part of the story from a different point of view. For instance, tell how another character might have viewed the events.				Narration
✠ Old Story New, Week 69 ✠ UD: Simply Christian, Ch. 13		✠ Great Divorce, Ch. 8		Other
📚 Literature: 1: Five Little Peppers and How They Grew, Ch. 15 2: This Week: A Wonder-Book for Girls and Boys: The Paradise of Children 3: The Princess and the Goblin, Ch. 21 4: This Week: Tanglewood Tales, The Dragon's Teeth	📚 Literature: 5: Around the World in 80 Days, Ch. 17-18 6: The Adventures of Sherlock Holmes, Ch. 2 7: Northanger Abbey, Ch. 21 8: A Double Story, Ch. 4	📚 Book of English Verse, No. 864-865 ✠ Church History: Book of Common Prayer Biography, pp. 60-70 ✠ 100 Events, A.D. 1966 ✠ Science and Religion Lecture 2		Literature

Preschool and Lower Grammar	
✏ Pathways: Path 1, Day 2 A. Kindergarten Gems B. C. McCloskey—Make Way for Ducklings D. Random House Poetry, p. 208	Pathways
✏ 3-D pipe cleaner art Have your little one put the ends of pipe cleaners into the holes of a colander to make a sculpture. Develops fine motor skills.	Activity

Week 33

	GRAMMAR	DIALECTIC	RHETORIC
BIBLE	✦ PLAN 1: Journey Through the Bible, pp. 362-363 ✦ PLAN 2: What the Bible Is All About, 2 Timothy		
	✦ LG: TBB: Jesus is Arrested and Crucified; Jesus is Risen ✦ UG: Egermeier's, 3 stories	✦ LD: Hurlbut's, 2 stories ✦ UD: Golden's, 2 stories	
LANGUAGE ARTS	Choose appropriate level of one of the following: ⸙ Reading Lessons Through Literature, next list and story ⸙ Prepared dictation from ELTL, Spelling Wisdom, or today's reading ⸙ Your own grammar program		⸙ UR: WGRP, keyboarding. (3 days)
MATH	Choose appropriate level of one of the following:		
	✎ Math-U-See, page D ✎ Miquon/Singapore Math ✎ Your own math program		✎ Math-U-See, page D ✎ Your own math program
GEOGRAPHY	🌐 Reading, choose one of the following: A. United States: Moccasin Trail, Ch. 17 B. Nevada: Mustang: Wild Spirit of the West, Ch. 8		
SCIENCE	Choose one spine, one or more core reading selections, and optional reading as desired.		
	⚛ Core reading: 1. Isaac Newton for Kids, Ch. 6 2. Insiders Inventions, pp. 32-37	⚛ Core reading: 1. Uncle Albert and the Quantum Quest, Ch. 5 2. Waves, Ch. 2	⚛ Spine: SHSPhys, Week 12 Manga Relativity, pp. 130-140 ⚛ Core reading: The Elegant Universe, Ch. 11
	⚛ Optional extra reading, topic: Theory of Relativity and Einstein Simon Bloom, Ch. 33-35 Albert Einstein by Kathleen Krull		

Day 4

GRAMMAR	DIALECTIC	RHETORIC	
♪♫ Term 3 Composer: Choose between Shostakovich, Britten, Leon Kirchner			ACTIVITIES
⚛ GSA The World of Light and Sound, Lesson 18 ⚛ 201 Awesome Experiments, 189-190		⚛ Physics Lab 🎨 Great Art Writing	
✑ Oral or written narration; LG students can draw a picture from the reading and tell about the picture. Suggested subject: science.		✑ Written narration for science or Bible.	NARRATION
✢ Old Story New, Week 69			
	↺ UD: The Art of Argument: Create an ad or an argument using this week's fallacy ↺ UD: Science Matters, pp. 256-270	↺ UR: Classical English Rhetoric, 1/4 Ch. 17	OTHER
📚 Suggested read-aloud: The Neverending Story, Ch. 16			LITERATURE

PRESCHOOL AND LOWER GRAMMAR	
✐ Pathways: Path 3 A. Burgess Flower Book, Ch. 38 B. Gooney Bird Greene, Ch. 5 C. The Magic School Bus And the Science Fair Expedition D. Random House Poetry, p. 209	PATHWAYS
✐ Zipper board Glue zippers to a board for your toddler to practice zipping and unzipping. You can also add scrap fabric with snaps, buttons, and holes for lacing, too.	ACTIVITY

Week 33

	GRAMMAR	DIALECTIC	RHETORIC
BIBLE	Choose one of the following plans: ✛ PLAN 1: Journey Through the Bible, pp. 364-365 ✛ PLAN 2: What the Bible Is All About, Titus		
LANGUAGE ARTS	Choose appropriate level of one of the following: ❡ English Lessons Through Literature, Lesson 99 Reading Lessons Through Literature, phonogram review ❡ Rod and Staff English, Lesson 115 Copywork/Commonplace Book ❡ Your own grammar program		❡ A Rulebook for Arguments, Ch. 43-44 ❡ LR: The Power in Your Hands, 1 lesson ❡ LR: Rod and Staff 10, L. 109
MATH	Choose appropriate level of one of the following: ✎ Math-U-See, page E ✎ Miquon/Singapore Math ✎ Your own math program		✎ Math-U-See, pages E & H ✎ Your own math program
GEOGRAPHY	🌐 Mapping: Western Europe 🌐 Reading, choose one of the following: A. United States: Moccasin Trail, Ch. 18 B. Nevada: Mustang: Wild Spirit of the West, Ch. 9		🌐 Kilimanjaro Diaries, Ch. 9-10
HISTORY	Choose one spine, one or more core reading selections, and optional reading as desired.		
	♟ Spine: ♟ Core reading: 1. Who Was Nelson Mandela, Ch. 7 2. Neil Armstrong, Ch. 10 3. Journey to Jo'burg, Ch. 6	♟ Spine: ♟ Core reading: 1. Red Scarf Girl, Ch. 8 2. Warriors Don't Cry, Ch. 9	♟ Spine: America, 1/4 of Ch. 34 World Empires, Missions, Wars, Unit 9 Week 3 ♟ Core reading: 1 & 2. Les Miserables, 14 pages LR: 1 & 2. Philosophy Book, through Fanon UR: 1 & 2. Think, 1/2 Ch. 6 1. 1984, Ch. 2 2. Ender's Game, Ch. 6

Day 5

GRAMMAR	DIALECTIC	RHETORIC	
♪♪ Term 3 Composer: Choose between Shostakovich, Britten, Leon Kirchner			ACTIVITIES
🎨 Art Lesson: Choose appropriate level of one of the following:			
🎨 I Can Do All Things	🎨 Lamb's Book of Art II	🎨 How Great Thou ART I or II	
🎨 Lamb's Book of Art I	🎨 Feed My Sheep	🎨 Book of Many Colors	
☞ Oral or written narration; LG students can draw a picture from the reading and tell about the picture. Suggested subject: geography.		☞ Oral or written narration for history or geography.	NARRATION
✠ Old Story New, Week 69			OTHER
📚 Suggested read-aloud: The Neverending Story, Ch. 17			LITERATURE
📚 Literature: 1: Five Little Peppers and How They Grew, Ch. 16 2: This Week: A Wonder-Book for Girls and Boys: The Paradise of Children 3: The Princess and the Goblin, Ch. 22 4: This Week: Tanglewood Tales, The Dragon's Teeth	📚 Literature: 5: Around the World in 80 Days, Ch. 19-20 6: The Adventures of Sherlock Holmes, Ch. 3 7: Northanger Abbey, Ch. 22 8: A Double Story, Ch. 5	📚 Book of English Verse, No. 866-867 ✠ Church History: Book of Common Prayer Biography, pp. 70-80 ✠ Science and Religion Lecture 3	

PRESCHOOL AND LOWER GRAMMAR

✏️ Pathways: Path 1, Day 3 A. Kindergarten Gems B. 50 Famous Stories C. McCloskey— Blueberries for Sal D. Random House Poetry, p. 210	PATHWAYS
🎨 Art Lesson: Choose one of the following Barry Stebbing art books for you little one to do art like the big kids: Art and the Bible for Children, Baby Lamb's Book of Art, Joseph the Canada Goose, or Little Annie's Art Book.	ACTIVITY

Created to mark the 50th Anniversary of the launch of Sputnik
Image by Gregory R Todd. License: CC BY-SA 3.0; via Wikimedia Commons.

History Through Art: Sputnik 1

The year 1957 saw a world divided between two bitterly opposed superpowers: the United States and the Soviet Union. Both nations were enormous, with vast armies and horrifyingly destructive weapons at their disposal. The two sides hated each other intensely. Nuclear missiles, weapons capable of wiping out a city in an instant, were on constant standby. The only thing saving the world from the horrors of a massive Russian-American war was the fact that the two sides were roughly equal—neither side wanted to risk a fight because neither side was sure it could win. The tension was nearly broken with disastrous results in 1957 during what has been called the Sputnik crisis.

Sputnik itself wasn't a very threatening object. Only the size of a beach ball, it was largely just a metal ball with radio antennae sticking off of it. The Soviet Union succeeded in launching it into a low orbit around the Earth, becoming the first group of humans in the planet's history to launch a satellite into orbit.

While Sputnik was a tremendous step forward for science, it threatened to end the fragile peace between Russia and America. Because Russia had succeeded in launching an object into space first, it began to be perceived that Russia possessed superior technology—and thus, might win a war.

Fortunately, Sputnik triggered not a global apocalypse but instead a golden age of science. In response to the first satellite, the United States founded NASA—the National Aeronautics and Space Administration—with the intent to match their rivals in space exploration. NASA began launching satellites and shuttles of their own. Both sides rushed to prove their superiority by launching things into outer space, competing in what has come to be known as the Space Race. Sputnik was just the first lap of a race that would end with increasingly large parts of the solar system explored and the first astronauts setting foot on the Moon.

Moccasin Trail

Barrels

Sally tells Dan'l to get the barrels from the shed. A barrel is a container, usually for storing some sort of liquid. Traditionally, barrels were made of wood, but modern barrels can be made of aluminum, stainless steel, or even plastic. A barrel, sometimes called a cask, can be a specific unit of measurement as well. For instance, in the United Kingdom, a barrel of beer is specifically 36 imperial gallons. A wine barrel is 26 imperial gallons.

Barrels are still used in winemaking. Constructed from oak, the barrels will hold the wine as it ages and ferments. The wood used in its construction will lend a specific flavor to the beverage. In addition to winemaking, wooden barrels are also used to hold and age whiskey and beer.

Someone who makes barrels is known as a cooper. Other names for barrels may be buckets, tubs, hogsheads, firkins, kegs, or puncheons. Oil is also stored and traded in barrels of oil which are 42 U. S. gallons or 34.9 imperial gallons. This measurement originated in Pennsylvania at some of the earliest sites of oil discovery and extraction and allowed British and American oil merchants to use the same unit of measurement in oil trading.

Soap Making

Sally plans to make soap. Soap is a salty, fatty acid normally used for cleaning. It is made from vegetable or animal oils and fats. Extremely alkaline soaps can be made with a chemical called lye, which can be obtained from ashes; it can burn the skin if too much is added. The history of soap-making dates back to at least Egyptian times; written records from 2,200 BC have a formula for making soap consisting of water, ash, and cassia oil.

Through Roman times and the Middle Ages soap making continued. By 800 AD, Medieval Spain was the leading soap maker in the west. Modern soap making continues on a grand scale in the industrial age with liquid soaps gaining in popularity although they were not invented until this century. Many people also make soap as a cottage industry in their homes and their specialty, fragrance designer soaps can fetch much larger prices than their industrial counterparts.

Ants

Tom tells Jim that he's "jumpy as a prairie dog in an anthill." You might think that we human beings are the rulers of Earth. We're the ones who build cities, after all. We're the ones who have farms and armies and tools and societies. A lot of humans think that way. But imagine our surprise to realize that ants, the little specks of bug we find crawling on our picnics, do all the same things we do—and more!

Ants live in colonies that can hold anywhere from hundreds to millions of individual workers, all scurrying around the nest to perform one of the hundreds of jobs necessary for the colony's survival. Some ant workers stack dirt on the surface, forming an anthill. Some venture into the dangerous wilderness to gather food, like crumbs that people drop on the floor. Some take food that has already been gathered and feed it to the larvae, who will someday grow into workers

In soap making, the lye is dissolved in water. This can be dangerous—note the safety gloves. This photo was originally created for the students of the Soapmaking Studio, specifically to demonstrate pouring lye into water for solvation in order to make soap. Photo by Certified Lye. License: CC BY-SA 3.0; via Wikimedia Commons.

themselves. And one single ant, the queen, lives at the center of the colony and lays the eggs. She is vital to the colony's future.

Some ants have truly remarkable means of making sure they always have food available. A few species have been found that have special fungus farms deep underground, and they harvest the fungus for food. A few others herd aphids atop tall plants, scaring away their predators and collecting sweet dew from them like a human farmer would milk a cow. Ants are among the most sophisticated and civilized creatures in the animal kingdom.

Mustang: Wild Spirit of the West

Pencils

Annie's father presents her a bill of sale for Hobo, complete with a sharpened pencil so that she can sign it. A pencil is a utensil used for writing or art. It's made from a solid core of pigment or graphite inside a protective casing, usually wood. A modern pencil does not contain "lead" but rather a mixture of graphite and clay. The casing protects the core from being broken or from smudging the user's hand and work surface. The pencil works by a process of physical abrasion with the paper, wearing away at the solid core and leaving a trail. This is different from a pen which leaves a trail of ink behind and stains the paper.

Pencils came to America from Europe before the American Revolution. Benjamin Franklin advertised pencils for sale in his newspaper. Cabinetmakers often made pencils on the side, and their methods and styles were kept as closely guarded trade secrets. In 1858, a man named Hymen Lipman received the first patent for a pencil with an eraser on the end, which was considered a novel idea at the time.

Contracts

A bill of sale is a contract. A contract is a formal agreement, often legally binding, between two or more people. Contract law is an entire field in Western legal culture, with lawyers practicing just how to word and write these contracts to serve the best interests of their clients. A contract will be offered by one party and accepted by the other. These are formal terms, and often a contract is signed before witnesses.

All cultures have their version of a contract, and the concept dates back to the earliest of civilizations. Breaking a contract could have serious ramifications, up to and including death. Men lost entire fortunes and sometimes even their liberty when circumstances forced them to break contracts. Even today, breaking a contract can be financially ruinous. The court system rules that a contract, legally entered into by parties who were competent, is binding until both parties agree to end the contract. As a result, contract law is serious business, and nobody enters into one without protecting themselves from the repercussions or including a method to legally get out of the contract.

Optical Illusions

Annie and her mother practice fixing her hair to give "an optical illusion to [her] out-of-line features." An optical illusion is a visually perceived image that is different from reality. The information gathered by the human eye is processed in the brain, and the brain interprets the information that it receives. Normally, this process of interpretation by the brain helps us to better visualize the world around us. However, in the case of optical illusions, the brain is tricked into seeing things that do not reflect reality accurately. Optical illusions can depend on the brain's ability to pick out images, such as the famous rabbit-duck illusion. A viewer who looks at the picture will either see a rabbit or a duck, but both are evident in the picture.

Some animals have incorporated optical illusions into their natural camouflage, such as the spots of a young deer, called a fawn, or the stripes of the tiger. These are intended to break up the image of the animal and prevent the brain from immediately identifying what it is looking at.

Optical illusion. Squares A and B are exactly the same color of gray. You can use a color picker to verify this. © Copyright 1995 by Edward H. Adelson. Used by permission. Via Wikimedia Commons.

Week 34 Signposts

P/K & LG Activity Supplies:

Day 1:
• Origami paper

Day 3:
• Water-safe
• Plastic bin (or sink)

Day 4:
• Beans

Science Experiment Supplies:

• Scissors
• Ruler
• String
• Small plastic garbage bag
• Small washer

• 2-quart glass bowl
• Scissors
• Ruler
• Sewing thread
• Masking tape
• Sewing needle
• Bar magnet

UD, Science Matters:

On pages 287-288 of *Science Matters*, Hazen states: "The question of whether life begins at conception comes up constantly in the debate over abortion rights in the United States. This is not a scientific question, but a legal, moral, and ethical one. It illustrates an important point about what science can and cannot do. Science is very good at answering quantitative questions about how the universe works, but cannot provide answers to some important questions about how we should behave as individuals or as a society."

Here, Hazen shows his bias; there was no other reason to bring up the abortion debate in order to discuss human reproduction. Moreover, there's a serious flaw in his logic in this paragraph. The question of whether or not life begins at conception is definitely a quantitative question about how the universe works. Science can and does tell us whether or not something is alive and, if so, what species it is. Science tells us that an unborn child is indeed human; its DNA makes this indisputable. Science tells us that from the moment of conception, an unborn child is alive because it meets the scientific criteria for life: it uses food for energy, it responds to stimuli, it grows, and, as a species, it is capable of reproduction. To argue otherwise is to deny objective scientific evidence.

Instead, it is important to understand that this is a philosophical and ideological argument. Since science tells us that an unborn child is both alive and human, then we must recognize what the true question is in the abortion debate, a question which is key to many other issues in our society from war to capital punishment to self-defense: At what point and under what circumstances is it acceptable to kill a human being?

Any quest for Truth means facing the difficult questions head-on instead of trying to put them in a more comfortable light. To do otherwise is intellectually dishonest.

Week 34

	GRAMMAR	DIALECTIC	RHETORIC
BIBLE	Choose one of the following plans: ✛ PLAN 1: Journey Through the Bible, pp. 366-367 ✛ PLAN 2: Journey Through the Bible, pp. 380-385		
LANGUAGE ARTS	Choose appropriate level of one of the following: ❡ English Lessons Through Literature, Lesson 100 　Reading Lessons Through Literature, phonogram review ❡ Rod and Staff English, Lesson 116 　Copywork/Commonplace Book ❡ Your own grammar program		❡ LR: The Power in Your Hands, 1 lesson ❡ UR: WGRP, finishing. (5 days) ❡ LR: Rod and Staff 10, L. 110
MATH	Choose appropriate level of one of the following: ✎ Math-U-See, Video and page A ✎ Miquon/Singapore Math ✎ Your own math program		✎ Math-U-See, Video and page A ✎ Your own math program
GEOGRAPHY	🌐 50 States, Review Southern 🌎 Reading, choose one of the following: 　A. United States: Moccasin Trail, Ch. 19 　B. Nevada: Mustang: Wild Spirit of the West, Ch. 10		🌎 Kilimanjaro Diaries, Ch. 11
HISTORY	Choose one spine, one or more core reading selections, and optional reading as desired. ♟ Spine: SOTW, Ch. 39.1 ♟ Core reading: 　1. Who Was Nelson Mandela, Ch. 8 　2. Neil Armstrong, Ch. 11 　3. Journey to Jo'burg, Ch. 7	♟ Spine: SOTW, Ch. 39.1 ♟ Core reading: 　1. Red Scarf Girl, Ch. 9 　2. Warriors Don't Cry, Ch. 10	♟ Spine: 　Western Civ, 1/4 of Ch. 29 　World Empires, Missions, Wars, Unit 9 Week 4 ♟ Core reading: 　1 & 2. Les Miserables, 14 pages 　1. 1984, Ch. 3 　2. Ender's Game, Ch. 7

Day 1

GRAMMAR	DIALECTIC	RHETORIC	
♪♪ Term 3 Composer: Choose between Shostakovich, Britten, Leon Kirchner ⧗ Timeline/Book of Centuries			ACTIVITIES
☞ Oral or written narration; LG students can draw a picture from the reading and tell about the picture. Suggested subject: history.		☞ Written narration for history or geography.	NARRATION
✝ Old Story New, Week 70 ☏ UD: Economics in One Lesson, Ch. 22		✝ Great Divorce, Ch. 9	OTHER
📚 Literature: 1: Five Little Peppers and How They Grew, Ch. 17 2: This Week: A Wonder-Book for Girls and Boys: The Three Golden Apples 3: The Princess and the Goblin, Ch. 23 4: This Week: Tanglewood Tales, Circe's Palace	📚 Literature: 5: Around the World in 80 Days, Ch. 21-22 6: The Adventures of Sherlock Holmes, Ch. 4 7: Northanger Abbey, Ch. 23 8: A Double Story, Ch. 6	📚 Book of English Verse, No. 868-870 ✝ Church History: Book of Common Prayer Biography, pp. 80-90 ✝ Science and Religion Lecture 4	LITERATURE
PRESCHOOL AND LOWER GRAMMAR			
✏ Pathways: Path 1, Day 1 A. Kindergarten Gems B. C. 20th—The Story of Ferdinand D. Random House Poetry, p. 211			PATHWAYS
✏ Origami Try some origami. Some projects are quite simple, and you can find instructions online. Here's a website to get you started: www.origami-fun.com/origami-for-kids.html You can also find YouTube.com videos with detailed instructions.			ACTIVITY

Week 34

	GRAMMAR	DIALECTIC	RHETORIC
BIBLE	Choose one of the following plans: ✚ PLAN 1: Journey Through the Bible, pp. 368-369 ✚ PLAN 2: What the Bible Is All About, Hebrews		
	✚ LG: TBB: Jesus Returns ✚ UG: Egermeier's, 2 stories	✚ LD: Hurlbut's, 1 story ✚ UD: Golden's, 3 stories	
LANGUAGE ARTS	Choose appropriate level of one of the following: ❡ Reading Lessons Through Literature, next list and story ❡ Prepared dictation from ELTL, Spelling Wisdom, or today's reading ❡ Rod and Staff English, Lesson 117 ❡ Your own grammar program		❡ UR: WGRP, finishing. (5 days)
MATH	Choose appropriate level of one of the following:		
	✎ Math-U-See, page B ✎ Miquon/Singapore Math ✎ Your own math program		✎ Math-U-See, page B ✎ Your own math program

GEOGRAPHY	🌐 Reading, choose one of the following:
	   A. Germany: An Elephant in the Garden, Part 1 Ch. 1
	   B. Nevada: Mustang: Wild Spirit of the West, Ch. 11
			🌐 Geography for Dummies, 1/2 of Ch. 17

SCIENCE	Choose one spine, one or more core reading selections, and optional reading as desired.		

	⚛ Core reading:
	   1. Isaac Newton for Kids, Ch. 7
	   2. Insiders Inventions, pp. 38-43
		⚛ Core reading:
		   1. Uncle Albert and the Quantum Quest, Ch. 6
		   2. Waves, Ch. 3
			⚛ Spine:
			   Physics for Dummies, Ch. 18
			
			⚛ Core reading:
			   The Elegant Universe, Ch. 12

	⚛ Spine: Quark Chronicles: Physics, Ch. 16		

Day 2

	GRAMMAR	DIALECTIC	RHETORIC	
♪♪ Term 3 Composer: Choose between Shostakovich, Britten, Leon Kirchner 🎨 Art Lesson: Choose appropriate level of one of the following:				ACTIVITIES
🎨 I Can Do All Things 🎨 Lamb's Book of Art I	🎨 Lamb's Book of Art II 🎨 Feed My Sheep	🎨 How Great Thou ART I or II 🎨 Book of Many Colors		
⚛ GSA The World of Light and Sound, Lesson 19		🎨 Great Art, Lecture 34		
✐ Oral or written narration; LG students can draw a picture from the reading and tell about the picture. Suggested subject: Bible.		✐ Oral or written narration for science or Bible.		NARRATION
✚ Old Story New, Week 70				
	❧ UD: The Art of Argument, Fallacy 28 ❧ UD: Science Matters, pp. 271-285	❧ UR: Classical English Rhetoric, 1/4 Ch. 17		OTHER
📚 Suggested read-aloud: The Neverending Story, Ch. 18				LITERATURE
PRESCHOOL AND LOWER GRAMMAR				
✏ Pathways: Path 2 A. Little Wanderers, Ch. 34-35 B. Burgess Seashore Book, Ch. 37 C. D. Random House Poetry, p. 212				PATHWAYS
🎨 Art Lesson: Choose one of the following Barry Stebbing art books for you little one to do art like the big kids: Art and the Bible for Children, Baby Lamb's Book of Art, Joseph the Canada Goose, or Little Annie's Art Book.				ACTIVITY

Week 34

	GRAMMAR	DIALECTIC	RHETORIC
BIBLE	Choose one of the following plans: ✝ PLAN 1: Journey Through the Bible, pp. 370-372 ✝ PLAN 2: What the Bible Is All About, James		

LANGUAGE ARTS	Choose appropriate level of one of the following:
	
	¶ English Lessons Through Literature, Lesson 101
	  Reading Lessons Through Literature, phonogram review
	
	¶ Rod and Staff English, Lesson 118
	  Copywork/Commonplace Book
	
	¶ Your own grammar program
			¶ Essential Literary Terms, 3-4 pages
			
			¶ LR: The Power in Your Hands, 1 lesson
			
			¶ UR: WGRP, finishing. (5 days)
			
			¶ LR: Rod and Staff 10, L. 111

MATH	Choose appropriate level of one of the following: ✎ Math-U-See, page C ✎ Miquon/Singapore Math ✎ Your own math program		✎ Math-U-See, page C ✎ Your own math program

GEOGRAPHY	🌐 50 States, Review Southwest
	
	🌐 Reading, choose one of the following:
	  A. Germany: An Elephant in the Garden, Ch. 2
	  B. Nevada: Mustang: Wild Spirit of the West, Ch. 12
			🌐 Kilimanjaro Diaries, Ch. 12

HISTORY	Choose one spine, one or more core reading selections, and optional reading as desired.		

	♟ Spine: SOTW, Ch. 39.2
	
	♟ Core reading:
	  1. Who Was Nelson Mandela, Ch. 9
	  2. Neil Armstrong, Ch. 12
	  3. Journey to Jo'burg, Ch. 8
		♟ Spine: SOTW, Ch. 39.2
		
		♟ Core reading:
		  1. Red Scarf Girl, Ch. 10
		  2. Warriors Don't Cry, Ch. 11
			♟ Spine:
			  America, 1/4 of Ch. 34
			  World Empires, Missions, Wars, Unit 9 Week 4
			
			♟ Core reading:
			  1 & 2. Les Miserables, 14 pages
			  1. 1984, Ch. 4
			  2. Ender's Game, Ch. 8

Day 3

Grammar	Dialectic	Rhetoric	
♪♪ Term 3 Composer: Choose between Shostakovich, Britten, Leon Kirchner			Activities
☛ Oral or written narration; could be a group project. Tell something you learned from the story, or tell about how the story made you understand something in a new way.			Narration
✚ Old Story New, Week 70 ✚ UD: Simply Christian, Ch. 14		✚ Great Divorce, Ch. 10	Other
📚 Literature: 1: Five Little Peppers and How They Grew, Ch. 18 2: This Week: A Wonder-Book for Girls and Boys: The Three Golden Apples 3: The Princess and the Goblin, Ch. 24 4: This Week: Tanglewood Tales, Circe's Palace	📚 Literature: 5: Around the World in 80 Days, Ch. 23-24 6: The Adventures of Sherlock Holmes, Ch. 5 7: Northanger Abbey, Ch. 24 8: A Double Story, Ch. 7	📚 Book of English Verse, No. 871-874 ✚ Church History: Book of Common Prayer Biography, pp. 90-112 ✚ Science and Religion Lecture 5	Literature
PRESCHOOL AND LOWER GRAMMAR			
✏ Pathways: Path 1, Day 2 A. Kindergarten Gems B. C. McCloskey— "The Doughnuts" D. Random House Poetry, p. 213			Pathways
✏ Sink or float Fill the sink or a plastic bin with water. Have a variety of water-safe objects ready. See which ones sink and which ones float.			Activity

Week 34

	GRAMMAR	DIALECTIC	RHETORIC
BIBLE	Choose one of the following plans: ✠ PLAN 1: Journey Through the Bible, pp. 373-375 ✠ PLAN 2: Journey Through the Bible, pp. 386-391		
	✠ LG: TBB: A Net Full of Fish; Jesus Goes to Heaven ✠ UG: Egermeier's, 2 stories	✠ LD: Hurlbut's, 1 story ✠ UD: Golden's, 3 stories	
LANGUAGE ARTS	Choose appropriate level of one of the following: ❡ Reading Lessons Through Literature, next list and story ❡ Prepared dictation from ELTL, Spelling Wisdom, or today's reading ❡ Your own grammar program		❡ UR: WGRP, finishing. (5 days)
MATH	Choose appropriate level of one of the following: ✎ Math-U-See, page D ✎ Miquon/Singapore Math ✎ Your own math program		✎ Math-U-See, page D ✎ Your own math program
GEOGRAPHY	🌍 Reading, choose one of the following: A. Germany: An Elephant in the Garden, Ch. 3 B. Nevada: Mustang: Wild Spirit of the West, Ch. 13		
SCIENCE	Choose one spine, one or more core reading selections, and optional reading as desired.		
	⚛ Core reading: 1. Isaac Newton for Kids, Ch. 8 2. Insiders Inventions, pp. 44-49	⚛ Core reading: 1. Uncle Albert and the Quantum Quest, Ch. 7 2. Relativity and Quantum Mechanics, Ch. 1	⚛ Spine: Manga Relativity, pp. 141-151 ⚛ Core reading: The Elegant Universe, Ch. 13
	⚛ Optional extra reading, topic: Quantum Physics and Its Weirdness Simon Bloom, Ch. 36-37		

Day 4

Grammar	Dialectic	Rhetoric	
♪♪ Term 3 Composer: Choose between Shostakovich, Britten, Leon Kirchner			Activities
⚛ GSA The World of Light and Sound, Lesson 20 ⚛ 201 Awesome Experiments, 191-192		🎨 Great Art Writing	
↪ Oral or written narration; LG students can draw a picture from the reading and tell about the picture. Suggested subject: science.		↪ Written narration for science or Bible.	Narration
✟ Old Story New, Week 70			
	✂ UD: The Art of Argument: Create an ad or an argument using this week's fallacy ✂ UD: Science Matters, pp. 286-300	✂ UR: Classical English Rhetoric, 1/4 Ch. 17	Other
📚 Suggested read-aloud: The Neverending Story, Ch. 19			Literature
Preschool and Lower Grammar			
✏ Pathways: Path 3 A. Burgess Flower Book, Ch. 39 B. Gooney Bird Greene, Ch. 6 C. D. Random House Poetry, pp. 214-215			Pathways
✏ Sprout beans You can sprout just a couple of beans or a whole pot of beans. To sprout just a couple of beans, first soak the beans overnight. Then, get a paper towel damp but not dripping. Place the paper towel inside a plastic bag, and place the bean on the towel. The bean will begin to sprout over a period of days. Make sure to keep the paper towel damp. If you eat beans, you can sprout them before cooking which unlocks additional nutrition from the beans. First, soak the beans overnight. If you do this in Mason jars, you can observe the amount of water that the beans absorb overnight. Rinse the beans, and leave them in the colander over a bowl to catch drips. Cover the beans with a cloth. Rinse them morning and evening for one to three days and sprouts will appear. Cook as usual.			Activity

Week 34

	GRAMMAR	DIALECTIC	RHETORIC
BIBLE	Choose one of the following plans: ✠ PLAN 1: Journey Through the Bible, pp. 376-377 ✠ PLAN 2: What the Bible Is All About, 1 Peter		

LANGUAGE ARTS	Choose appropriate level of one of the following:
	
	❡ English Lessons Through Literature, Lesson 102
	    Reading Lessons Through Literature, phonogram review
	
	❡ Rod and Staff English, Lesson 119
	    Copywork/Commonplace Book
	
	❡ Your own grammar program
			❡ A Rulebook for Arguments, Ch. 45
			
			❡ LR: The Power in Your Hands, 1 lesson
			
			❡ LR: Rod and Staff 10, L. 112

MATH	Choose appropriate level of one of the following: ✎ Math-U-See, page E ✎ Miquon/Singapore Math ✎ Your own math program		✎ Math-U-See, pages E & H ✎ Your own math program
GEOGRAPHY	🌍 Mapping: Eastern Europe		
	🌍 Reading, choose one of the following: B. Nevada: Mustang: Wild Spirit of the West, Ch. 14		🌍 Kilimanjaro Diaries, Ch. 13
HISTORY	Choose one spine, one or more core reading selections, and optional reading as desired.		

	♟ Spine:
	
	♟ Core reading:
	    1. Who Was Nelson Mandela, Ch. 10
	    2. Neil Armstrong, Ch. 13
	    3. Journey to Jo'burg, Ch. 9
		♟ Spine:
		
		♟ Core reading:
		    1. Red Scarf Girl, Ch. 11
		    2. Warriors Don't Cry, Ch. 12
			♟ Spine:
			    America, 1/4 of Ch. 34
			    World Empires, Missions, Wars, Unit 9 Week 4
			
			♟ Core reading:
			    1 & 2. Les Miserables, 14 pages
			    LR: 1 & 2. Philosophy Book, through Derrida
			    UR: 1 & 2. Think, 1/2 Ch. 7
			    1. 1984, Ch. 5
			    2. Ender's Game, Ch. 9

Day 5

Grammar	Dialectic	Rhetoric	
♪♪ Term 3 Composer: Choose between Shostakovich, Britten, Leon Kirchner			ACTIVITIES
🎨 Art Lesson: Choose appropriate level of one of the following:			
🎨 I Can Do All Things	🎨 Lamb's Book of Art II	🎨 How Great Thou ART I or II	
🎨 Lamb's Book of Art I	🎨 Feed My Sheep	🎨 Book of Many Colors	
👁 Oral or written narration; LG students can draw a picture from the reading and tell about the picture. Suggested subject: geography.		👁 Oral or written narration for history or geography.	NARRATION
✙ Old Story New, Week 70 ❧ UD: Economics in One Lesson, Ch. 23			OTHER
📚 Suggested read-aloud: The Neverending Story, Ch. 20			LITERATURE
📚 Literature: 1: Five Little Peppers and How They Grew, Ch. 19 2: This Week: A Wonder-Book for Girls and Boys: The Three Golden Apples 3: The Princess and the Goblin, Ch. 25 4: This Week: Tanglewood Tales, Circe's Palace	📚 Literature: 5: Around the World in 80 Days, Ch. 25-26 6: The Adventures of Sherlock Holmes, Ch. 6 7: Northanger Abbey, Ch. 25 8: A Double Story, Ch. 8	📚 Book of English Verse, No. 875-877 ✙ Church History: Book of Common Prayer Biography, pp. 112-124 ✙ Science and Religion Lecture 6	
PRESCHOOL AND LOWER GRAMMAR			
✐ Pathways: Path 1, Day 3 A. Kindergarten Gems B. C. McCloskey— Burt Dow, Deep-Water Man D. Random House Poetry, p. 216			PATHWAYS
🎨 Art Lesson: Choose one of the following Barry Stebbing art books for you little one to do art like the big kids: Art and the Bible for Children, Baby Lamb's Book of Art, Joseph the Canada Goose, or Little Annie's Art Book.			ACTIVITY

Vostok I capsule used by Yuri Gagarin in first space flight, on display at the RKK Energiya Museum outside of Moscow. Photo by SiefkinDR. License: CC BY-SA 3.0; via Wikimedia Commons.

History Through Art: Yuri Gagarin

During the Space Race, America and Russia raced to be the first nations to achieve great feats of space exploration. At the beginning of the race, an early lead was won by the Soviet Union. First they launched the first satellite—Sputnik—and before long, they launched the first man—Yuri Gagarin.

Yuri Gagarin was a cosmonaut, the Russian equivalent to an astronaut. In 1961, Gagarin was chosen for a risky project. He was chosen to be the sole man on board the Vostok spacecraft which was intended to launch a human being into space for a full orbit around the earth before returning him back to the ground. A lot could go wrong. The tiniest miscalculation could cause his craft to overheat and explode before leaving the atmosphere. Even if it got into space, the smallest error could send Vostok hurtling into the depths of space. A single loose screw would mean certain doom with no chance of rescue.

Despite the odds, Russian engineering handled the challenge beautifully. Gagarin's words upon liftoff have become famous throughout Russia: "Poyekhali"—"Let's go." The Vostok spacecraft entered space without difficulty and returned Gagarin safely to Earth.

50th Anniversary Stamp in Ukraine. Image is in the public domain; via Wikimedia Commons.

Not all Russian space projects were successes, however. One of Gagarin's close friends died when a launch went terribly wrong years later. He had tried to persuade his friend to let him fly in his place, knowing that the Russian government would work harder to make sure the spacecraft was well-engineered if a national hero was onboard. His friend refused; the ship exploded, and Gagarin was officially forbidden from taking part in any further space missions. Somewhat ironically, he passed away in 1968 after the fatal crash of the jet he was piloting. Despite the tragic ending to his life, Yuri Gagarin will be remembered as the first human being to have visited the void above the night sky.

An Elephant in the Garden

Nurses

The narrator of the story is a nurse in a nursing home. Nursing is a healthcare profession which focuses on the care of people so they can gain, maintain, or recover their health. Nurses tend to work differently than doctors and practice in a much wider diversity of areas. In modern times, nurses have various credentials and authority depending upon their level of certification and their specific field.

In ancient times, nurses were traditionally male, but during the World Wars in Europe, men were doctors and soldiers while women tended to the wounded. This led to a post-war belief that nursing was a traditionally female profession, which had never historically been the case. During Medieval times, monks and nuns both maintained hospices where they cared for the sick and wounded. However, during the Reformation of the 16th century, these organizations were largely dismantled by Protestants, often by force.

Today, nurses operate both in and out of hospital environments, and it is a profession which is always in need of more people, male or female.

Nursing Homes

Within human society, some people begin to require constant care and support in order to live a safe and healthy life. The elderly, for instance, may slowly lose their health and the ability to take care of themselves as they grow older. The mentally disabled often have similar problems. When circumstances such as these arise, people may require a place to live where they can also receive medial care.

For this purpose, nursing homes have been established.

Registered nurses and nursing assistants make up the bulk of a nursing home's staff, as the people who live in the building may require care that requires a professional's touch. The residents require many things, from the basics of room and board to specific services like assisted bathing.

Prior to the Industrial Revolution, families would take care of their elderly grandparents themselves. When the world was industrialized, however, normal people had less time to spend taking care of the elderly, so the government took over. Nowadays there are both publicly and privately funded institutions for the purpose of nursing the needy.

Phonographs

Lizzie says that her family had had a gramophone. The phonograph was invented in 1877 specifically for the recording and reproduction of sound. Sound travels in waveforms which can be etched or impressed onto the surface of a rotating cylinder or disc with the latter being called a record. To recreate the sound, the surface needs to be rotated at the same speed as it was recorded, and a needle will trace the groove. As the surface is rotated, the needle will vibrate and reproduce the recorded sound.

Florence Nightingale was an influential figure in the development of modern nursing. No uniform had been created when Florence Nightingale was employed during the Crimean War. Both nursing role and education were first defined by Florence Nightingale. Photo circa 1860. Image is in the public domain; via Wikimedia Commons.

The device was invented in 1877 by Thomas Edison. Other inventors had produced multiple devices to record sounds but Edison's phonograph was the first to be able to play back the recorded sound. By the 1890s, inventor Emile Berliner had produced a device which had moved from cylinders to flat discs with a groove which ran to the center. Music and speech recorded on these discs were the dominant form of speech and music reproduction throughout most of the 20th century. The type of musical signal they produced was known as analog, and it was the predecessor to the modern digital recordings of today.

Malt

Annie and her father splurge on malted milk. The word malt refers to germinated cereal grains that have been dried through a special process known as malting. The grains are soaked in water until they start to germinate. Immediately, this process is halted by drying them with hot air. The malted grains have had their starches partially turned into sugars by special enzymes created during the malting process within the grain. The expertise required in making different types of malts comes from knowing when to halt the germination process to get the precise amount of sugars.

Malted grains are used to make many things ranging from beer and whiskey to candy. It is an ancient process dating back to the beginning of agriculture. Evidence exists of malted grains being used in ancient Egypt, Sumeria, and China. In Persian countries, they still make a sweet paste from malted wheat grains, and it is part of common family gatherings. In the United States, there is a special drink called a malted milkshake which contains ice cream, milk, and malted grains.

Mining

Mr. Richards tells Annie that he used to be a miner. Mining is the extraction of minerals or other substances from the earth. Ores, valuable stones, and gems are found in deposits in the earth's surface, and miners are those who dig for them. Any substance that is not grown on a farm or in the wild or made in a factory is gained through mining.

Humans have been mining in the earth since prehistoric times. As our technology has increased, mines have become more productive, but they are also more problematic in terms of their effects on the landscape. Entire mountains are removed in search of coal or gold, leaving gaping holes and landslides. Toxic chemicals are released into rivers and streams as by-products of the mining industry. As a result, governments have begun to regulate the mines and to force mine owners to clean up the pollution as part of the cost of mining.

For the men and women who work in the mines, it can be a dangerous profession, even today. A collapse of the mine can trap people below ground where they will either die from lack of food and water or suffocate when the air runs out. Working with heavy equipment in the dimly lit underground can also lead to crippling injuries. Invisible dangers such as toxicity can leave long-lasting diseases and ailments on those who work the mines.

Opera

Annie and Charley drive past Piper's Opera House. An opera is a form of art with singers and musicians. Together, they put on a dramatic show with singing. Two different types of singing are common. Recitative is a style similar to speech while arias are more melodic. Opera combines theatre with its own special style of music. It has all of the scenery, acting, and costumes of the theatre, but it's often accompanied by an orchestra. Opera started in Italy at the end of the 16th century and is a part of the Western music tradition. Operas are usually performed in an opera house and are traditionally considered a fine art.

Different cultures have different opera styles and also their own famous national operas. Many operas celebrate or reflect upon national identities and special events and have been used as a method of propaganda throughout the centuries. Different types of opera singers have different voice ranges such as soprano, tenor, and bass. The singers have a lot of volume, their style having been developed to be heard over the sound of the orchestra in the times before speakers and microphones. The phrase, "It ain't over until the fat lady sings," rose to a colloquialism from the end of Richard Wagner's German opera *Der Ring des Nibelungen*, where a woman playing a valkyrie appears in a winged helmet with a shield and spear.

The Atlanta Opera's *Lucia di Lammermoor* Season 2011/12. Image cropped. Photo by Tim Wilkerson for The Atlanta Opera. License: CC BY-SA 3.0; via Wikimedia Commons.

P/K & LG Activity Supplies:

Day 1:
- Pattern blocks

Day 3:
- Toilet paper tubes
- Construction paper
- Markers
- Yarn (optional)

Day 4:
- Clay

Science Experiment Supplies:

- Pencil
- 3-ounce paper cup
- 2 magnets with holes in the middle

- Masking tape
- Bar magnets, several different sizes
- Box of small paper clips

Week 35

	GRAMMAR	DIALECTIC	RHETORIC
BIBLE	Choose one of the following plans: ✛ PLAN 1: Journey Through the Bible, pp. 378-381 ✛ PLAN 2: What the Bible Is All About, 2 Peter		
LANGUAGE ARTS	Choose appropriate level of one of the following: ¶ English Lessons Through Literature, Lesson 103 Reading Lessons Through Literature, phonogram review ¶ Rod and Staff English, Lesson 120 Copywork/Commonplace Book ¶ Your own grammar program		¶ LR: The Power in Your Hands, 1 lesson ¶ UR: WGRP, finishing. (5 days) ¶ LR: Rod and Staff 10, L. 113
MATH	Choose appropriate level of one of the following: ✎ Math-U-See, Video and page A ✎ Miquon/Singapore Math ✎ Your own math program		✎ Math-U-See, Video and page A ✎ Your own math program
GEOGRAPHY	🌎 50 States, Review Rocky Mountain 🌎 Reading, choose one of the following: A. Germany: An Elephant in the Garden, Part 2 Ch. 1 B. Nevada: Mustang: Wild Spirit of the West, Ch. 15		🌎 Kilimanjaro Diaries, Ch. 14
HISTORY	Choose one spine, one or more core reading selections, and optional reading as desired. ♟ Spine: SOTW, Ch. 40.1 ♟ Core reading: 1. MTH Heroes for All Times, Ch. 6 2. Neil Armstrong, Ch. 14 3. Journey to Jo'burg, Ch. 10	♟ Spine: SOTW, Ch. 40.1 ♟ Core reading: 1. Red Scarf Girl, Ch. 12 2. Warriors Don't Cry, Ch. 13	♟ Spine: Western Civ, 1/4 of Ch. 30 ♟ Core reading: 1 & 2. Les Miserables, 14 pages 1. 1984, Ch. 6 2. Ender's Game, Ch. 10

Day 1

GRAMMAR	DIALECTIC	RHETORIC	
♪♫ Term 3 Composer: Choose between Shostakovich, Britten, Leon Kirchner ⧗ Timeline/Book of Centuries			ACTIVITIES
☞ Oral or written narration; LG students can draw a picture from the reading and tell about the picture. Suggested subject: history.		☞ Written narration for history or geography.	NARRATION
✣ Old Story New, Week 71 ❀ UD: Economics in One Lesson, Ch. 24		✣ Great Divorce, Ch. 11	OTHER
📚 Literature: 1: Five Little Peppers and How They Grew, Ch. 20 2: This Week: A Wonder-Book for Girls and Boys: The Miraculous Pitcher 3: The Princess and the Goblin, Ch. 26 4: This Week: Tanglewood Tales, The Pomegranate Seeds	📚 Literature: 5: Around the World in 80 Days, Ch. 27-28 6: The Adventures of Sherlock Holmes, Ch. 7 7: Northanger Abbey, Ch. 26 8: A Double Story, Ch. 9	📚 Book of English Verse, No. 878-880 ✣ Church History: Book of Common Prayer Biography, pp. 124-136 ✣ Science and Religion Lecture 7	LITERATURE
PRESCHOOL AND LOWER GRAMMAR			
✐ Pathways: Path 1, Day 1 A. Kindergarten Gems B. C. 20th—"The Sneetches" D. Random House Poetry, p. 217			PATHWAYS
✐ Pattern block scoop Have your child scoop up a pile of pattern blocks, then have him sort them and count how many of each he has.			ACTIVITY

Week 35

	GRAMMAR	DIALECTIC	RHETORIC
BIBLE	Choose one of the following plans: ✠ PLAN 1: Journey Through the Bible, pp. 382-383 ✠ PLAN 2: Journey Through the Bible, pp. 392-397		
	✠ LG: TBB: The Holy Spirit Comes ✠ UG: Egermeier's, 2 stories	✠ LD: Hurlbut's, 1 story ✠ UD: Golden's, 3 stories	
LANGUAGE ARTS	Choose appropriate level of one of the following: ❡ Reading Lessons Through Literature, next list and story ❡ Prepared dictation from ELTL, Spelling Wisdom, or today's reading ❡ Rod and Staff English, Lesson 121 ❡ Your own grammar program		
MATH	Choose appropriate level of one of the following:		
	✎ Math-U-See, page B ✎ Miquon/Singapore Math ✎ Your own math program		✎ Math-U-See, page B ✎ Your own math program
GEOGRAPHY	🌐 Reading, choose one of the following: A. Germany: An Elephant in the Garden, Ch. 2 B. Nevada: Mustang: Wild Spirit of the West, Ch. 16		🌐 Geography for Dummies, 1/2 of Ch. 18
SCIENCE	Choose one spine, one or more core reading selections, and optional reading as desired.		
	⚛ Core reading: 1. Isaac Newton for Kids, Ch. 9 2. Insiders Inventions, pp. 50-55	⚛ Core reading: 1. Uncle Albert and the Quantum Quest, Ch. 8 2. Relativity and Quantum Mechanics, Ch. 2	⚛ Spine: SHSPhys, Week 13 Physics for Dummies, Ch. 19 ⚛ Core reading: The Elegant Universe, Ch. 14
	⚛ Spine: Quark Chronicles: Physics, Ch. 17		

Day 2

Grammar	Dialectic	Rhetoric	
♪ Term 3 Composer: Choose between Shostakovich, Britten, Leon Kirchner			Activities
🎨 Art Lesson: Choose appropriate level of one of the following:			
🎨 I Can Do All Things	🎨 Lamb's Book of Art II	🎨 How Great Thou ART I or II	
🎨 Lamb's Book of Art I	🎨 Feed My Sheep	🎨 Book of Many Colors	
⚛ GSA The World of Light and Sound, Lesson 21		🎨 Great Art, Lecture 35	
➘ Oral or written narration; LG students can draw a picture from the reading and tell about the picture. Suggested subject: Bible.		➘ Oral or written narration for science or Bible.	Narration
✠ Old Story New, Week 71			Other
	☙ UD: The Art of Argument, Review 6	☙ UR: Classical English Rhetoric, 1/4 Ch. 18	
	☙ UD: Science Matters, pp. 301-315		
📚 Suggested read-aloud: The Neverending Story, Ch. 21			Literature

Preschool and Lower Grammar	
✏ Pathways: Path 2 A. Little Wanderers, Ch. 36-37 B. Burgess Seashore Book, Ch. 38 C. D. Random House Poetry, p. 218	Pathways
🎨 Art Lesson: Choose one of the following Barry Stebbing art books for you little one to do art like the big kids: Art and the Bible for Children, Baby Lamb's Book of Art, Joseph the Canada Goose, or Little Annie's Art Book.	Activity

Week 35

	GRAMMAR	DIALECTIC	RHETORIC
BIBLE	Choose one of the following plans: ✠ PLAN 1: Journey Through the Bible, pp. 384-385 ✠ PLAN 2: What the Bible Is All About, 1 John		

LANGUAGE ARTS	Choose appropriate level of one of the following:
	
	❡ English Lessons Through Literature, Lesson 104
	    Reading Lessons Through Literature, phonogram review
	
	❡ Rod and Staff English, Lesson 122
	    Copywork/Commonplace Book
	
	❡ Your own grammar program
			❡ Essential Literary Terms,
			   3-4 pages
			
			❡ LR: The Power in Your
			   Hands, 1 lesson
			
			❡ LR: Rod and Staff 10, L. 114

MATH	Choose appropriate level of one of the following: ✎ Math-U-See, page C ✎ Miquon/Singapore Math ✎ Your own math program		✎ Math-U-See, page C ✎ Your own math program

GEOGRAPHY	🌍 Reading, choose one of the following:
	   A. Germany: An Elephant in the Garden, Ch. 3
	   B. Nevada: Mustang: Wild Spirit of the West, Ch. 17
			🌍 Kilimanjaro Diaries,
			   Ch. 15

HISTORY	Choose one spine, one or more core reading selections, and optional reading as desired.		

	♟ Spine: SOTW, Ch. 40.2
	
	♟ Core reading:
	  1. MTH Heroes for All
	  Times, Ch. 2
	  2. Neil Armstrong, Ch. 15
	  3. Journey to Jo'burg,
	  Ch. 11
		♟ Spine: SOTW, Ch. 40.2
		
		♟ Core reading:
		  1. Red Scarf Girl, Ch. 13
		  2. Warriors Don't Cry,
		  Ch. 14
			♟ Spine:
			  Western Civ, 1/4 of Ch. 30
			
			♟ Core reading:
			  1 & 2. Les Miserables,
			  14 pages
			  1. Animal Farm, Ch. 1-2
			  2. Ender's Game, Ch. 11

Day 3

	Grammar	Dialectic	Rhetoric	
♪♪ Term 3 Composer: Choose between Shostakovich, Britten, Leon Kirchner				Activities
☞ Oral or written narration; could be a group project. Choose a scene from your book. Write it as a play and act it out.				Narration
✛ Old Story New, Week 71 ✛ UD: Simply Christian, Ch. 15		✛ Great Divorce, Ch. 12		Other
📚 Literature: 1: Five Little Peppers and How They Grew, Ch. 21 2: This Week: A Wonder-Book for Girls and Boys: The Miraculous Pitcher 3: The Princess and the Goblin, Ch. 27 4: This Week: Tanglewood Tales, The Pomegranate Seeds	📚 Literature: 5: Around the World in 80 Days, Ch. 29-30 6: The Adventures of Sherlock Holmes, Ch. 8 7: Northanger Abbey, Ch. 27 8: A Double Story, Ch. 10	📚 Book of English Verse, No. 881-883 ✛ Church History: Book of Common Prayer Biography, pp. 136-148 ✛ Science and Religion Lecture 8		Literature
Preschool and Lower Grammar				
🖉 Pathways: Path 1, Day 2 A. Kindergarten Gems B. C. McCloskey— Lentil D. Random House Poetry, p. 219				Pathways
🖉 Toilet-paper roll people Collect the cardboard tubes from toilet-paper. Children can glue construction paper around the tubes for clothes, draw faces, add yarn for hair, etc.				Activity

Week 35

	GRAMMAR	DIALECTIC	RHETORIC
BIBLE	Choose one of the following plans: ✠ PLAN 1: Journey Through the Bible, pp. 386-387 ✠ PLAN 2: What the Bible Is All About, 2 John		
	✠ LG: TBB: The First Church; The Lame Man ✠ UG: Egermeier's, 2 stories	✠ LD: Hurlbut's, 1 story ✠ UD: Golden's, 3 stories	
LANGUAGE ARTS	Choose appropriate level of one of the following: ❡ Reading Lessons Through Literature, next list and story ❡ Prepared dictation from ELTL, Spelling Wisdom, or today's reading ❡ Your own grammar program		
MATH	Choose appropriate level of one of the following:		
	✎ Math-U-See, page D ✎ Miquon/Singapore Math ✎ Your own math program		✎ Math-U-See, page D ✎ Your own math program

GEOGRAPHY	🌎 Reading, choose one of the following:
	    A. Germany: An Elephant in the Garden, Part 3 Ch. 1
	    B. Nevada: Mustang: Wild Spirit of the West, Ch. 18		

SCIENCE	Choose one spine, one or more core reading selections, and optional reading as desired.		

	⚛ Core reading:
	    1. Isaac Newton for Kids, Ch. 10
	    2. Insiders Inventions, pp. 56-61
		⚛ Core reading:
		    1. Uncle Albert and the Quantum Quest, Ch. 9
		    2. Relativity and Quantum Mechanics, Ch. 3
			⚛ Spine: SHSPhys, Week 13 Manga Relativity, pp. 152-162
			
			⚛ Core reading:
			    The Elegant Universe, Ch. 15

	⚛ Optional extra reading, topic: String Theory Simon Bloom, Ch. 38-39		

Day 4

Grammar	Dialectic	Rhetoric	
♪♪ Term 3 Composer: Choose between Shostakovich, Britten, Leon Kirchner			ACTIVITIES
⚛ GSA The World of Light and Sound, Lesson 22 ⚛ 201 Awesome Experiments, 193-194		🎨 Great Art Writing	
☞ Oral or written narration; LG students can draw a picture from the reading and tell about the picture. Suggested subject: science.		☞ Written narration for science or Bible.	NARRATION
✠ Old Story New, Week 71			OTHER
	∞ UD: The Art of Argument: Write a narration on fallacies of clarity ∞ UD: Science Matters, pp. 316-330	∞ UR: Classical English Rhetoric, 1/4 Ch. 18	
📚 Suggested read-aloud: The Neverending Story, Ch. 22			LITERATURE
PRESCHOOL AND LOWER GRAMMAR			
✐ Pathways: Path 3 A. Burgess Flower Book, Ch. 40 B. Gooney Bird Greene, Ch. 7 C. The Magic School Bus And the Climate Challenge D. Random House Poetry, p. 220			PATHWAYS
✐ Clay day Make regular time for you little ones to play with modeling clay.			ACTIVITY

Week 35

	GRAMMAR	DIALECTIC	RHETORIC
BIBLE	Choose one of the following plans: ✙ PLAN 1: Journey Through the Bible, pp. 388-389 ✙ PLAN 2: What the Bible Is All About, 3 John		
LANGUAGE ARTS	Choose appropriate level of one of the following: ❡ English Lessons Through Literature, Lesson 105 　　Reading Lessons Through Literature, phonogram review ❡ Rod and Staff English, Lesson 123 　　Copywork/Commonplace Book ❡ Your own grammar program		❡ A Rulebook for Arguments, Appendix I ❡ LR: The Power in Your Hands, 1 lesson ❡ LR: Rod and Staff 10, L. 115
MATH	Choose appropriate level of one of the following: ✏ Math-U-See, page E ✏ Miquon/Singapore Math ✏ Your own math program		✏ Math-U-See, pages E & H ✏ Your own math program
GEOGRAPHY	🌎 Mapping: Caribbean 🌎 Reading, choose one of the following: 　　B. Nevada: Mustang: Wild Spirit of the West, Ch. 19		🌎 Kilimanjaro Diaries, Ch. 16
HISTORY	Choose one spine, one or more core reading selections, and optional reading as desired. ♟ Spine: SOTW, Ch. 41.1 ♟ Core reading: 　1. MTH Heroes for All Times, Ch. 3 　3. Journey to Jo'burg, Ch. 12	♟ Spine: SOTW, Ch. 41.1 ♟ Core reading: 　1. Red Scarf Girl, Ch. 14 　2. Warriors Don't Cry, Ch. 15	♟ Spine: ♟ Core reading: 　1 & 2. Les Miserables, 14 pages 　LR: 1 & 2. Philosophy Book, through Cixous 　UR: 1 & 2. Think, 1/2 Ch. 7 　1. Animal Farm, Ch. 3-4 　2. Ender's Game, Ch. 12

Day 5

	Grammar	Dialectic	Rhetoric	
	♪♪ Term 3 Composer: Choose between Shostakovich, Britten, Leon Kirchner			Activities
	🎨 Art Lesson: Choose appropriate level of one of the following:			
	🎨 I Can Do All Things	🎨 Lamb's Book of Art II	🎨 How Great Thou ART I or II	
	🎨 Lamb's Book of Art I	🎨 Feed My Sheep	🎨 Book of Many Colors	
	👉 Oral or written narration; LG students can draw a picture from the reading and tell about the picture. Suggested subject: geography.		👉 Oral or written narration for history or geography.	Narration
	✠ Old Story New, Week 71			Other
	📖 Suggested read-aloud: The Neverending Story, Ch. 23			Literature
	📖 Literature: 1: Five Little Peppers and How They Grew, Ch. 22 2: This Week: A Wonder-Book for Girls and Boys: The Miraculous Pitcher 3: The Princess and the Goblin, Ch. 28 4: This Week: Tanglewood Tales, The Pomegranate Seeds	📖 Literature: 5: Around the World in 80 Days, Ch. 31-32 6: The Adventures of Sherlock Holmes, Ch. 9 7: Northanger Abbey, Ch. 28 8: A Double Story, Ch. 11	✠ Church History: Book of Common Prayer Biography, pp. 148-159 ✠ Science and Religion Lecture 9	

Preschool and Lower Grammar

✏️ Pathways: Path 1, Day 3 A. Kindergarten Gems B. C. McCloskey— "Ever So Much More So" D. Random House Poetry, p. 221	Pathways
🎨 Art Lesson: Choose one of the following Barry Stebbing art books for you little one to do art like the big kids: Art and the Bible for Children, Baby Lamb's Book of Art, Joseph the Canada Goose, or Little Annie's Art Book.	Activity

Astronaut Buzz Aldrin on the moon. Photo by Astronaut Neil Armstrong of NASA, who can be seen in Aldrin's visor. Photo is in the public domain; via Wikimedia Commons.

History Through Art: Apollo 11

"That's one small step for man, one giant leap for mankind." With these words, the astronaut Neil Armstrong stepped off a shuttle and onto the white powdery surface of the Moon, becoming the first Earthling in the history of the universe to do so.

The Apollo 11 mission was launched from Florida in 1969, during the peak of the international struggle called the Space Race. During this period, Russia and the United States competed to prove their superiority by launching probes, animals, and eventually people into the dark void of outer space, and—sometimes—returning them safely to Earth. Failure to prove superiority could mean war, a brutal nuclear war the likes of which the planet had never seen. Both countries considered it imperative to win.

By landing on the moon, the United States effectively won the Space Race once and for all. The mission succeeded in allowing astronauts to conduct a twenty-minute walk on the moon's surface, collecting rocks and even leaving an American flag planted in the lunar soil.

The full crew of Apollo 11 consisted of Neil Armstrong, Edwin "Buzz" Aldrin, and Michael Collins. The crew had a playful side to them not often discussed in press releases, such as when they nicknamed the two spacecraft that made up the mission "Charlie Brown" and "Snoopy." They were widely celebrated upon their return to Earth, and rightly so. As Neil Armstrong put it, they had most certainly taken a massive leap for mankind.

An Elephant in the Garden

Cabbage

Although Marlene had loved potatoes best, she would also eat cabbage leaves. A cabbage is a leafy **biennial** plant, one which blooms and produces seeds in its second year. Although cabbage takes two years to grow, it is normally picked in the first year. Cabbage which is specifically being grown for seed will be allowed to persist through to the second year. Cabbage can be green or purple, and it is recognizable due to its dense leaves and rounded head. It is closely related to broccoli and brussels sprouts. Many different varieties of cabbage exist, and a mature cabbage head will range from one to nine pounds.

It is difficult to know exactly where cabbage developed, but they most likely came from somewhere in Europe before 1,000 BC. Cabbage is popular and widespread across many European cuisines, and by the Middle Ages, it was featuring prominently on the tables of both the upper and lower classes. It is not difficult to grow but requires very healthy soil and some care as it is prone to pests and diseases.

Air Raid

The family had heard the sound of the air-raid sirens. Flying is an incredible power to have, as any bird could tell you, if birds could talk. You can travel faster than anything on the ground, speeding over obstacles that would slow down or stop anything else. Airplanes have made quite a few human activities far easier by harnessing the power of flight—including, unfortunately, the activities of war.

An air raid is an attack by aircraft on targets on the ground, to destroy things valuable to the enemy. This can take a number of different forms. In an air strike, specific military targets are attacked, like fortresses or groups of enemy soldiers. Strategic bombing consists of air raids directed against an enemy nation's ability to wage war. Airplanes engaging in strategic bombing will drop bombs on anything the enemy can use, such as factories, laboratories, and in many cases, the people of the country themselves.

Juggling

Karli had juggled snow balls. Juggling is a physical skill used for recreation, entertainment, or sport. People who juggle are called jugglers, and they perform alone or with groups of other entertainers. The most common form is called toss juggling where one or more objects are tossed into the air and manipulated at the same time using one or both hands. Commonly, these objects will be balls

Lexington Barbecue Festival 2008, street juggler on stilts working his craft.
Photo by Dennis Brown. License: CC BY 3.0; via Wikimedia Commons.

or fruit, but sometimes jugglers will use more dramatic items such as knives or flaming torches. As a form of entertainment, juggling dates back to the earliest recorded history and across all cultures. Wall paintings in Egyptian tombs show whole troops of jugglers with suggestions of religious significance. In the Middle Ages, religious authorities frowned upon the type of traveling performers who juggled, called gleemen. They were accused of having poor morals, and it was believed they corrupted the innocent.

Today, street performers can often be seen juggling in return for donated cash. Often they will mix their juggling with other forms of entertainment such as dancing, singing, or telling jokes. Jugglers may also perform at parties or as part of circus and carnival acts.

Mustang: Wild Spirit of the West

Foghorn

Annie says she can hear Zeke's foghorn voice as she reads his note. A foghorn is a loud, audio signal which is meant to warn vehicles of hazards. Typically used on ships or shoreline structures such as lighthouses, the foghorn will sound to alert all other vessels within sound range to hazards such as rocky shores or other boats. They are especially used during the times of dense fog which often occurs along the seashores at night. Without such a signal, a ship might crash upon the rocks and sink.

For as long as man has been sailing upon the sea, some form of fog signal has been used. In ancient times, it might be a loud bell or gong to alert ships that they were nearing the shore. Watchfires were often left burning, but in heavy daytime fogs, they could not easily be seen until it was too late. A more modern foghorn signal is divided into two notes: a high and a low. The inventor of the first steam-powered foghorn was Robert Foulis, a Scotsman who is said to have heard his daughter playing a piano in the distance. In the fog, he noticed the low notes were more easily heard over the distance, and he designed the foghorn to produce the low-frequency sound.

Telephone Switchboard

Annie hears Mr. Baring say hello to Ruthie at the switchboard. A telephone switchboard was a series of switches which enabled a public telephone network to operate. Because of the way electrical signals moved over phone lines, an operator had to manually make a connection on a circuit in order to connect two people who wished to talk. In most urban areas, a center where numerous operators sat in front of switchboards had been established to handle the phone traffic. In 1888, an automatic switchboard system was created, and it began to manually replace the operators. In rural areas, the transition was much slower, and the telephone switchboard and its operator became a fixture of rural culture.

Today, all the switching of physical line phones and cellphones is managed by electronic, automated means. The occasional large building such as a hotel or office may retain a operator to manage calls and speak to customers, but even that is continuing to be replaced by more automation and recorded messages.

Cowboy Boots

Jim Wright ends his talk with, "You bet your cowboy boots I am!" Cowboy boots are a type of riding boot worn by the cowboys of the American West. They are normally made from cow leather, but they can be made out of more expensive, exotic hides such as alligator or ostrich. They have a heel and a rounded or pointed toe and no laces. There are two modern styles of cowboy boot, the classic and the roper. The classic comes up to at least mid-calf while the roper stops below the middle of the calf and has a more squared-off heel.

Specialized riding boots have been around for as long as people have been riding horses, and up until the industrial age, the boots were made by hand in different styles depending upon the riding culture. The earliest cowboy boots were heavily influenced by the cowboy riders from Spain who were called *vaquero*. Today, cowboy boots have a style unrelated to their function as riding boots.

Women's boots on a display rack at Joe's Boot Shop in Clovis, New Mexico. Many boots for both sexes are highly decorated and are not meant to be worn while actually riding a horse but are worn to be fashionable while identifying with ranching culture. Photo by Pete unseth. License: CC BY-SA 3.0; via Wikimedia Commons.

P/K & LG Activity Supplies:

Day 1:
- Tempera or finger paint
- Gallon-size zip top bag

Day 3:
- Food coloring
- Celery stalks, Nappa cabbage leaves, or flowers

Day 4:
- 45 uniform objects (popsicle sticks, spindles, etc.)
- Containers large enough to hold 10 of the objects

Science Experiment Supplies:

- Modeling clay
- Coin
- Toothpick
- Balloon

- Scissors
- Ruler
- Sewing thread
- Small paper clip
- Cellophane tape
- Book
- Magnet
- Compass

Rhetoric: This week: Find an example of a literary technique from Essential Literary Terms and discuss it. How did the author use this technique? Why do you think the author used it? Write a paper, complete with introduction and conclusion.

Rhetoric, Physics:

Physics lab on Day 4.

Week 36

	GRAMMAR	DIALECTIC	RHETORIC
BIBLE	Choose one of the following plans: ✚ PLAN 1: Journey Through the Bible, pp. 390-391 ✚ PLAN 2: What the Bible Is All About, Jude		

LANGUAGE ARTS	Choose appropriate level of one of the following:
	
	❡ English Lessons Through Literature, Lesson 106
	   Reading Lessons Through Literature, phonogram review
	
	❡ Rod and Staff English, Lesson 124
	   Copywork/Commonplace Book
	
	❡ Your own grammar program
			❡ LR: Rod and Staff 10, L. 116

MATH	Choose appropriate level of one of the following: ✎ Math-U-See, Video and page A ✎ Miquon/Singapore Math ✎ Your own math program		✎ Math-U-See, Video and page A ✎ Your own math program

GEOGRAPHY	🌎 50 States, Review Pacific Coast
	
	🌎 Reading, choose one of the following:
	   A. Germany: An Elephant in the Garden, Ch. 2
	   B. Nevada: Mustang: Wild Spirit of the West, Ch. 20
			🌏 Kilimanjaro Diaries,
			   Ch. 17

HISTORY	Choose one spine, one or more core reading selections, and optional reading as desired.
	
	♟ Spine: SOTW, Ch. 41.2
	
	♟ Core reading:
	   1. MTH Heroes for All Times, Ch. 4
	   2. YWWT Apollo 13, pp. 5-13
	   3. Journey to Jo'burg, Ch. 13
		♟ Spine: SOTW, Ch. 41.2
		
		♟ Core reading:
		   1. Red Scarf Girl, Ch. 15
		   2. Warriors Don't Cry, Ch. 16
			♟ Spine:
			   Western Civ, 1/4 of Ch. 30
			
			♟ Core reading:
			   1 & 2. Les Miserables, 14 pages
			   1. Animal Farm, Ch. 5-6
			   2. Ender's Game, Ch. 13

Day 1

Grammar	Dialectic	Rhetoric	
♪♪ Term 3 Composer: Choose between Shostakovich, Britten, Leon Kirchner ⧗ Timeline/Book of Centuries			ACTIVITIES
☞ Oral or written narration; LG students can draw a picture from the reading and tell about the picture. Suggested subject: history.		☞ Written narration for history or geography.	NARRATION
✛ Old Story New, Week 72 ℭℬ UD: Economics in One Lesson, Ch. 25		✛ Great Divorce, Ch. 13	OTHER
📚 Literature: 1: Five Little Peppers and How They Grew, Ch. 23 2: This Week: A Wonder-Book for Girls and Boys: The Chimæra 3: The Princess and the Goblin, Ch. 29 4: This Week: Tanglewood Tales, The Golden Fleece	📚 Literature: 5: Around the World in 80 Days, Ch. 33-34 6: The Adventures of Sherlock Holmes, Ch. 10 7: Northanger Abbey, Ch. 29 8: A Double Story, Ch. 12	✛ Church History: Book of Common Prayer Biography, pp. 159-170 ✛ Science and Religion Lecture 10	LITERATURE

Preschool and Lower Grammar

✎ Pathways: Path 1, Day 1 A. Kindergarten Gems B. C. 20th—The Story of Little Babaji D. Random House Poetry, p. 222	PATHWAYS
✎ Paint bag writing tablet Add tempera or finger paint to a zip-top bag. You need enough paint to make a thin layer over the entire surface of the bag. Remove air from the bag and close it. Spread the paint through the bag. Now your little one can "write" in the paint using a finger or a cotton swab. See example here: www.lets-explore.net/blog/2009/10/paint-bag-writing/	ACTIVITY

Week 36

	GRAMMAR	DIALECTIC	RHETORIC
BIBLE	Choose one of the following plans: ✦ PLAN 1: Journey Through the Bible, pp. 392-393 ✦ PLAN 2: What the Bible Is All About, Revelation		
	✦ LG: TBB: A Changed Man; Paul's Journeys ✦ UG: Egermeier's, 2 stories	✦ LD: Hurlbut's, 2 stories ✦ UD: Golden's, 2 stories	
LANGUAGE ARTS	Choose appropriate level of one of the following: ❡ Reading Lessons Through Literature, next list and story ❡ Prepared dictation from ELTL, Spelling Wisdom, or today's reading ❡ Rod and Staff English, Lesson 125 ❡ Your own grammar program		❡ Essential Literary Terms, This week: Find an example of a literary technique from Essential Literary Terms and discuss it.
MATH	Choose appropriate level of one of the following: ✎ Math-U-See, page B ✎ Miquon/Singapore Math ✎ Your own math program		✎ Math-U-See, page B ✎ Your own math program
GEOGRAPHY	🌎 Reading, choose one of the following: A. Germany: An Elephant in the Garden, Ch. 3 B. Nevada: Mustang: Wild Spirit of the West, Ch. 21		🌎 Geography for Dummies, 1/2 of Ch. 18
SCIENCE	Choose one spine, one or more core reading selections, and optional reading as desired.		
	⚛ Core reading:	⚛ Core reading: 1. Uncle Albert and the Quantum Quest, Ch. 10 2. Relativity and Quantum Mechanics, Ch. 4	⚛ Spine: SHSPhys, Week 14 ⚛ Core reading:
	⚛ Spine: Quark Chronicles: Physics, Ch. 18		

Day 2

	Grammar	Dialectic	Rhetoric	
♪♫ Term 3 Composer: Choose between Shostakovich, Britten, Leon Kirchner 🎨 Art Lesson: Choose appropriate level of one of the following:				Activities
🎨 I Can Do All Things 🎨 Lamb's Book of Art I	🎨 Lamb's Book of Art II 🎨 Feed My Sheep	🎨 How Great Thou ART I or II 🎨 Book of Many Colors	
⚛ GSA The World of Light and Sound, Lesson 23		🎨 Great Art, Lecture 36	
☛ Oral or written narration; LG students can draw a picture from the reading and tell about the picture. Suggested subject: Bible.		☛ Oral or written narration for science or Bible.	Narration
✠ Old Story New, Week 72			Other
	෪ UD: The Art of Argument, Appendix A ෪ UD: Science Matters, pp. 331-346	෪ UR: Classical English Rhetoric, 1/4 Ch. 18	
📚 Suggested read-aloud: The Neverending Story, Ch. 24			Literature

Preschool and Lower Grammar	
🖋 Pathways: Path 2 A. Little Wanderers, Ch. 38 B. Burgess Seashore Book, Ch. 39-40 C. D. Random House Poetry, p. 223	Pathways
🎨 Art Lesson: Choose one of the following Barry Stebbing art books for you little one to do art like the big kids: Art and the Bible for Children, Baby Lamb's Book of Art, Joseph the Canada Goose, or Little Annie's Art Book.	Activity

Week 36

	GRAMMAR	DIALECTIC	RHETORIC
BIBLE	Choose one of the following plans: ✠ PLAN 1: Journey Through the Bible, pp. 394-395 ✠ PLAN 2: The Story, Ch. 31		
LANGUAGE ARTS	Choose appropriate level of one of the following: ❡ English Lessons Through Literature, Lesson 107 Reading Lessons Through Literature, phonogram review ❡ Rod and Staff English, Lesson 126 Copywork/Commonplace Book ❡ Your own grammar program		❡ LR: The Power in Your Hands, 1 lesson ❡ LR: Rod and Staff 10, L. 117
MATH	Choose appropriate level of one of the following: ✎ Math-U-See, page C ✎ Miquon/Singapore Math ✎ Your own math program		✎ Math-U-See, page C ✎ Your own math program
GEOGRAPHY	🌐 Reading, choose one of the following: A. Germany: An Elephant in the Garden, Part 4 Ch. 1 B. Nevada: Mustang: Wild Spirit of the West, Ch. 22		🌐 Kilimanjaro Diaries, Ch. 18
HISTORY	Choose one spine, one or more core reading selections, and optional reading as desired.		
	♟ Spine: SOTW, Ch. 42.1 ♟ Core reading: 1. MTH Heroes for All Times, Ch. 5 2. YWWT Apollo 13, pp. 14-21 3. Journey to Jo'burg, Ch. 14	♟ Spine: SOTW, Ch. 42.1 ♟ Core reading: 1. Red Scarf Girl, Ch. 16 2. Warriors Don't Cry, Ch. 17	♟ Spine: Western Civ, 1/4 of Ch. 30 ♟ Core reading: 1 & 2. Les Miserables, 14 pages 1. Animal Farm, Ch. 7-8 2. Ender's Game, Ch. 14

Day 3

Grammar	Dialectic	Rhetoric	
♪♪ Term 3 Composer: Choose between Shostakovich, Britten, Leon Kirchner			ACTIVITIES
☞ Oral or written narration; could be a group project. Choose a favorite passage to read aloud to your family. If other family members may read the book, be careful not to choose a passage with spoilers!			NARRATION
✠ Old Story New, Week 72 ✠ UD: Simply Christian, Ch. 16		✠ Great Divorce, Ch. 14	OTHER
📚 Literature: 1: Five Little Peppers and How They Grew, Ch. 24 2: This Week: A Wonder-Book for Girls and Boys: The Chimæra 3: The Princess and the Goblin, Ch. 30 4: This Week: Tanglewood Tales, The Golden Fleece	📚 Literature: 5: Around the World in 80 Days, Ch. 35-36 6: The Adventures of Sherlock Holmes, Ch. 11 7: Northanger Abbey, Ch. 30 8: A Double Story, Ch. 13	✠ Church History: Book of Common Prayer Biography, pp. 170-180 ✠ Science and Religion Lecture 11	LITERATURE

Preschool and Lower Grammar

✎ Pathways: Path 1, Day 2 A. Kindergarten Gems B. C. McCloskey— Time of Wonder D. Random House Poetry, p. 224	PATHWAYS
✎ Water movement Put about an inch and a half of water into two jars. Add different colors of food coloring to each. Make it a nice, dark color. Place stalks of celery, Nappa cabbage leaves, or flowers in each jar. Observe the changes throughout the day.	ACTIVITY

Week 36

	GRAMMAR	DIALECTIC	RHETORIC
BIBLE	Choose one of the following plans: ✛ PLAN 1: Journey Through the Bible, pp. 396-397 ✛ PLAN 2: Journey Through the Bible, pp. 398-402		
	✛ LG: TBB: Earthquake in Prison; Jesus is Coming ✛ UG: Egermeier's, 3 stories	✛ UD: Golden's, 3 stories	
LANGUAGE ARTS	Choose appropriate level of one of the following: ❡ Reading Lessons Through Literature, next list and story ❡ Prepared dictation from ELTL, Spelling Wisdom, or today's reading ❡ Your own grammar program		
MATH	Choose appropriate level of one of the following: ✏ Math-U-See, page D ✏ Miquon/Singapore Math ✏ Your own math program		✏ Math-U-See, page D ✏ Your own math program
GEOGRAPHY	🌐 Reading, choose one of the following: A. Germany: An Elephant in the Garden, Ch. 2 B. Nevada: Mustang: Wild Spirit of the West, Ch. 23		
SCIENCE	Choose one spine, one or more core reading selections, and optional reading as desired.		
	⚛ Core reading:	⚛ Core reading:	⚛ Spine: SHSPhys, Week 14 Manga Relativity, pp. 163-end ⚛ Core reading:
	⚛ Optional extra reading, topic: Hypothetical Theory of Everything Simon Bloom, Ch. 40-41 G: Magic School Bus and the Science Fair Expedition by Joanna Cole		

Day 4

GRAMMAR	DIALECTIC	RHETORIC	
♪♫ Term 3 Composer: Choose between Shostakovich, Britten, Leon Kirchner			ACTIVITIES
⚛ GSA The World of Light and Sound, Lesson 24 ⚛ 201 Awesome Experiments, 195-196		⚛ Physics Lab 🎨 Great Art Writing	ACTIVITIES
☞ Oral or written narration; LG students can draw a picture from the reading and tell about the picture. Suggested subject: science.		☞ Written narration for science or Bible.	NARRATION
✚ Old Story New, Week 72			OTHER
	☙ UD: The Art of Argument, Appendix B	☙ UR: Classical English Rhetoric, 1/4 Ch. 18	
📚 Suggested read-aloud: The Neverending Story, Ch. 25			LITERATURE

PRESCHOOL AND LOWER GRAMMAR

✎ Pathways: Path 3 A. Burgess Flower Book, Ch. 41-42 B. C. The Magic School Bus And the Electric Field Trip D. Random House Poetry, p. 225	PATHWAYS
✎ Counting 1-10 Have 10 containers and 45 objects. The traditional Montessori activity has 45 spindles with a box that has 10 compartments, but you can do this with popsicle sticks and cups. Label the containers 0-9. The child puts 0 objects in the first cup, 1 object in the second cup, etc., all the way up to 9.	ACTIVITY

Week 36

	GRAMMAR	DIALECTIC	RHETORIC
BIBLE	Choose one of the following plans: ✛ PLAN 1: Journey Through the Bible, pp. 398-401		
LANGUAGE ARTS	Choose appropriate level of one of the following: ❡ English Lessons Through Literature, Lesson 108 　Reading Lessons Through Literature, phonogram review ❡ Rod and Staff English, Lesson 127 　Copywork/Commonplace Book ❡ Your own grammar program		❡ A Rulebook for Arguments, Appendix II ❡ LR: The Power in Your Hands, 1 lesson ❡ LR: Rod and Staff 10, L. 118
MATH	Choose appropriate level of one of the following:		
	✎ Math-U-See, page E ✎ Miquon/Singapore Math ✎ Your own math program		✎ Math-U-See, pages E & H ✎ Your own math program
GEOGRAPHY	🌎 Mapping: North America		
	🌎 Reading, choose one of the following: 　A. Germany: An Elephant in the Garden, Ch. 3 　B. Nevada: Mustang: Wild Spirit of the West, Ch. 24		🌎 Kilimanjaro Diaries, Ch. 19 - Epilogue
HISTORY	Choose one spine, one or more core reading selections, and optional reading as desired.		
	♟ Spine: SOTW, Ch. 42.2 ♟ Core reading: 　1. MTH Heroes for All Times, Ch. 6 　2. YWWT Apollo 13, pp. 22-29 　3. Journey to Jo'burg, Ch. 15	♟ Spine: SOTW, Ch. 42.2 ♟ Core reading: 　1. Red Scarf Girl, Ch. 17 - Epilogue 　2. Warriors Don't Cry, Ch. 18 - Epilogue	♟ Spine: ♟ Core reading: 　1 & 2. Les Miserables, 14 pages 　LR: 1 & 2. Philosophy Book, through Zizek 　UR: 1 & 2. Think, Ch. 8 　1. Animal Farm, Ch. 9-10 　2. Ender's Game, Ch. 15

Day 5

	Grammar	Dialectic	Rhetoric	
	♪♪ Term 3 Composer: Choose between Shostakovich, Britten, Leon Kirchner			ACTIVITIES
	🎨 Art Lesson: Choose appropriate level of one of the following:			
	🎨 I Can Do All Things 🎨 Lamb's Book of Art I	🎨 Lamb's Book of Art II 🎨 Feed My Sheep	🎨 How Great Thou ART I or II 🎨 Book of Many Colors	
	☞ Oral or written narration; LG students can draw a picture from the reading and tell about the picture. Suggested subject: geography.		☞ Oral or written narration for history or geography.	NARRATION
	✠ Old Story New, Week 72 ℃℧ UD: Economics in One Lesson, Ch. 26			OTHER
	📚 Suggested read-aloud: The Neverending Story, Ch. 26			
	📚 Literature: 1: Five Little Peppers and How They Grew, Ch. 25 2: This Week: A Wonder-Book for Girls and Boys: The Chimæra 3: The Princess and the Goblin, Ch. 31-32 4: This Week: Tanglewood Tales, The Golden Fleece	📚 Literature: 5: Around the World in 80 Days, Ch. 37 6: The Adventures of Sherlock Holmes, Ch. 12 7: Northanger Abbey, Ch. 31 8: A Double Story, Ch. 14	✠ Church History: Book of Common Prayer Biography, pp. 180-194 ✠ Science and Religion Lecture 12	LITERATURE

PRESCHOOL AND LOWER GRAMMAR

✏ Pathways: Path 1, Day 3 A. Kindergarten Gems B. C. McCloskey—One Morning in Maine D. Random House Poetry, p. 226	PATHWAYS
🎨 Art Lesson: Choose one of the following Barry Stebbing art books for you little one to do art like the big kids: Art and the Bible for Children, Baby Lamb's Book of Art, Joseph the Canada Goose, or Little Annie's Art Book.	ACTIVITY

An artist's concept portrays a NASA Mars Exploration Rover on the surface of Mars. Image by NASA/JPL/Cornell University, Maas Digital LLC. Image in the public domain; via Wikimedia Commons.

History Through Art: Mars Rovers

Did you know that Mars is the only known planet to be entirely populated by robots? It's true. While one of our closest neighbors is a barren, desolate desert, mankind has not missed the opportunity to extend our reach and explore farther and farther into the heavens. On Mars, we seek to accomplish that goal by sending robots equipped with wheels and cameras.

The Mars Exploration Rover Mission consists of two rovers, named Spirit and Opportunity. The car-sized robots were sent to Mars to carry out the research that scientists couldn't do from Earth, namely, investigating Martian rocks and soil. It sounds boring, but one of the main goals of the mission was to find out whether the rocks and dirt of Mars had been exposed to water in the past because if there had been water on Mars, it's possible that there had been life there as well.

235

The question of whether life has ever existed on Mars is still up for debate, but the rovers did help to make the discovery that water had flowed on our planetary neighbor in the distant past. But that isn't where their work ended! While it was thought that the rovers would only be able to last a couple of years at most on the red planet before breaking down, at the time of this writing they've been going strong for nearly thirteen years.

An Elephant in the Garden

Pacifism

Lizzie says that her mother had always been a pacifist. Pacifism is a belief which stands opposed to war and other types of violence. The word was first used by the French peace advocate Emile Arnaud and has been adopted by other advocates since. It is a core philosophy in Buddhism and there are many pacifistic beliefs evident in Christianity, including in the words of Jesus Christ Himself.

The belief in pacifism is a wide spectrum belief, meaning that different people have different ways of adhering to it. Some take a stance against war while others take a stance advocating that violence should only ever be done in self-defense. Extreme pacifists believe that no violence should be done whatsoever, even in the defense of self or others.

In many countries, including the United States, pacifists have been arrested and even imprisoned for protesting wars. Ammon Hennacy was a famous Christian pacifist who was thrown in prison for refusing to fight in several American wars. He took such a firm stance against it that he refused to even earn enough money to be taxed by the government because he did not want his labors to be used to harm others.

Compasses

Lizzie says that they would not have made it without Peter and the compass. A magnetic compass is a device used for navigational aid as it always points to magnetic north. It was first developed in the Song Dynasty of China around the 11th century, but by the 14th century, it was being used by European ships. Compasses are still used today, and you can even get one on your cellphone. While this may seem like a simple device, it was revolutionary in that sea navigation prior to its invention was largely done by sighting landmarks. It allowed the use of maps and navigation away from land. Without the compass, there would have been no discovery of the Americas or the Age of Discovery where sea-bound merchants spread out from Europe to navigate the world.

A compass works by lightly suspending a pin or small rod with a bit of magnetic lodestone attached. The lodestone, a naturally occurring magnetic ore, will align itself with the earth's magnetic field and pull the pin towards magnetic north, which is very near to what we refer to as the north pole. It is a trustworthy navigational aid except in areas full of lodestone in the ground or when it is surrounded by large amounts of metal.

Parachutes

Soldiers had come looking for the parachutists. The problem with flying is that it's very easy to stop flying. If you stop flying in midair due to some sort of accident, then you start falling. Falling from a great height is not a fun experience, as you likely know very well by now. A fall from a height as high as an airplane flies can be deadly.

Fortunately for fliers, an invention called the parachute is a great way of making a fall a lot less of a lethal nuisance. The name comes from the French words *para* and *chute*, which mean "protection against" and "fall" respectively. That's exactly what a parachute does. When activated, a parachute bloats up to catch the air while in mid-fall, falling much more slowly and gently in the same way that a feather or a dandelion seed does. Gravity has a constant rate of acceleration, which means that everything falls at the same rate of acceleration, no matter its mass. However, the design of the parachute, as well as the feather and the dandelion seed, creates **drag**, a type of friction. This friction with the air slows the object, making it fall more slowly.

United States Army paratroopers training in a jump at Fort Brag, North Carolina, USA. Photo by Jonas N. Jordan, U.S. Army Corps of Engineers. Image is in the public domain; via Wikimedia Commons.

Parachutes aren't 100% reliable, as they can malfunction, but they definitely make falling from a great height much safer—to the extent that some people called skydivers take special flights so they can jump out of planes with their parachutes on, just for the thrill of it.

Mustang: Wild Spirit of the West

Pony Express

Annie mentions that mustangs were used by the Pony Express in the rough, mountain regions. In 1859, a company was formed known as the Central Overland California and Pikes Peak Express Company. This cumbersome name was shortened and popularized as the Pony Express. A series of relay stations from Saint Joseph, Missouri, all the way to California provided fresh horses and riders at each station, spaced roughly ten miles apart. The growing wealth of distant California due to the gold rush had brought wealthy investors and businessmen to the west who needed to maintain contact with the east. The Pony Express proved that it was possible.

Though the stations only operated for a brief 19 months. During the operation, the only serious disruption of operations was due to the Paiute War in Nevada. The Paiute Indian tribe's violence along the route caused the Pony Express to halt deliveries briefly in May of 1860.

By 1861, the telegraph had become sufficiently widespread to replace the Pony Express as a fast—and less dangerous—means of communication between East and West. But in that short amount of time, the rugged Pony Express riders became romanticized and entered into the cultural history and lore of the American West.

Propeller Aircraft

Robert O'Brien charters a Piper Cub plane to fly over the ranges to find some wild horses. Propeller aircraft function by having a set of blades which rotate around a central hub. The blades rotate fast enough to create both lift and thrust in a forward direction, allowing the plane to move and fly. Most common is the tractor design of propeller which puts the rotating blades in front of the engine. This provides better airflow to the propeller and keeps the weight forward for better distribution. The earliest propeller designs were powered by man, usually riding a bicycle to turn the blades. Later, propeller designs moved large dirigibles or balloons.

Classic Fighters 2015 - Piper PA-18 Super Cub ZK-BOY, a modified bush plane. Photo by Oren Rozen. License: CC BY-SA 3.0; via Wikimedia Commons.

Though jet aircraft can travel much faster, propeller aircraft are still the main in aviation today. They are robust and can use conventional fuels instead of the more expensive and difficult to produce jet fuel. Propeller aircraft are also easier to repair and service without requiring a special set of skills and tools, which may not be available in more remote and rural airports. Many small, private planes are propeller aircraft.

Congressional Bills

Annie's bill was being heard in Congress. In an institution like the United States federal government, there is perhaps no more important job than the making of laws. The Founding Fathers wanted to make sure that the government did a balanced job of making fair but effective laws. To ensure this, they made a government that requires multiple different groups of politicians to agree before new laws can be made.

The lawmaking process begins with a bill which is introduced in one of the Houses of Congress and submitted for review. The Houses of Congress are the Senate and the House of Representatives. If the bill is voted on and approved in the House it starts off in, it is passed to the other legislative House. If one House votes against the bill, it will die and never become a law. If both Houses vote to pass it, the bill is brought before the President of the country, who can either sign it with his name or veto it, either passing it into law or putting an end to the whole idea. A veto can be overruled by congress, but this seldom happens. It would require all of Congress to be opposed to the President, which isn't at all common.

Appendix A: English Lessons Through Literature Lists

All the literature selections suggested herein are in the public domain in the United States of America and are probably available at your local library. The complete texts can also be found online from Project Gutenberg (www.gutenberg.org) and/or the Baldwin Project (www.mainlesson.com). Most are available as audio books, and free audio book versions may be found online from LibriVox (www.librivox.org).

Level 1

Beatrix Potter Stories
The twenty Beatrix Potter stories do not follow the order of any particular published edition of her work.

Just So Stories by Rudyard Kipling
One of the stories, "How the Leopard Got His Spots," contains a racial slur near the end. Please pre-read to determine the best way to deal with this for your family.

Five Children and It by Edith Nesbit

The Jungle Book by Rudyard Kipling

Pinocchio by C. Collodi

The Orange Fairy Book by Andrew Lang (seven stories)

The Velveteen Rabbit by Margery Williams

Five Little Peppers and How They Grew by Margaret Sidney

Level 2

The Wonderful Wizard of Oz by L. Frank Baum

The Blue Fairy Book by Andrew Lang (13 stories)

Peter Pan by J. M. Barrie

The Wind in the Willows by Kenneth Grahame

Alice's Adventures in Wonderland by Lewis Carroll

Through the Looking-Glass and What Alice Found There by Lewis Carroll

A Wonder-Book for Girls and Boys by Nathaniel Hawthorne

Level 3

The Story of Doctor Dolittle by Hugh Lofting
There is a racially sensitive portion of this book in chapters eleven and twelve. My understanding is that the Dover Children's Thrift Classics edition of the book is an altered version which changes this part to better respect modern sensibilities. Parents can read the original chapters online to determine whether or not the altered version is desired.

The Marvelous Land of Oz by L. Frank Baum

Beautiful Stories from Shakespeare by E. Nesbit
There are many children's versions of Shakespeare's plays, modern versions such as those by Bruce Coville and Leon Garfield, as well as others in the public domain such as those by Charles and Mary Lamb. Choose the ones you like best. We prefer Bruce Coville's picture books. Modern versions can often be found at the local library.

The Secret Garden by Frances Hodgson Burnett

The Princess and the Goblin by George McDonald

Level 4

The Book of Dragons by E. Nesbit

Black Beauty by Anna Sewell

Ozma of Oz by L. Frank Baum

"The Reluctant Dragon" by Kenneth Grahame, part of the book *Dream Days* by Kenneth Grahame on Gutenberg.org.

Heidi by Johanna Spyri

Tanglewood Tales by Nathaniel Hawthorne

Level 5

"The Ransom of Red Chief" by O. Henry

"The Gift of the Magi" by O. Henry

The Emerald City of Oz by L. Frank Baum

The Adventures of Tom Sawyer by Mark Twain

The Happy Prince and Other Tales by Oscar Wilde

Little Women by Louisa May Alcott

Around the World in Eighty Days by Jules Verne

Level 6

At the Back of the North Wind by George MacDonald

White Fang by Jack London

The Patchwork Girl of Oz by L. Frank Baum

Otto of the Silver Hand by Howard Pyle

The Adventures of Sherlock Holmes by Sir Arthur Conan Doyle

Level 7

"Rip Van Winkle" by Washington Irving

"The Legend of Sleepy Hollow" by Washington Irving

"The Raven" by Edgar Allan Poe

"The Tell-Tale Heart" by Edgar Allan Poe

"The System of Dr. Tarr and Professor Fether" by Edgar Allan Poe

The Black Arrow by Robert Louis Stevenson

A Christmas Carol by Charles Dickens

The Canterville Ghost by Oscar Wilde

The Tin Woodman of Oz by L. Frank Baum

Northanger Abbey by Jane Austen

Level 8

The Importance of Being Earnest by Oscar Wilde

The Misanthrope by Moliere (I found an online version here: https://ebooks. adelaide.edu.au/m/moliere/misanthrope/index.html. There's also a Dover Thrift Edition, in both paperback and ebook editions, which is very reasonably priced.)

Glinda of Oz by L. Frank Baum

Cyrano de Bergerac by Edmond Rostand

20,000 Leagues Under the Sea by Jules Verne

A Double Story by George MacDonald (It's also called *The Wise Woman* and *The Lost Princess*, but *A Double Story* is the title on Gutenberg.)

Appendix B: Literature Suggestions by Grade

Here are a few books which my children have enjoyed at approximately these ages. It's intended merely to give you a starting point for finding non-twaddle for your younger readers.

2nd Grade

The Littles by John Peterson

The Last Little Cat by Meindert DeJong

Nim's Island by Wendy Orr

Ramona the Brave by Beverly Cleary

Henry and Ribsy by Beverly Cleary

Encyclopedia Brown, Boy Detective by Donald J. Sobol

Stuart Little by E. B. White

Emily's Runaway Imagination by Beverly Cleary

3rd Grade

The Toothpaste Millionaire by Jean Merrill

Red Sails to Capri by Ann Wei

Ginger Pye by Eleanor Estes

4th Grade

Little Pilgrim's Progress by Helen L. Taylor

Charlie and the Chocolate Factory by Roald Dahl

The Borrowers by Mary Norton

Dealing with Dragons by Patricia C. Wrede

How to Train Your Dragon by Cressida Cowell

Harry Potter by J. K. Rowling

The Discontented Ghost by Scott Corbett

Appendix C: Pathways Schedule

Pathways is a two-year adjustable reading program for preschoolers and early elementary. Each schedule includes up to 180 days of reading, depending on which path(s) you choose.

Path 1 is three-days per week; it is scheduled on Day 1, Day 3, and Day 5. Paths 2 and 3 are each only one-day per week; Path 2 is scheduled on Day 2, and Path 3 is scheduled on Day 4. Do Paths 2 and 3 only, and you have a two-day per week program. Do one of them with Path 1, and you have four days per week. Do both with Path 1, and you have five days per week.

Each path has up to four readings per day—A, B, C, and D—so you can also determine how many books you want to include each day.

Public Domain Books

The core of the reading is in the public domain. These books may be found at www.gutenberg.org, www.mainlessson.com, or www.archives.org. As public domain history books often include questionable content, the lists are weighted towards science. The James Baldwin books are more legend than history, but they will acquaint the young child with famous names and other time periods. The science in these books is usually in story form.

The 1A fairy tale books are the only books which will ever appear in more than one path. Extra stories from these are used as filler.

1A	Fairy Tales
1B	Science (Clara Dillingham Pierson books) and History (James Baldwin books)
2A	Science (Margaret W. Morley)
2B	Science (Thornton Burgess; some selections are copyrighted)
3A	Science (Thornton Burgess)
3B	Chapter Books (some selections are copyrighted)

Most of the poetry is in copyrighted books. I recommend the poetry collections from www.amblesideonline.org if you'd prefer a free option.

Copyrighted Books

I've included a selection of more modern books for people who have either the budget or a good public library. I invite you to use this as a starting place. Focus on picture books that your library has, or skip scheduled chapter books to continue another series that you love.

1C	Picture Books
2C	Chapter Books
3B	Chapter Books
3C	Mixed
D	Poetry

How to Use This Program

First choose how many books you want to read, and how many days per week you want to read. Then, choose the corresponding paths.

If you are a new homeschooler, or if you have difficulty reading aloud—a skill which requires practice—then I recommend starting small. Do Path 1, which is three-days per week, and choose two or three books within the path. As the year goes on, you may find that you're reading more than three-days per week, and so you will finish before the school year is over. If this happens, start back at the beginning and do either Path 2 or 3. Paths that you don't use during the school year can also be used as a summer reading program. The schedule flexes around you rather than expecting you to flex around the schedule.

The book lists appear on the following pages. Below is a six-week schedule from Year 1 which will hopefully illustrate more fully how the program works. You can download the entire program from my Lulu store. Year 1 is scheduled in the Ancient and Revolution books. Year 2 is scheduled in the Medieval and Modern books.

Pathways, Year 1

English Lessons Through Literature Level 0

WEEK		PATH 1, DAY 1	PATH 2	PATH 1, DAY 2	PATH 3	PATH 1, DAY 3
1	A.	For the Children's Hour	Seed Babies, Ch. 1	For the Children's Hour	Burgess Animal Book, Ch. 1	For the Children's Hour
	B.	50 Famous People	Burgess Bird Book, Ch. 1	Among the Farmyard People	My Father's Dragon, Ch. 1	50 Famous People
	C.	20th—Madeline	Winnie-the-Pooh, Ch. 1	Madeline's Rescue	S&N—The Berenstain Bears' Almanac, pp. 1-29	Madeline and the Bad Hat
	D.	The Real Mother Goose—2 poems	World of Christopher Robin—3 poems	The Real Mother Goose—2 poems	A Child's Garden of Verses—1 poem	The Real Mother Goose—2 poems
2	A.	For the Children's Hour	Seed Babies, Ch. 2	For the Children's Hour	Burgess Animal Book, Ch. 2	For the Children's Hour
	B.	Among the Farmyard People	Burgess Bird Book, Ch. 2	50 Famous People	My Father's Dragon, Ch. 2	Among the Farmyard People
	C.	20th—Chicka Chicka Boom Boom	Winnie-the-Pooh, Ch. 2	Madeline and the Gypsies	S&N—The Berenstain Bears' Almanac, pp. 30-62	Madeline in London
	D.	The Real Mother Goose—3 poems	World of Christopher Robin—3 poems	The Real Mother Goose—3 poems	A Child's Garden of Verses—1 poem	The Real Mother Goose—3 poems
3	A.	For the Children's Hour	Seed Babies, Ch. 3	For the Children's Hour	Burgess Animal Book, Ch. 3	For the Children's Hour
	B.	50 Famous People	Burgess Bird Book, Ch. 3	Among the Farmyard People	My Father's Dragon, Ch. 3	50 Famous People
	C.	20th—Swimmy	Winnie-the-Pooh, Ch. 3	Madeline's Christmas	S&N—The Berenstain Bears' Nature Guide, pp. 63-95	People by Peter Spier
	D.	The Real Mother Goose—3 poems	World of Christopher Robin—3 poems	The Real Mother Goose—3 poems	A Child's Garden of Verses—2 poems	The Real Mother Goose—3 poems
4	A.	For the Children's Hour	Seed Babies, Ch. 4	For the Children's Hour	Burgess Animal Book, Ch. 4	For the Children's Hour
	B.	Among the Farmyard People	Burgess Bird Book, Ch. 4-5	50 Famous People	My Father's Dragon, Ch. 4	Among the Farmyard People
	C.	20th—A Chair for My Mother	Winnie-the-Pooh, Ch. 4	20th— Goodnight Moon	S&N—The Berenstain Bears' Nature Guide, pp. 96-126	Milly-Molly-Mandy, Ch. 1
	D.	The Real Mother Goose—3 poems	World of Christopher Robin—2 poems	The Real Mother Goose—3 poems	A Child's Garden of Verses—2 poems	The Real Mother Goose—3 poems
5	A.	For the Children's Hour	Seed Babies, Ch. 5	For the Children's Hour	Burgess Animal Book, Ch. 5	For the Children's Hour
	B.	50 Famous People	Burgess Bird Book, Ch. 6	Among the Farmyard People	My Father's Dragon, Ch. 5	50 Famous People
	C.	20th—The Snowy Day	Winnie-the-Pooh, Ch. 5	Milly-Molly-Mandy, Ch. 2	S&N—The Berenstain Bears' Science Fair, pp. 127-157	Milly-Molly-Mandy, Ch. 3
	D.	The Real Mother Goose—3 poems	World of Christopher Robin—2 poems	The Real Mother Goose—3 poems	A Child's Garden of Verses—2 poems	The Real Mother Goose—3 poems
6	A.	For the Children's Hour	Seed Babies, Ch. 6	For the Children's Hour	Burgess Animal Book, Ch. 6	For the Children's Hour
	B.	Among the Farmyard People	Burgess Bird Book, Ch. 7	50 Famous People	My Father's Dragon, Ch. 6	Among the Farmyard People
	C.	20th—"The Letter"	Winnie-the-Pooh, Ch. 6	Milly-Molly-Mandy, Ch. 4	S&N—The Berenstain Bears' Science Fair, pp. 158-190	Milly-Molly-Mandy, Ch. 5
	D.	The Real Mother Goose—3 poems	World of Christopher Robin—2 poems	The Real Mother Goose—3 poems	A Child's Garden of Verses—2 poems	The Real Mother Goose—3 poems

Year A and Year B Books

The following books are included in both years of the program. Most of these books and stories are included in anthologies and author collections, making them more affordable for those who wish to purchase some of the books.

1C Books

The 20th Century Children's Book Treasury

Madeline by Ludwig Bemelmans
Chicka Chicka Boom Boom by Bill Martin, Jr., and John Archambault
Swimmy by Leo Lionni
A Chair for My Mother by Vera B. Williams
Goodnight Moon by Margaret Wise Brown
The Snowy Day by Ezra Jack Keats
"The Letter" by Arnold Lobel
Freight Train by Donald Crews
Make Way for Ducklings by Robert McCloskey
A Million Fish...More or Less by Patricia C. McKissack
A Boy, a Dog and a Frog by Mercer Mayer
Millions of Cats by Wanda Gág
Guess How Much I Love You by Sam McBratney
Alexander and the Terrible, Horrible, No Good, Very Bad Day by Judith Viorst
Curious George by H. A. Rey
I Hear, I See, and I Touch by Helen Oxenbury
Miss Nelson Is Missing! by Harry Allard
Titch by Pat Hutchins
Where the Wild Things Are by Maurice Sendak
"The Cat Club" by Esther Averill
Sylvester and the Magic Pebble by William Steig
Good Night, Gorilla by Peggy Rathmann
Mike Mulligan and His Steam Shovel by Virginia Lee Burton
Stevie by John Steptoe
The Tub People by Pam Conrad
"In Which Pooh Goes Visiting..." by A. A. Milne
Bedtime for Frances by Russell Hoban
"The Stinky Cheese Man" by Jon Scieszka
The Story of Babar by Jean de Brunhoff
The Berenstain Bears and the Spooky Old Tree by Stan and Jan Berenstain
"The Elves in the Shelves" by Joan Aiken
Ten, Nine, Eight by Molly Bang Stellaluna by Janell Cannon
D.W. the Picky Eater by Marc Brown
Petunia by Roger Duvoisin
First Tomato by Rosemary Wells
Amelia Bedelia by Peggy Parish
I Am a Bunny by Ole Risom

Harry the Dirty Dog by Gene Zion
Whose Mouse Are You? by Robert Kraus
Owen by Kevin Henkes
The Story of Ferdinand by Munro Leaf
"The Sneetches" by Dr. Seuss
The Story of Little Babaji by Helen Bannerman

Harper Collins Treasury of Picture Book Classics:

Goodnight Moon
Caps for Sale
Harold and the Purple Crayon
Crictor
A Baby Sister for Frances
Leo the Late Bloomer
William's Doll
If You Give a Mouse A Cookie
George Shrinks
Baby Says
From Head to Toe
Pete's Pizza

Mad About Madeline

The Complete Adventures of Curious George

Mike Mulligan and More by Burton

Mike Mulligan and His Steam Shovel
The Little House
Katy and the Big Snow
Maybell the Cable Car

Make Way for McCloskey

Make Way for Ducklings
Blueberries for Sal
"The Doughnuts"
Burt Dow, Deep-Water Man
Lentil
"Ever So Much More So"
Time of Wonder
One Morning in Maine

Individual Titles

Choo Choo by Virginia Lee Burton
Calico the Wonder Horse by Virginia Lee Burton
People by Peter Spier

3C Books

The Berenstain Bears' Big Book of Science and Nature (S&N)
The Berenstain Bears' Almanac
The Berenstain Bears' Nature Guide

The Berenstain Bears' Science Fair
The Magic School Bus At the Waterworks
The Magic School Bus Inside the Earth
The Magic School Bus Inside the Human Body
The Magic School Bus Lost in the Solar System
The Magic School Bus On the Ocean Floor
The Magic School Bus In the Time of the Dinosaurs
The Magic School Bus Inside a Hurricane
The Magic School Bus Inside a Beehive
The Magic School Bus And the Electric Field Trip
The Magic School Bus Explores the Senses
The Magic School Bus And the Science Fair Expedition
The Magic School Bus And the Climate Challenge

Year A Titles

Public Domain Books:

1A	For the Children's Hour by Carolyn S. Bailey
1B	Among the Farmyard People by Clara Dillingham Pierson
	Among the Pond People by Clara Dillingham Pierson
	Among the Night People by Clara Dillingham Pierson
	50 Famous People by James Baldwin
2A	Seed Babies by Margaret W. Morley
	The Bee People by Margaret W. Morley
2B	The Burgess Bird Book by Thornton Burgess
3A	The Burgess Animal Book by Thornton Burgess
3B	My Father's Dragon by Ruth Stiles Gannett

Copyrighted Books:

1C	The Travels of Babar
	Babar the King
	Babar and His Children
	Babar and Father Christmas
	Babar and the Wully-Wully
	Adele and Simon
	Adele and Simon in America
	Milly-Molly-Mandy's Adventures
2C	Winnie-the-Pooh by A. A. Milne
	The House at Pooh Corner by A. A. Milne
	Beezus and Ramona by Beverly Cleary
	Ramona the Pest by Beverly Cleary
3B	Pippi Longstocking
	Betsy-Tacy
3C	Is This a House for Hermit Crab? by Megan McDonald
	Wild About Books by Judy Sierra

Amazing Grace by Mary Hoffman
Zin! Zin! Zin! A Violin by Lloyd Moss
The Little Red Lighthouse and the Great Gray Bridge
by Hildegarde H. Swift
How Much Is a Million? by David M. Schwartz
Sophie And Lou by Petra Mathers
Animal Cafe by John Stadler
Mummies Made in Egypt by Aliki
Digging Up Dinosaurs by Aliki
Paul Bunyan, a Tall Tale by Steven Kellogg
Mufaro's Beautiful Daughters: An African Tale
by John Steptoe
One Small Blue Bead by Byrd Baylor
The Patchwork Quilt by Valerie Flournoy
Barn Dance! by Bill Martin Jr.
Alexander, Who Used to Be Rich Last Sunday
Alexander, Who's Not (Do You Hear Me? I Mean It!) Going to Move

D   The Real Mother Goose
The World of Christopher Robin: The Complete When
We Were Very Young and Now We Are Six by A. A. Milne
A Child's Garden of Verses by Robert Louis Stevenson

Year B Titles

Public Domain Books:

1A   Kindergarten Gems by Agnes Taylor Ketchum
1B   Among the Forest People by Clara Dillingham Pierson
       Among the Meadow People by Clara Dillingham Pierson
       50 Famous Stories Retold by James Baldwin
2A   Little Wanderers by Margaret W. Morley
3A   The Burgess Flower Book by Thornton Burgess
3B   Little House in the Big Woods by Laura Ingalls Wilder
       (public domain in Canada; available in most U.S. libraries)

Copyrighted Books:

1C   The Story About Ping
       How to Make an Apple Pie and See the World
       The Salamander Room
       The Bee Tree
       Owl Moon
       The Runaway Bunny
       There's No Such Thing as a Dragon by Jack Kent
       The Paper Bag Princess by Robert Munsch
       Strega Nona by Tomie dePaola
       The Night Pirates by Peter Harris

Beatrice's Goat by Page McBrier
The Colors of Us by Karen Katz
Anno's Magic Seeds by Mitsumasa Anno
A Year at Maple Hill Farm
The Hundred Dresses
James Herriot's Treasury for Children (JH)
2B   The Burgess Seashore Book by Thornton Burgess
2C   A Bear Called Paddington
More About Paddington
Paddington Helps Out
A Mouse Called Wolf
3B   TumTum and Nutmeg
Gooney Bird Greene
3C   Corduroy by Don Freeman
What's Smaller Than a Pygmy Shrew? by Robert E. Wells
Cloudy with a Chance of Meatballs by Judi Barrett
The Classic Tales of Brer Rabbit by Joel Chandler Harris
Henry Huggins by Beverly Cleary
D   The Random House Book of Poetry for Children

Appendix D: Prepared Dictation Instructions

In prepared dictation, children type or write a passage after studying it for five to ten minutes. The basic process was described by Charlotte Mason in her book *Home Education*. We combine the method with analyzing words according to phonograms and spelling rules.

I know that dictation can sound like a huge, time consuming exercise, especially with multiple children. It's not. We do prepared dictation twice a week, on the "off" days from grammar. First, I try to have my boys read through the spelling rules at least once each week, and we make an effort to analyze words that illustrate the different rules. (If they don't appear naturally through the passages we study, then we occasionally spend some time exploring a rule rather than a passage.) Then, each of my boys studies his passage for about ten minutes. He chooses, sometimes with my help, two or three words to analyze. A passage should not have more than three or four unknown words to be studied, though there's nothing wrong with analyzing extra words. He adds these to his Spelling Journal, analyzing each word syllable by syllable.

The Spelling Journal organizes words according to phonogram or spelling rule, and it is a free download on my site. The Spelling Journal can help identify problem spelling areas. Also, having children read through their Spelling Journals occasionally can help reinforce lessons from their previous studies. If you prefer to avoid printing out workbooks, then you could use the Spelling Journal as a template for creating a Spelling Journal in a composition book.

Dictations may be written or typed. My boys type their dictations. The spelling and grammar checks are turned off in our word processing program, and we increase the font size to 20+ points so that I can read over their shoulders. I read the exercises while each boy takes his turn at the keyboard. I stand behind them so that I can make sure they don't make any mistakes. When a mistake is made, we correct immediately. After the dictation, we analyze, or re-analyze, the missed word. Most weeks, there are no missed words from any of my boys.

Beginners can start with just a sentence or two, while older children can type or write up to several paragraphs. We use a variety of sources, including Aesop's fables, literature, Bible verses, poetry, and even my children's free reading choices. It's important to avoid passages which contain incorrect grammar, which many modern books do. However, I've found that dictation goes easier when the child is studying a passage he loves.

Appendix E: Montessori Three-Period Lesson

Dr. Montessori recommended the Seguin lesson for teaching language, a technique named after Dr. Edouard Seguin. The Seguin lesson has three parts. First, the child is shown new vocabulary in a concrete way. Second, the parent asks, "Where is _____?" and the child shows the parent. And third, the parent asks, "What is this?"

This method can be used for any sort of vocabulary development, using cards or objects in the environment. Two things of different sizes can show big and small. Laminated cards or picture books can be used to show colors, animals, or objects of any sort. The lesson should include at least two things so the child can make a comparison.

The first colors I taught my daughter at age two and a half were red and yellow. She called it "the yellow game" and asked for it periodically. I had not created any manipulatives to work with her, so I pointed towards fabric boxes on a bookshelf. I pointed to the first and said, "This is red." Being two, she immediately repeated me. Then I pointed to the yellow box and said, "This is yellow." Again, she repeated me. We pointed towards each of them a few times and said the names of the colors.

At this point, I turned the game around and said, "Show me red." At first, she showed me only the red box that I had shown her. Later, she showed me the other red box on the shelf. And on subsequent days, she began to look for other examples of red on the book shelf. I also asked her to show me yellow, and we gradually started adding in other colors.

Use of laminated cards or spindles as used in Montessori color matching games makes the game more predictable, as you won't have a mischievous toddler searching all over for the room for "red." However, the game does not have to be the same way every time. Since many of my daughter's toys are brightly colored, we spontaneously played "the yellow game" regularly.

The third part of the game comes later, when the child really knows the information. The parent points to red, whether the card or book, the spindle, or the fabric box on the shelf, and says, "What color is this?" If the child has the answer, then he's absorbed this vocabulary. If not, then continue on with "the yellow game."

It is true that many toddlers, especially when they have older siblings, do not need to be taught colors or animal names. I have five children, and I only ever taught the first one to count to ten. The others began counting spontaneously between the ages of two and four. Toddlers will often pick up the names of colors and shapes in the same way. So if it's not actually necessary for language acquisition, why should we do it?

To me, the first and foremost answer is that it's an enjoyable way to interact with my toddler. It's fun for both of us. There are many parents who love getting down on the floor and playing in all sorts of creative ways with their toddlers, but sadly, I've never been one of them. For those of use missing the "play" gene, these are ways for us to interact in meaningful ways with our little ones.

The second reason is that there's a difference between picking things up passively, through toddler osmosis, and actively acquiring information. The toddler can learn that the acquisition of knowledge is an enjoyable process. Furthermore, later lessons can grow out of these beginning games rather than coming as a shock to the young child who's never had to do anything but play.

And third, we can take this game to a new level. With a set of base ten blocks, with the units put away since they're choking hazards, the toddler can learn the names of tens, hundreds, and thousands in a concrete way. Consider the ease of teaching place value to the child for whom these concepts are as common as red, blue, and yellow.

Learning the Phonograms

In the same way that children can acquire language for common objects and colors, they can also learn the sounds of letters and groups of letters, called phonograms. As adults, we see learning to read as a skill for older children, and so we wait. However, to the very young child, learning the sounds of the phonograms is just another naming game. They absorb language easily at early ages, and they like to play repetitious naming games. Both of these traits are an advantage in learning to read.

Have a set of phonogram cards, and start with the one-letter phonograms—the letters of the alphabet. Present two cards to the child, three to a child who has been doing this for a time. Tell him the name of each phonogram, including all of its sounds, and have him repeat them. Then say, "Where is _____?" Do this a couple of times for each phonogram, then put these cards away and bring out two or three more cards. My three-year old daughter and I can go through roughly twelve to fifteen phonograms in a session.

If your child has the coordination necessary, you can add a multi-sensory dimension to these lessons. The child can say the sound(s) of each phonogram as he air writes the phonograms in the air with his hand or elbow; make sure the motion includes moving the shoulder for the benefit of including gross motor control. The child can also say the sound(s) of each phonogram as he writes the phonogram with his finger in a sand or salt tray, or he could trace a letter that the parent has made in the sand tray. He can also trace the sandpaper letters with his finger and/or trace the phonogram cards with his finger as he says the sounds. In these ways, the child learns to both read and write each phonogram.

Eventually, he will have fully absorbed the knowledge, and he will know and be able to say the sounds the phonograms make when he sees them. Then, he is truly on the path to reading.

A free file of extras as well as notebooking pages for Quark Chronicles can be downloaded here:

http://barefootmeandering.com/site/wayfarers-extras/

Please note that this file is only for those who have purchased Wayfarers, so please don't share it. You will need the following password and username to access the page and then to download the files.

Username: wayfarers
Password: 47Tp6(WCP?Z6

Manufactured by Amazon.ca
Bolton, ON